The
Far East

By
CHESTER A. BAIN

FOURTH EDITION

1965

LITTLEFIELD, ADAMS & CO.
TOTOWA, NEW JERSEY

Preface

The Far East is intended to serve both as a supplementary guide for students taking courses in world history and as a convenient review book for those studying the Far East. While not intended as a substitute for a textbook, it may be used as a condensed text.

Special credit for the successful completion of both the first and revised editions of this book goes to my wife, June W. Bain, whose training as editor and teacher have proven invaluable. I also extend my gratitude to the numerous librarians who have patiently served me over the years.

The fourth edition remains the same in form through chapter 13 as the third edition with some minor revisions and new bibliographies. The chapters covering the post World War II period, however, have been extensively revised and expanded.

C. A. B.

CONTENTS

CHAPTER

Period	World Setting	China Political	China Cultural
5000 B.C.	Emergence of Sumer & Egypt into age of metal		Neolithic Culture Cultivation of wheat Domestication of animals
4000	Indus Valley civilization		Primitive Animism
3000		Legendary Emperors Huang Ti	Bronze Age Culture—beginning in Wei and Hwang Ho Valleys
	Egypt—Old Kingdom		Potter's wheel
2000	Sargon I	Legendary Founding of Hsia Dynasty by Yü (2205 B.C.)	
1900	Egypt—Middle Kingdom Hammurabi		
1800			Development of written characters
1700	Hyksos Invasion of Egypt	Shang Dynasty (1700-1122 B.C.)	Silk Culture
1600		Beginning of historical period Many feudal states	
1500			Advanced Bronze Age Shell currency
1400			
1300	Egyptian Empire Amenhotep III		Development of cities
1200			
1100			Fine metal and jade work Bamboo slip books
	Phoenician Alphabet	Chou Dynasty (1122-256 B.C.)	
1000	Solomon	Development of traditional Chinese government and Civil Service System	
900	Assyrian Conquest		Wet rice
800			
700	Sargon II	Feudal Period	
600			Golden Age of literature Laotze
500	Persian Wars Pericles		Confucius
400	Plato and Aristotle		
300	Alexander the Great		Mencius Round coins
200		Ch'in Dynasty (221-207 B.C.) Shih Huang-ti	Beginning of Iron Age Building of Great Wall Burning of the Books
100		Western Han Dynasty (206 B.C.-9 A.D.)	Contacts with Roman Empire, Parthia, and Bactria
0	Julius Caesar Christ	Hsin (9 A.D.-23 A.D.)	Introduction of Buddhism Pottery glazing
100 A.D.	Augustus	Eastern Han (23 A.D.-220 A.D.)	Invention of paper Cultivation of tea
200	Diocletian	*Dark Ages*	Kite, water mill, sedan chair, compass, first use of coal, introduction of dice
300		Three Kingdoms 220-265 Six Dynasties 317-589 Feudal Warfare	
400		Colonization of South China	
	Justinian		Nestorian Christianity
500	Mohammed		
600	Pope Gregory the Great	Sui Dynasty (590-618)	Construction of Grand Canal Civil Service Examinations
700	Battle of Tours (732)	T'ang Dynasty (618-907) Imperial Expansion	Zoroastrianism Mohammedanism Fire Works
800	Charlemagne Alfred the Great of England		Porcelain Invention of block printing
900			
		Five Dynasties (907-960)	Foot binding
1000	Crusades (1095-1291)	Sung Dynasty (960-1279)	First book printed from wood blocks Movable type Chair

X

Period	Japan Political	Japan Cultural	Minor Countries of East Asia
5000 B.C.			
	Age of		
4000	Deities		
3000	and	Gradual migration	
2000	Legendary	of Japanese people	
1900	Heroes	from Asia via Korea	
1800		and from East Indies	
1700		via islands in path	
1600		of Japanese current	
1500			
1400			
1300			
1200			
1100			Legendary founding of Ki Dynasty in Korea (1122 B.C.)
1000			
900			
800			
700			
600	Legendary date of Jimmu Jenno (660 B.C.) First Emperor	Late Neolithic Culture	
500			
400		Beginning of introduction of Bronze Age culture from China via Korea	Migration of Thais into Indo-China
300			Hindu settlements in Cambodia and Burma Large Chinese migration to Korea End of Ki Dynasty in Korea
200			Shih Huang-ti conquers Tonking & Annam Hindu settlements in Java
100			Han domination in North Korea and Tonking Kingdoms of Paikché, Kokuli, and Silla in Korea
0	Probable date of Jimmu Tenno (40-10 B.C.)	Primitive animism developing into Shinto	First Japanese envoy to China
100 A.D.			
200	Age of Clans (Yamato Era)		
300			Japanese invade Korea; Paikché, Silla, and Imma become Japanese vassals (391)
400			
500	Soga Clan domination	Migration of Korean craftsmen and farmers to Japan	Silla drives Japanese from Imma (527)
600	Shotoko Regent Kamatari Great Reform (645)	Buddhism brought from Korea Adoption of Chinese writing and literature	Japan withdraws from Korea (622) Rise of Kingdom of Sri Vishaya First kingdom of Tibet (T'u-fan)
700	Nara Period (710-784)	Beginning of Japanese literature and art	First united kingdom of Cambodia T'ang Dynasty reannexes Korea Prome dominates South Burma
800	Heian Era (784-1185) Fujiwara Regents (858-1160)	Kojiki and Nihongi, first Japanese histories (712-720) Rapid cultural advance at court in literature, music, and art	First Burmese ambassadors to China Construction of city of Angkor Than in Cambodia
900	Taira and Minamoto struggle for power	Pillow Book	Independent kingdom of Annam established
1000			Rise of Burmese Kingdom of Pagan (1044)

Period	World Setting	China Political	China Cultural
1100			Gunpowder used in warfare Chuttsi—Neo-Confucianism
1200	Magna Charta		State Socialism; Social experiments
1300		Mongol (Yüan) Dynasty (1279-1368 A.D.)	Marco Polo Lamaism Favored Use of abacus
1350			Spherical Trigonometry Drama and fiction
1400		Ming Dynasty (1368-1644)	Trading missions sent to Indies, India, Arabia, and Africa
1425			Chinese ships forbidden to leave China
1450	Printing in Europe		Confucianism again official faith
1475			Renaissance in painting
	Columbus discovers America		Conservatism and lack of originality in literature
1500			
1525		Russians cross Amur River	Indian corn and tobacco
1550		Portuguese receive Macao (1557)	
1575			
	Shakespeare		
1600			
1625			
	30 Years War	Manchu (Ch'ing) Dynasty (1644-1912)	Imposition of queue
1650	Louis XIV		Continuance of Ming cultural traditions
1675		All ports opened to trade (1685) Treaty of Nerchinsk (1689)	Opium smoking Introduction of European science by missionaries
1700			Hoppo System
1725		Treaty of Kiakhta (1727) with Russia	First prohibition of opium trade (1729) Drama and novel flourish Literary Inquisition (1744-88)
1750	Age of Enlightenment	Foreign trade confined to Canton (1757)	Co Hong established
1775	Industrial Revolution	Macartney Embassy (1793)	Increased opium consumption
1800	Napoleon I	Amherst Mission (1816)	Second opium ban (1800)
1825			
1835		Opium War (1839-42)	
		Treaty of Wanghia (1844) Taiping Rebellion (1848-65)	Rapid increase of foreign trade
1845			
1855		Arrow War and Treaty Revision (1858-1860)	
	Napoleon III		Tungwen College 1865
1865	Franco-Prussian War		Railroad Construction
1875			Yung Wing Educational Mission (1872)
1885			
1895		Foreign land grabs Boxer Rebellion Open Door Policy	
1905		Manchu reform Constitution of 1908	Intermarriage permitted between Chinese and Manchu
	World War I	Revolution of 1911	Educational reforms Acceleration of Westernization
1915			Hu Shih's literary renaissance San Min Chu I
1925		Kuomintang Victory (1927) Japanese Invasion	New Life Movement
1935	World War II		
1945		Communist China (1949)	

TIME CHART

Period	Japan Political	Japan Cultural	Minor Countries of East Asia
1100	Kamakura Shogunate (1185-1333) Established by Minamoto Yoritomo	Growth of feudalism New Buddhist sects: Zen, Shinron, Shingon & Nichren	Height of Sri Vishaya power (1180)
1200	Hojo become regents for Minamoto Shoguns. Government by indirection.	Bushido (Code of the Warrior) Hara-kiri Development of the No drama	Founding of Madjapahit in East Indies Mongol expansion pushes Thais south into Indo-China
1300			Kublai Khan conquers Pagan Rise of Singosari; fall of Sri Vishaya
1350	Ashikaga Period (1336-1568) Feudal warfare	Court life follows Nara and Heian patterns Tea Ceremony introduced Monasteries become cultural centers	Ava and Pegu dominate Burma Repeated Siamese invasions of Cambodia (1350-1460)
1400			Annam annexed by China (1406-1428) Introduction of Islam to E. Indies
1425			Angkor abandoned by Cambodians as Monkhmer Empire collapses
1450			Collapse of Madjapahit Empire Champa annexed by Annam (1471)
1475			
1500			Albuquerque seizes Malacca (1511)
1525			Magellan reaches Philippine Islands Japanese invade Korea
1550	Oda Nobunaga (1568-1582)	Portuguese arrive Francis Xavier	Tabin Shwehti of Toungoo becomes King of Burma
1575	Hideyoshi (1582-1598)		First Spanish settlement in the Philippines Dutch take Batavia, Java, and Malacca
1600	Tokugawa Shogunate (1600-1868); founded by Ieyasu Tokugawa	Christianity banned (1612) Shimabara Revolt Buddhism official religion Dutch at Deshima	
1625	Exclusion policy (1639)		
1650		Shift from rice to money economy	
1675		Rise of middle class	
1700		Drama flourishes; popular theater develops	
1725		Official encouragement of scholarly studies Mabuchi (1697-1769)	Tibetan revolt crushed by China (1725)
1750		Motoori Norinaga (1730-1801) Historical studies emphasize position of Emperor	
1775			
1800		Introduction of Western language	British occupy Dutch East Indies during Napoleonic Wars
1825			First Anglo-Burmese War (1824-26)
1835		Rice riots	
1845			Culture system in Dutch E. Indies
1855	Perry visit, Treaty of Kanagawa		Mongkut, Progressive King of Siam (1851-1868) French occupy Cochin China (1859)
1865	Resignation of Shogun (1867)	First newspaper	José Rizal (1861-1896)—Philippine leader French protectorate over Cambodia (1867)
1875	Restoration (1868) Constitutional Imperial administration Mutsuhito (1867-1912)	Shinto becomes official cult Western fashions introduced Complete religious liberty (1873) Railroad construction	Taewungun—Regent in Korea Tonking War
1885	Feudalism abolished (1871) Constitution (1889) Sino-Japanese War (1894-5)	Rapid industrialization First political parties Western education	Korean insurrection of 1883 British annex last of Burma (1885)
1895	War with Russia (1904-5)	Tokyo Imperial University Heavy industry; textiles	Aguinaldo, Philippine leader United States annexes Philippines (1899)
1905			Korea annexed by Japan
1915			
1925	Expansion into Manchuria	Rise of military nationalism	
1935	Pearl Harbor and war with United States & Allied Powers		United States of Indonesia formed under Dutch Crown Burma, Philippines, Korea independent
1945	Military occupation		Viet-Mihn Revolt in Indo-China South Korea invaded by North Korea and Chinese Communists

CHAPTER I
Ancient Chinese History and Culture

RACIAL GROUPS

The population of China is composed of several branches of the Mongoloid race who speak numerous languages and dialects. The Chinese Republic established in 1912 officially recognized five major races. The flag adopted in that year had five stripes, each representing one race: red for the Chinese, yellow for the Manchus, blue for the Mongols, white for the Turkis, and black for the Tibetans. Among other racial groups found in considerable numbers in China, the Koreans in the north and the Shans in the south are closely related to the Chinese.

Intermingling of Racial Groups. With many races living in proximity, it was natural that intermarriage should take place. This was especially true of the north which was subjected to repeated conquests by wild tribes from inner Asia.

Location of the Groups. The Chinese are the predominant race throughout the older provinces of China, while the Mongols predominate in outer Mongolia, the Tibetans in Tibet, the Turkis in Sinkiang. Most Manchus have been absorbed, except for some groups north of the Great Wall.

Racial Difference. The Chinese people vary from the north to the south in physical characteristics and temperament much as the Europeans vary from the large and light-complexioned Scandinavians to the smaller and darker Mediterraneans.

PREDYNASTIC PERIOD

Prehistoric Man in China. According to some historians the Chinese people first migrated from central Asia to the upper Yellow River Valley some time between 3000 B.C. and 2500 B.C.

However, recent archeological discoveries have led us to believe that the Chinese might have arrived in north China many thousands of years earlier.

PEKING MAN. Remains of manlike creatures indicate that humans inhabited north China as long ago as the early Pleistocene Era (Ice Ages). This was established by the discovery in 1928 of skeletal remains of a type of man known as *Sinanthropus Pekinensis* or Peking Man.

Primitive Civilizations. The ancestors of the modern Chinese became progressively more civilized, largely by their own efforts. Far removed from the civilizations of India, Egypt, and Mesopotamia, the Chinese accumulated increasing knowledge of how to gain a living from the earth by methods other than hunting. Grains were cultivated, and the pig and the dog were domesticated. Black pottery came into use, and a primitive shell money. Soon, in addition to inventing and improving tools and utensils, the Chinese began to develop a distinctive political life. By 2200 B.C. the legendary period of Chinese history emerges.

LEGENDARY PERIOD (2200-1700 B.C.). For information regarding this period, we must rely on Chinese legends and myths. They attribute the creation of heaven, earth, and human civilization to the great Pan Ku, twelve heavenly sovereigns, and nine human sovereigns. Huang Ti, the Yellow Emperor, supposedly ruled about 2700 B.C., and introduced the study of astronomy and silk culture. The early legends also report the existence of the Hsia Dynasty from about 2200 B.C. to 1700 B.C. However, as no material remains have been discovered from this period, there is no certainty the Hsia Dynasty actually existed.

EARLY DYNASTIES

Shang Dynasty (c. 1700 - 1122 B.C.). The Shang dynasty, according to legends, followed the Hsia. We have no accurate dates for the Shang, but we do have evidence of its existence. It is not improbable that many of the occurrences and discoveries described in the myths, such as the development of Chinese writing and silk culture, actually occurred under the Shang, or even later.

EXTENT OF SHANG EMPIRE. The Shang empire, which probably represented the maximum extent of the expansion of the Chinese race, covered most of the Hwang and Huai river valleys and extended north to the Pei River and south to the Yangtze. Thus it included most of modern Shantung, Hopei, Kansu, Honan, Shansi, Shensi, and Anhui provinces.

SHANG CULTURE. By the end of the Shang dynasty, the Chinese had reached a high level of civilization. The wheel was used, large buildings were constructed, and religion had already begun to be linked with the worship of ancestors. The highest god was Shang Ti.

THE FALL OF THE SHANG. Surrounding the Shang empire lived less civilized clans related to the Chinese. The most powerful of these, the Chou clans of the upper Wei valley, conquered the Shang.

Chou Dynasty (c. 1122 - 256 B.C.). The Chou dynasty, the longest in China's history, is usually divided into three periods: Early Chou (1122 - 771 B.C.); Middle Chou (771 - 474 B.C.); and Late Chou (473 - 256 B.C.). Under the Early Chou emperors, Chinese rule was extended over most of the Yellow River Valley. After the conquest, the Chou, ruling from their capital near Sian, parceled much of the empire out as fiefs to relatives and military aids. While strong kings sat on the Chou throne, the vassals remained loyal, but gradually the lords of the fiefs began to defy central authority and to war among themselves. The Middle Chou was a feudal period in which the emperors could exert authority only in a priestly capacity as religious arbiters. Despite the lack of central authority, however, the Chinese empire continued to expand southward. In the Middle and Late Chou, the state of Wu, Yüeh and Ch'u appeared in the Yangtze Valley. The Late Chou history is largely concerned with the struggle between these new southern states and the Wei Valley state of Ch'in. Out of this struggle emerged the Ch'in dynasty.

CHOU CULTURE. While the Middle and Late Chou were periods of political turmoil, they were also periods of cultural progress. The Late Chou is considered the classical age of China, for it produced the great teachers, Confucius, Lao Tzu, Mo Ti, Mencius, Chuang Tzu, and Yang Chu. During the Chou dynasty, China emerged from the Bronze Age into the early Iron Age. The arts and crafts improved greatly. Agriculture was aided by the introduction of the ox-drawn plow and irrigation.

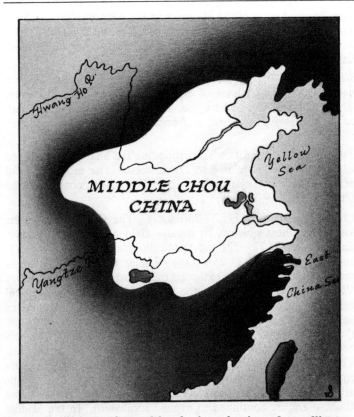

Economic life was changed by the introduction of metallic money and by the development of an urban society. During this period, the main elements of China's family system were adopted, and the philosophers implanted the ceremonies and ideas that have dominated Chinese society ever since.

LAO TZU (c. 604-531 B.C.) and CONFUCIUS (551-479 B.C.). The two Chinese who have most molded Chinese character are Lao Tzu, father of Taoism, and Confucius, founder of Confucianism. These two systems are closely interwoven into Chinese social and political life. Lao Tzu, in his *Tao Te Ching,* advocated a profound and negative pacifism. Man should seek to master not others but himself. Victory in life is gained not by striving but by achieving spiritual harmony by following the Tao, or the Way. Lao Tzu's teachings were corrupted by later generations until Taoism became a system of magic and witchcraft. Today the Taoist priest is the village necromancer. K'ung Fu-tzu, or Confucius, advocated a more positive way of life. A practical statesman in an age of strife, Confucius looked back at the "good old days" for guidance in statecraft and life. He sought to bring order by inducing men to follow a central harmony or golden mean in all their actions. Individuals were to be governed by rules of conduct regulating the mutual relationship between (1) ruler and subject, (2) parent and child, (3) husband and wife, (4) older brother and younger brother, and (5) friend and friend. Basic to the Confucian system is filial piety or family loyalty. Son must honor and obey father, but father must present an example of good conduct to son. Confucius believed man was naturally good but self-control was required to restrain the passions that led to evil. Confucianism became China's state religion as well as an ethical guide for the Chinese in everyday living.

Ch'in Dynasty (221 - 207 B.C.). **Shih Huang-ti.** The turbulent era of the late Chou was brought to an end by the conquest of all the warring states by Prince Cheng of Ch'in, who thereafter took the title of Shih Huang-ti.

INTERNATIONAL DEVELOPMENTS. Shih Huang-ti and his chief minister, Li Ssu, reorganized the government of China, replacing the old feudal structure with a centralized bureaucracy controlled by the emperor. In order to achieve political, cultural, and economic unity in China, Shih Huang-ti encouraged internal improvements such as the standardization of weights and measures, tools, and the gauges of wagons; the construction of irrigation projects and canals; the building of the Great Wall to protect the northern frontier; and peasant ownership of land. In a further effort to eradicate the feudal past, Shih Huang-ti ordered that all books be destroyed except those dealing with medicine, divination, and agriculture.

FALL OF THE CH'IN. The ambitious emperor resorted to forced labor on a large scale, to increased taxation, and to issuance of harsh laws. These severe measures and the hatred of the scholars due to the burning of the books, built up bitter resentment against Shih Huang-ti. However, a rebellion did not occur until after Shih Huang-ti's death in 210 B.C. Civil war was ended by the rise of General Liu Pang to the emperor's throne as Kao Tsu, the first Han emperor.

Han Dynasty (206 B.C. - 220 A.D.). The Han dynasty roughly parallels the centuries of the greatness of Rome. The Han empire was about equal to Rome's in both area and population, but the Han had the advantage of cultural and political unity which Rome never accomplished. So great and rich was the Han empire that the Chinese still like to call themselves the Sons of Han.

DIVISION INTO WESTERN AND EASTERN HAN. The Han dynasty was divided into two periods, for there was a brief interlude from A.D. 9-23 in which the Hsin controlled China. The periods before and after the Hsin are commonly called the Western and Eastern Han from the location of the capital in each period.

EXTENSION OF HAN EMPIRE. Under the Han, China's great and powerful empire extended from southern Manchuria and Korea in the north to Annam and Tonkin in the south, and from the Pacific on the east to the Pamir Mountains in the west.

HAN CULTURE. Scholars quickly revived most of the learning temporarily lost in the burning of the books by Shih Huang-ti. The discovery of paper encouraged literary productions; music, painting, and sculpture were improved with new techniques; agriculture was enriched by such additions as crop rotation with leguminous plants, and better harness for draft animals; trade was encouraged by the great extension of China's boundaries; pottery glazing was discovered; the calendar was improved; and the seismograph was invented to register earthquakes.

DECLINE OF THE HAN. Under the Eastern Han emperors the dynasty declined, and control of the country fell into the hands of corrupt court eunuchs who were increasingly entrusted with important duties. In the end the eunuchs destroyed the Han dynasty by a palace revolution. The disintegration of the empire, however, began almost before its conquests were completed. China was too large for any but the strongest central authority to hold together. Also, while the Chinese in the highly cultured interior forgot the arts of war, the frontier barbarians remained virile and warlike. The fall of the Han resembles in some respects the fall of the Roman Empire. Both events were accompanied by barbarian invasions that brought ruin to high civilizations. In place of the previous large empires, there developed numerous barbarian kingdoms, each of which tried to imitate the empire it had helped to destroy. The result in both cases was a period termed the Dark Ages.

PERIOD OF DARKNESS (220-590 A.D.)

The Three Kingdoms (220 - 265 A.D.). In the period immediately following the collapse of the Han, there were three kingdoms in China: Wei, in the north; Wu, in the southeast; and Shu, in the southwest. The three states struggled for control of China until, in 280, Wei emerged to found the Tsin dynasty, which continued a shady existence until A.D. 420. The unification of China under the Tsin was short-lived. The new state was not only plagued with internal strife, but also had to face waves of Turkic, Mongol, and Hunnish invaders, who set up a series of states ruling over varying portions of China.

The Six Dynasties (317 - 590 A.D.). During this period, the Yangtze Valley region remained under Chinese rule. The period is called the Six Dynasties by the Chinese because of the six states that successively centered about Nanking.

Hsiung Nu Invaders. One of the most important of the invading barbarian groups are the Hsiung Nu, who are generally believed to be the people called the Huns by the Europeans. The Hsiung Nu ruled at least four states during China's Dark Ages.

Progress in the Dark Ages. Despite the bloodshed and political anarchy during these 400 years, the Chinese continued their territorial expansion and cultural progress. Buddhism became an important Chinese religion, while Confucianism was weakened by the collapse of the central government that normally fostered it. Taoism, first taught as a philosophical way of life, was transformed into a religion by copying many of the ceremonials and doctrines of Buddhism. The use of tea was begun, the wheelbarrow, the water mill, the sedan chair, and the kite were invented, or at least came into prominence. It is also possible that coal was first used as a fuel at this time and that the compass was discovered. Dice were introduced into China either by barbarian tribesmen or by Buddhist visitors from India, while glassmaking was imported from Parthia.

LATER DYNASTIC HISTORY
(590 - 1644 A.D.)

Sui Dynasty (590 - 618 A.D.). The Duke of Sui brutally seized power, and after gaining control of most of China proper, he assumed the title of Emperor Yang Chien in 589. Yang Chien's son and murderer, Yang Ti, extended China's sway over Indo-China, but failed in his attempt to conquer Korea.

FALL OF THE SUI. The Sui Dynasty ended, as it began, in violence, but efforts toward reuniting China bore fruit under their successors, the T'ang dynasty. The downfall of the Sui was caused primarily by foreign wars, which prevented consolidating of their hold on China proper, and by large-scale use of forced labor on building projects and in construction of the Grand Canal.

T'ang Dynasty (618-907 A.D.). The early T'ang emperors not only warded off strong attacks by frontier tribes, but also pushed the Chinese borders deep into Mongolia and southern Manchuria. Korea was made a vassal state, and the Turkish tribes of the Tarim Basin recognized Chinese suzerainty.

REORGANIZATION OF GOVERNMENT. The T'ang rulers codified the laws, redivided China into provinces, and revived the centralized bureaucratic government. To provide educated officials, a system of civil service examinations was inaugurated. Civil service examinations may have been used as early as Chou, and some Han emperors used competitive examinations occasionally to choose worthy officials; but not until the T'ang were they used on a large scale for all offices of state.

MATERIAL PROGRESS. Under the early T'ang, prosperity was greatly stimulated. The T'ang redistributed much land that had gone out of cultivation in the Dark Ages. Public works were improved and commerce was encouraged. The wealth of the T'ang empire attracted traders by sea and by land from all of Asia. Ch'ang-an, the T'ang capital, was probably the largest and most beautiful city of the world with its two million population.

INVENTIONS. During this time, the Chinese produced the first gunpowder, which they used for a long period of time only for fireworks. The discovery of block printing seems to have resulted around 600 A.D. from the need for duplicating the religious works of the Buddhists and Taoists. The first known printed book dates from 868 A.D.

RELIGIOUS DEVELOPMENTS. As the result of the large influx of foreign traders, new religions were introduced into China. Nestorians, Christians, Moslems, Manicheans, and Zoroastrians were found in large numbers, especially in the trading centers. The most influential of all alien religions was Buddhism, which reached such power that the T'ang emperors finally considered it necessary to place all religions under state control, if not to suppress them outright. To combat the alien influences, the T'ang encouraged a revival of Confucianism which, as the official state religion, developed great power.

CULTURE UNDER THE T'ANG. The T'ang era produced many illustrious scholars and artists. Li Po, Wang Wei, and Tu Fu, who are among China's greatest poets, helped to make the reign of Emperor Ming Huang (712-756 A.D.) known as the Golden Age of Poetry. Two great encyclopedias, several excellent histories, and numerous superior works on science were written. Painting and sculpture were especially fostered by Taoism and Buddhism, but secular themes were also largely used. The production of porcelain was raised to the level of a fine art.

DECLINE OF THE T'ANG. As in the case of previous dynasties the gradual weakening of the central government resulted in barbarian encroachment and civil uprisings. The T'ang dynasty collapsed in the early tenth century, leaving China to suffer a half century of disunity.

The Five Dynasties (907-960 A.D.). The period following the T'ang is called the period of Five Dynasties and Ten Independent States. It was a time of decadence, with five houses successively ruling over the remnants of the T'ang empire. During this same period, adventurers and Mongol invaders set up a series of secession states. The most important invaders were the Mongol Khitans who moved into Mongolia and Manchuria.

FOOT BINDING. One example of the decadence of this period was the adoption of the custom of binding the feet of dancing girls to produce the excessively small "lily feet." This custom spread rapidly throughout all classes of society, and became so fixed that not until the late nineteenth and early twentieth centuries was it finally ended.

Sung Dynasty (960 - 1279 A.D.). Again it was a strong general, Chao K'uang-yin, that ended anarchy and founded a new imperial house, the Sung dynasty. So strong were the non-Chinese people north of the Great Wall, that the Sung won peace only by paying tribute to the barbarian chiefs. Two frontier states constantly threatened China: Hsi Hsia and Liao. Evenutally, the Sung fell before the greatest of the nomad leaders, Kublai Khan, the leader of the Mongol hordes.

MATERIAL PROGRESS. While China was not politically strong under the Sung, she was culturally progressive. Printing was improved by the development of movable type. Ceramics reached new peaks of artistry. The chair was introduced, and cotton came into general use. For the first time, gunpowder was used in warfare.

LITERATURE AND ARTS. The Sung period produced a number of illustrious philosophers who founded new schools of thought. Of these, Chu Hsi is best known for his eclectic neo-Confucianism which mingled elements of Taoism and Buddhism with Confucian doctrines. In addition to philosophy, the Sung writers excelled in science, mathematics, and history.

WANG AN-SHIH AND STATE SOCIALISM. The Sung minister Wang An-shih (1021-1086) was the first to introduce state socialism on an important scale into China. Under Wang, China experimented in such modern-sounding projects as state budgets, ever-normal granaries, government crop loans, equal redistribution of the land, and graduated taxation. In addition, this progressive official abolished conscript labor, improved the civil service examination system, and instituted compulsory military service in his reorganized army. These social experiments have influenced some western statesmen, and are said to have provided inspiration for portions of the New Deal agricultural program.

Yüan Dynasty (1279-1368 A.D.). The same Mongol hordes that destroyed the caliphate of the Moslems in the Near East and conquered Russia in Europe established the Yüan dynasty in China. The Mongol leader Jenghis Khan established a great central Asiatic empire, and at the time of his death in 1227, was preparing to attack China. Kublai, one of Jenghis' grandsons, was elected Grand Khan in 1260, the same year that Peking was named a secondary capital of the Mongol empire. It was not until 1279, however, that the last Sung army was defeated in southern China.

FOREIGN CONQUESTS. In 1274 and again in 1281, Kublai Khan made unsuccessful attempts to conquer Japan. In 1277, Burma was successfully invaded, but attempts to add Annam to the Mongol domain were frustrated. Diplomacy won Tibet for the Mongols, possibly as a reward for their adoption of Lamaism.

GOVERNMENT OF CHINA UNDER THE YÜAN. The Mongol emperors chose to rule China through the existing Chinese bureaucracy. Chinese were also used to administer many non-Chinese portions of the vast Mongol empire. To assure a plentiful supply of trained officials, the early Mongol rulers established schools in north China. Later the Yüan reorganized and improved the communication systems. Some of the socialistic policies of Wang An-shih were revived to provide state granaries, and state relief was furnished to the orphans, the sick, and the aged.

CULTURAL INNOVATIONS AND PROGRESS. Swarms of officials, traders, and missionaries moved into China from other parts of the Mongol empire, bringing new ideas, techniques, foods, medicines, and even musical instruments. Chinese mathematical knowledge was enriched by the adoption of the abacus and by the introduction of spherical trigonometry. New forms of art and architecture were adapted to Chinese styles. Progress in Chinese drama is amply evidenced by the 116 Yüan period plays still extant.

FALL OF THE MONGOL DYNASTY. After an unsuccessful attempt to import Christian missionaries, the Mongols were converted to Lamaism, the Tibetan form of Buddhism. Kublai and his successors gave great power to the Tibetan lamas in China, and this increased the hostility of the Chinese toward their alien rulers. Finally, in 1367 a Chinese, Chu Yüan-chang, raised the standard of revolt and drove out the last Mongol emperor. In the same year, Chu took the title of Hung Wu, first emperor of the Ming dynasty.

Ming Dynasty (1365 - 1644 A.D.). Under the Ming emperors, China again became a great nation in its own right. Nanking, located in central China, was logically chosen as the Ming capital.

CHINESE REACTION AGAINST ALIEN INFLUENCES. Emperor Hung Wu and his successors endeavored to eliminate by decree many of the alien influences brought into China under the Yüan. The lamas were driven from power, and other alien religions, including Christianity, were reduced in strength. Foreign garb was prohibited, and ancient Chinese costumes were revived.

EXPANSION UNDER EARLY MINGS. After defeating the Mongols, the Ming rulers expanded the borders of China to include Yünnan and Szechwan in the southwest and Manchuria as far north as the Amur River along the coast. Korea, Mongolia, and Burma became Chinese vassal states. By sending naval expeditions to southeastern Asia, the East Indies, India, Ceylon, Arabia, and even Africa, the Ming power made itself known and opened trade routes.

CLOSING OF CHINA'S DOORS. Just as the Ming reached the pinnacle of its power, when China was receiving tribute from lands as far away as Java and Ceylon, the doors of China were abruptly closed. The Chinese ships were forbidden to leave Chinese coastal waters. The great navy was allowed to disintegrate, leaving China's coasts easy prey to raids by the Japanese and by the Europeans that soon were exploring Eastern Asia.

MING GOVERNMENT. The early Ming emperors, in their desire to eliminate alien influences, revived the government of the early Chinese dynasties. The Hung Wu emperor redivided China into 13 provinces and set up 6 ministries of the central government. Civil service examinations were again made the key to government employment. He codified and revised the laws of China. Hung Wu and his successors pressed the improvement of agriculture, the cultivation of waste land, the extension of the canals and highways, and the restoration of public buildings.

MING CULTURE. While Hung Wu stimulated education by reviving the state examination system, he also narrowed the scope of scholarship by restricting the subject matter largely to classical Chinese literature. As a result, though Ming history and artistic production were large, it tended too much to imitation of classical pieces and classical themes. Though Hung Wu was reputed to have been a Buddhist monk, he nevertheless promoted Confucianism as the official faith. Taoism, which had been proscribed by the Yüan, regained strength under the Ming.

EUROPEAN INFLUENCES. During the Ming rule the "red-haired barbarians" of Europe first began to impinge in considerable numbers upon Chinese shores. There were two separate invasions: one by the merchants and another by the priests. The efforts of the traders were largely concentrated on the southern coast. Through the port of Canton, China began to trade regularly her silk, porcelain, and luxuries for European products and silver. The religious penetration occurred not only from the coast but also through the interior. While some Christians had worked successfully under the Yüan, the faith had been largely exterminated by the early Ming emperors. In the latter Ming period, however, the Roman Catholic church began to send missionaries.

JESUITS IN CHINA. Though other Christian orders were later represented, the Jesuits were first to arrive in China. The famous Spanish Jesuit, Francis Xavier, died in 1552 on the China coast after a successful mission in India and Japan. Matteo Ricci, an Italian, was more successful in China, where his great knowledge of mathematics and astronomy made him an important figure in the Ming court. Ricci was succeeded by other capable Jesuits, who reformed the Chinese calendar, corrected maps, and taught the Chinese to manufacture the cannon to fight the Manchus. Where others failed, the Jesuits were successful because they displayed great tolerance toward Chinese ancestor worship and other Confucian customs.

DECLINE OF THE MING. After 1456, the Ming rule deteriorated rapidly. Japanese pirates became so destructive that the Ming ordered all coastal population to withdraw thirty miles inland. Mingpo was burned, and in 1555 even Nanking was attacked. The vassal states Annam, Tibet, and Mongolia asserted their independence. Late in the sixteenth century, northern Manchuria threw off Chinese control. However, in 1592 and 1597, the Ming armies successfully fought off the Japanese armies numbering 200,000 men, which had been sent by Hideyoshi, the military dictator of Japan, to Korea for the purpose of conquering China.

Manchu or Ch'ing Dynasty (1644 - 1911 A.D.). The group of Jurchen Tartar tribes of Manchuria which are generally called Manchus began to assume important political power as early as 1599 when their leader Nurhachu successfully refused to continue tribute payments to the Ming. Only 17 years later, Nurhachu proclaimed himself emperor of the Ch'ing Dynasty and established his capital at Mukden. Nurhachu's son, Emperor Tái Tsung, continued the Manchu expansion, conquering Korea in 1627. The Ming were so weakened by famines, rebellions, and desertions, that they steadily lost province after province. Peking fell in 1644, though the last Ming general was not defeated until Formosa was subdued in 1683.

BIBLIOGRAPHY

Ch'u, T., *Law and Society in Traditional China*, 1961.

Cottrell, L., *Tiger of Ch'in; the Dramatic Emergence of China as a Nation*, 1962.

Cressey, G. B., *Land of the 500 Million: a Geography of China*, 1955.

de Bary, William T., compiler, *Sources of Chinese Tradition*, 1960.

Eberhard, W., *Conquerors and Rulers; Social Forces in Medieval China*, 1952.

Eberhard, W., *History of China*, 1950.

Fitzgerald, C. P., *China: A Short Cultural History*, 1950.

Goodrich, L. C., *A Short History of the Chinese People*, 1951.

Grousset, R., *Chinese Art and Culture*, Grove, 1959.

Grousset, R., *Rise and Splendour of the Chinese Empire*, 1958.

Hughes, E. R., and K. Hughes, *Religion in China*, 1950.

Latourette, K. S., *The Chinese, Their History and Culture*, 1957.

Lin, Y. T., *Imperial Peking; Seven Centuries of China*, 1961.

Liu, Wu-chi, *A Short History of Confucian Philosophy*, 1955.

McNair, H. F., ed., *China*, 1946.

Reischauer, E. O., and J. K. Fairbank, *East Asia: the Great Tradition*, 1960.

Seeger, E., *The Pageant of Chinese History*, 1947.

Thomas, E. D., *Chinese Political Thought*, 1927.

Waley, A., *Three Ways of Thought in Ancient China*, 1956.

Wilhelm, R., *Confucius and Confucianism*, 1931.

Wittfogel, K. A., *Oriental Despotism: a Comparative Study of Total Power*, 1957.

Wright, A. F., ed., *Studies in Chinese Thought*, 1953.

CHAPTER 2
Early Japanese History

RACIAL AND CULTURAL HERITAGE

Racial Origin. The Japanese people appear to be a racial mixture of Malay, Korean, Chinese, Mongolian, and aboriginal Ainu blood. This mixture expresses itself not only in physical appearance, but also in the Japanese language and culture.

CHINESE CULTURAL INFLUENCE. While the Chinese have always had a deep-seated pride in their culture, the Japanese have shown a readiness to throw theirs aside for an alien one, if convinced of its value. Through most of Japanese history, China has given Japan her basic tutoring in the arts, letters, government, religion, and philosophy.

AGE OF THE CLANS

Origin of Clan Rule. About 100 B.C. a warlike people, probably of Malay origin, pushed the original Ainu inhabitants northward out of Kyushu and southern Honshu. These early Japanese were divided into a number of independent clans, each headed by a chief claiming descent from a god. The chief of the more powerful Yamato clan claimed his descent from the sun goddess who gained supremacy among the Japanese deities.

JIMMU TENNO, FIRST EMPEROR. By virtue of this divine descent and of superior arms, the Yamato clan was able to bring the other clans into subjection. According to the earliest Japanese histories, the *Kojiki* (712 A.D.) and the *Nihongi* (720 A.D.), the first Yamato chieftain to dominate all the others and thus become first emperor was Jimmu Tenno. According to Japanese legends this occurred in 660 B.C., but some recent historians have estimated the date at around 40 B.C.

Rise of Soga Clan. Other clans constantly challenged the supremacy of the imperial clan. By the early sixth century A.D. the Soga clan succeeded in defeating all but the imperial clan. By his power, their chief was able to make himself the O-omi or hereditary Great Imperial Chieftain, actually ruling the kingdom while the emperor merely reigned. This began a pattern of dual government which is repeated many times in Japanese history.

EXPANSION INTO KOREA. During the fifth and sixth centuries, A.D., the Japanese extended their sway over portions of Korea despite clan warfare at home. In a memorial sent to the emperor of China in 478, the Japanese emperor boasted of his rule over several Korean kingdoms. By the end of the sixth century, however, the Japanese seem to have lost their foothold on the continent.

Courtesy of The New York Times

JAPANESE ISLANDS

Clan Age Culture. At the beginning of the clan age, Japanese culture was quite primitive. There was no written language, and the arts and crafts were scarcely more advanced than late Neolithic. Korea adopted Chinese writing, religion, and learning in the fourth century, and in the fifth and sixth centuries sent learned scholars to the Japanese. The Japanese aristocracy long continued to look upon writing as manual labor, with the result that their earliest records were kept by Chinese and Koreans until Prince Shotoku and other Japanese leaders led their subordinates to learn to read and write.

ERA OF REFORM

Regency of Shotoku Taishi. As the result of the assassination of the emperor by a Soga chief, rule of Japan passed to the imperial prince Shotoku Taishi, who became regent. Prince Shotoku, one of the few educated Japanese of his day, introduced into Japan Chinese political theory and Buddhism. In 604 A.D., he issued a code of moral laws which have been erroneously called Japan's first constitution. This code borrowed the Chinese idea of supreme power residing in the emperor. Shotoku sought to unify the Japanese people by changing their allegiance from clan to emperor, and his encouragement of Buddhism contributed to this end.

Taikwa (Great Reform). After Shotoku's regency, the Soga influence was revived until another educated Japanese, Kamatari, founder of the Fujiwara clan, overthrew the Soga clan in 645 A.D. Kamatari continued the introduction of Chinese ways into Japan. In 645, after consolidating his hold on the empire, Kamatari issued a series of reform edicts known collectively as the Taikwa or Great Reform. These attempted to transplant to Japan the political and economic institutions of the contemporary T'ang dynasty of China.

LAND REDISTRIBUTION. On the theory that all land was owned by the emperor, the Taikwa recalled all land for redistribution by the emperor. The nobles whose lands were confiscated and made subject to the imperial authority and taxation were compensated by imperial offices and salaries. The land was divided into new administrative units governed by imperial appointees. In actuality the Great Reform involved no change in the ruling class, for the great nobles, now appointed administrators over their former estates, continued to rule as before. The changes in land tenure affected the lower classes the most. The former serfs were freed to receive allotments of farm land on an equal basis. The lot of many was improved, but others lost land they had previously cultivated.

Taiho.   Between 701 and 704 A.D. another series of reform edicts, known as the Taiho (Great Treasure) was promulgated. The Taiho involved political reorganization of Japan, establishing a series of ministries of state similar to those of the Chinese. Beneath the Council of State, presided over by the chancellor, were the ministries of the Central Office, Ceremonies, Civil Affairs, Popular Affairs, War, Justice, National Treasury, and the Imperial Household.

FAILURE OF TAIHO. Unfortunately, this effort to introduce an elaborate bureaucracy into feudal Japan overlooked the fact that Japan lacked an educated class to direct it. Japan's aristocracy was one of birth and not of learning. Japanese aristocrats demanded and received high state offices though they were almost totally lacking in the necessary education to administer them effectively. Governmental efforts to encourage learning were little felt beyond the vicinity of the capital.

Reform in Japanese Culture.   The era of reform was characterized by a wholesale adoption of Chinese literature and art forms. The reformers introduced Sui and T'ang culture along with their political and economic systems. There was an interchange of scholars and artists between China, Korea, and Japan. Although Chinese characters were learned by the Japanese, they were ultimately given Japanese sounds. After an early avid study of Chinese literature, the Japanese produced a great literature of their own. Similarly in painting, architecture, and sculpture, the continental models were first borrowed and then modified by Japanese genius. Further, there was a general advancement of all the crafts, particularly in the introduction and development of metals and ceramics.

Nara Era (710 - 784). Prior to the Great Reforms, Japan had no fixed capital. To provide greater stability to the government, the first permanent capital was established at Nara in 710, where it remained until its transfer to Nagaoka in 784. Ten years later the capital was moved to Kyoto. So influential was this capital in disseminating Chinese civilization in Japan that it gives its name to one of the most productive periods of Japanese culture.

INFLUENCE OF CHINESE CULTURE. In addition to political and economic principles, Chinese literature and art were introduced. The courtiers at Nara quickly became infatuated with the new culture. But, except for the spreading of Buddhism, life outside the court remained largely unchanged. The court nobility (kuge) thus became quite distinct from the provincial administrators. During the Nara period the great Japanese histories, the *Nihongi* and *Kojiki,* were compiled. Other forms of literature, particularly poetry, also flourished, and the fine arts were richly patronized. Buddhism was enriched by the construction of beautiful temples and monasteries.

HEIAN ERA (784 - 1185)

Rise of the Fujiwara. The luxury of the court during the eighth century was a heavy burden on the land. The court nobles (kuge) were distracted from their duties, while the provincial nobles (buke) grew rich and powerful at the expense of the small farmers. In time the great provincial clans began battling for supremacy, and in 858, the Fujiwara gained dominance. Again, however, the imperial clan did not lose the throne. The Fujiwara leaders ruled with the title of Regent or Dictator, while the emperor was permitted to reign with little power.

CHILD EMPERORS. Usually during the Fujiwara period, a child of the imperial clan was made emperor and forced to accept a Fujiwara girl as his bride. When the emperor reached maturity he was unseated and succeeded by one of his infant children or near relatives, who in turn received a Fujiwara bride.

Displacement of the Fujiwara. As the Fujiwara regents usually named only their own clansmen to important state offices, great resentment grew among the leaders of the other clans. While provincial clans were increasing in power, the Fujiwara were succumbing to court luxuries. Finally, the Minamoto and the Taira, both branches of the imperial clan, began to challenge the Fujiwara. The central government gradually lost strength, and the feudal lords became almost independent. The

Taira and Minamoto fell to battling between themselves for supremacy. Although for a few years the Taira gained control of the emperor, in 1185 the Minamoto destroyed Taira power and took over the direction of government. The Minamoto chief took the title of Sei-i-tai Shogun (barbarian-defeating great general) and so founded the first shogunate or military dictatorship.

Culture in the Heian Era. During the ninth and tenth centuries, life at the Japanese court reached extremes of luxury and dilettantism rarely equalled in any age. Spending became a highly competitive art, and among the chief pastimes were poetry-writing contests. Not only did the court produce a tremendous volume of fine poetry, but also much excellent prose, most famous of which is *Genji Monogatori (The Tale of Genji)*. Music, dancing, painting, landscape gardening, and perfume smelling were also assiduously cultivated by the frivolous courtiers. The country as a whole, however, remained little influenced by the court life.

AGE OF THE FEUDAL BARONS

Kamakura Shogunate (1185 - 1333). The new government was called the Kamakura shogunate because the shogun's capital was at Kamakura, although the imperial capital remained at Kyoto. Under the shogunate, the emperor continued to be selected from the imperial line, but any emperor who attempted to rule as well as to reign was quickly replaced by a less ambitious relative.

GOVERNMENT BY INDIRECTION. The shogunate became an office hereditary in the line of the Minamoto chieftains. However, the shogun ruled only as long as his power was respected by the other war lords. Yoritomo, the first Kamakura shogun, was a strong ruler, but his son was not able to control the other powerful families. As a result, the shogunate fell under the domination of the leaders of the Hojo clan, who acted as regents for the incapable shoguns, who in turn were dictators controlling the emperor. Thus we have in effect a dictator who dictates to the dictator who rules for the emperor. While this was a complicated system, the Hojos gave Japan better government than it had seen for centuries, and in addition, it repelled two large-scale seaborne invasions of the Mongols in the thirteenth century.

Ashikaga Period (1336-1568). The struggle against the Mongols so weakened the Hojo clan that a revolt in 1333 brought the Kamakura shogunate to an end. The Ashikaga period which followed was an era of unbridled feudalism. The Ashikaga were never able to attain complete domination of Japan, and during the latter years of their rule they were almost as helpless as the emperor. The neglected emperors were themselves reduced to extreme poverty.

ASHIKAGA CULTURE. The courts of the Ashikaga shogunate followed the traditions established during the Nara and Heian periods. China continued to dominate Japanese arts. Poetry-writing and incense- and perfume-judging contests were favorite occupations of the courtiers, along with music, dancing, landscape gardening, and flower arrangement. During this period, the tea ceremony was introduced as an important social ritual. The monasteries had by this time also become important centers of culture and learning. Aside from the courts, the monasteries, and the seats of the feudal nobles, however, ignorance and poverty were almost universal.

Oda Nobunaga (1568 - 1582). The anarchy of the late Ashikaga period was terminated by the rise of a military triumvirate led by Oda Nobunaga, a minor feudal lord. By 1568, Nobunaga with the aid of his ally, Tokugawa Ieyasu, and his general, Toyotomi Hideyoshi, gained control of the central government. An effective government was created both by crushing the remaining feudal lords, and by defeating armies of warlike Buddhist monks.

Hideyoshi (1582 - 1598). At the time of his assassination in 1582, Nobunaga had extended his control over more than half of Japan. On his death, Hideyoshi was named kwampaku, or regent, by the helpless emperor. By 1587 the brilliant military leadership of Hideyoshi had broken all resistance.

INVASION OF KOREA. Hideyoshi envisioned the creation of a world empire including Korea, China, the Philippines, and probably India. However, his invasion of Korea in 1592 not only met with stiffer resistance than was expected on land, but also encountered a very strong Korean navy which at this time contained the first iron-clad warship known. In the midst of the war, Hideyoshi died, leaving his power to his son.

TOKUGAWA SHOGUNATE
(1600 - 1868)

Foundation of the Shogunate. Within two years after Hide-yoshi's death, Tokugawa Ieyasu rebelled, and after a great victory was named shogun by the emperor. But Ieyasu had to spend the next 15 years to complete his domination of Japan, and enjoyed peace only the last year of his life.

Tokugawa Wealth. In the process of conquering all Japan, Ieyasu confiscated the lands of the vanquished feudal lords. Even after rewarding his allies, the Tokugawa remained the greatest land holder in Japan.

Tokugawa Rule. The first three Tokugawa shoguns were strong enough to rule Japan personally, but after them, the actual power rested in the institution of the shogunate, which was dominated by a group of subordinate officeholders, rather than in the person of the shogun. We can best understand this form of indirect government by recalling that the family was the basic unit of Japanese society, and that the policy-making body of the family was the family council, although the eldest male might be the nominal head.

HIERARCHY OF RULE. The sequence of the ruling hierarchy of Japan under the Tokugawa can be explained as follows:

1. EMPEROR. The emperor was theoretically the temporal and spiritual ruler of Japan, but since the twelfth century, he had reigned without governing. He maintained a court in seclusion at Kyoto, almost forgotten by his subjects except for the shogun who exercised his power and supported him and his court nobles.

2. SHOGUN. Actual power was in the hands of the shogun, who was in theory named by the emperor, and who received his investiture from the imperial hands.

3. PRIVY COUNCIL AND SAMURAI. The shogun acted through a privy council which had jurisdiction over the feudal aristocracy. Actually the shogun and his privy councilors were often controlled by subordinate officeholders, the business samurai of the Tokugawa clan who were the real administrators.

4. DAIMYOS. Outside the shogun's government at Yedo (Tokoyo), the greatest power in Japan was invested in the daimyos or territorial nobles who ruled the territorial subdivisions

called daimyates. The original daimyos were appointed by the first Tokugawa shoguns, but subsequently these officers became hereditary feudal lords.

5. SAMURAI. The actual administration of the daimyates was handled by retainers of the daimyo, the samurai, who often controlled the daimyos as the shoguns controlled the emperor. The samurai thus were the true governing class of Japan, and they were also the fighting class, comparable to the medieval knights of Europe. However, the Japanese knight often was able to dominate his lord, because he was not only a formidable fighter, but also an educated administrator. This double usefulness made the samurai a highly privileged class by 1853. While the samurai were dependent upon their lords for their livelihood, the daimyo were dependent upon their samurai for their positions and power.

Tokugawa Economy. At the foundation of the Tokugawa shogunate, the Japanese economy was almost totally agrarian. Rice was the unit of exchange and the measure of wealth. The peasant was viewed as a rice-producing machine with no privileges of his own.

DIVERSIFICATION OF THE ECONOMY. The long peace enforced by Tokugawa rule encouraged the development of a money economy despite the shogun's efforts to discourage trade, partly in an effort to make Japan self-sufficient. The encouragement of silk growing developed the silk industry. The importation of the tallow tree from China brought about the foundation of a candle industry. Other industries resulted from the introduction of sugar cane and cotton culture, and the extension of tea cultivation. The new production encouraged manufacture, and increased manufacture stimulated wide-scale exchange of goods, which required money. Money was first imported from China and Korea, but in the seventeenth century a gold mint was established. Ultimately it became permissible to pay taxes in money, and finally even rice sold for currency.

RISE OF INDUSTRIAL CLASS. The increased demands for luxuries, stimulated by the prolonged peace, also encouraged the transition to a money economy. To satisfy the luxury demands, a new merchant and industrial class emerged in the growing towns.

MERGING OF THE CLASSES. Many merchants became wealthier than daimyos, although socially they ranked below the most destitute samurai. In time the merchant families bought their way into the aristocracy by intermarriage or adoption. By 1850, the samurai were much reduced in importance by this upstart business class that was supplanting them as administrators. The transition created social and political tensions that were reaching the breaking point when Perry forced Japan's doors open to trade.

RESULTS OF SOCIAL AND ECONOMIC CHANGE. The rise of the middle class weakened the Tokugawa shogunate. In addition, the tax system, geared to an agrarian economy, could no longer finance the government. The shift from rice to money for payment of taxes worked a hardship on the peasants, who were placed at the mercy of the rice brokers as well as of the feudal lords. This double exploitation, added to a succession of crop failures, caused a series of rural uprisings that further taxed the Tokugawa strength. The general economic dislocation also drove many peasants and samurai into outlawry.

EXCLUSION POLICY. As a result of the disturbances created earlier by disputes among Christian missionaries, the Tokugawa had ordered a rigid policy of exclusion of foreign commerce and influences. The Dutch were the only Europeans permitted to trade with Japan, and then only on a limited scale. While the exclusion policy gave Japan 200 years without foreign war, the governmental machine perfected by the first three Tokugawa shoguns kept internal peace. Tokugawa rule might have continued much longer except for the invasion of foreign warships and foreign ideas.

Revival of Rival Clans. Only by cooperation between several clans could the Tokugawa be overthrown. This possibility had been minimized by keeping each clan isolated by strips of Tokugawa lands. However, while the Tokugawa relaxed in the luxuries of Yedo and allowed their military efficiency to weaken, other clans improved their fighting power.

Revival of Learning. The samurai in time of peace maintained their fighting efficiency by constant practice of warlike games. To lead these warriors into peaceful occupations, the Tokugawa shoguns encouraged scholarly pursuits. As the Confucian classics were believed to be least likely to teach dangerous or revolutionary thoughts, schools of Confucian philosophy were established. But while the Confucian classics taught ethics that helped to pacify the samurai, they also taught the warriors that the highest loyalty was to the emperor and not to the shogun, who theoretically was only an official appointed by the emperor. This conflict of authority led many Japanese to study history and thus to learn that the shogun was an usurper of imperial power. Thus the emperor's prestige was increased, and he became a rallying point for all discontented daimyo and samurai.

Spread of Culture. The rise of the middle class led to the spread of the court culture among the new bourgeoisie. The result was a dilution. Japanese art forms lost some of their delicate refinement in the hands of the business class.

Western Learning. When the eighth shogun repealed the prohibition of foreign books in 1720, Japanese began to study western sciences and learning. Even before 1720, however, a few bold scholars had secretly imported western books.

RELIGIONS OF JAPAN

Buddhism. Buddhism has long been the principal religion of Japan though the rise of Shintoism as an official cult somewhat reduced Buddhist strength. Buddhism, introduced from China or Korea into Japan around 522 A.D., was officially encouraged by the Regent Shotoku Taishi (543-622). Although of foreign origin, Buddhism was greatly modified by the Japanese.

BUDDHIST SECTS. Over the centuries numerous sects were introduced from Korea or China or were created by native Japanese teachers. One of the first sects was Shingon (true word or mystic formula), which emphasized the utility of a beautiful ritual and the efficacy of talismans and charms. Zen Buddhism, introduced from China in the twelfth century, taught that salvation could be achieved only by stoical control of mind and body. This sect was well suited to the samurai, who cultivated military virtues and discipline. Jodo and Shinran Buddhism, founded in the twelfth century, taught that salvation could be granted only by the grace of Buddha, who has compassion for all who call upon him in true faith. Nichiren Buddhism, developed as an offshoot of Jodo, borrowed freely from Confucianism and

Shintoism, despite its extreme intolerance of other Buddhist sects.

Confucianism. Confucianism, first introduced by Shotoku and Kamatari, has never gained real popularity as a religion. But Confucian ethics and principles of human relations have become part of Japanese social order. Its influence is especially evident in the Bushido, or "way of the warrior," the guide for the samurai.

Shinto. Many Confucian elements such as the idea of the natural goodness of man have been absorbed by Japan's indigenous religion, Shinto, "the way of the gods." It was the Japanese religion prior to the introduction of Buddhism and Confucianism. Shinto mythology is incorporated in the *Kojiki* and *Nihongi,* both of which contain myths of the creation of Japan and of the Japanese gods. The earliest handbook of Shinto prayers and rites dates from the tenth century. The chief Shinto gods are the forces of nature, with the sun goddess at the head of the pantheon. In addition are the deified humans, such as great heroes of ancient Japanese history. Modern Shintoism is divided into numerous sects, ranging from the State sect to numerous smaller ones that are in some cases similar to Christian Science and other Protestant religions.

SACRED EMBLEMS. The most sacred objects of Shinto worship are the mirror, the sword, and the jewel which were supposed to have been handed down by the sun goddess to her grandson, Jimmu Tenno, the first emperor. These symbolize purity of soul, valour, and devotion to duty.

REVIVAL OF SHINTO. For a time, Shinto was so intermingled with Buddhism that it almost lost its separate identity. However, the intellectual pursuits during the Tokugawa shogunate revived interest in Shinto as a purely native religion closely connected with the imperial household. Thus the Shinto revival contributed to the restoration of the emperor to temporal and spiritual supremacy.

CHRISTIANITY IN JAPAN

Early Reception of Christianity. Japan was in the last throes of the feudal anarchy of the Ashikaga when the Portuguese accidentally discovered Japan in 1542. During the following 50 years of Portuguese monopoly of trade with the islands, Christianity was introduced and flourished. In 1549, Francis Xavier, with three fellow Jesuits, came to preach. Some of the southern daimyos who were eager for trade encouraged the conversion of their subjects and retainers, sometimes forcibly.

EXPANSION UNDER NOBUNAGA. When Oda Nobunaga was fighting his way to power against feudal lords and armies of Buddhist monks, he found the Christians strong enough to be of aid in suppressing Buddhist opposition to his rule. Under his and the daimyo's favor, the number of Christians increased to 150,000 by 1582.

SUPPRESSION UNDER HIDEYOSHI. Until he completed his conquest of Kyushu, Hideyoshi continued the friendly policy. Then, in 1587 for reasons not definitely known, he suddenly issued an edict accusing the Christian priests of illegal conduct and ordering them to depart on short notice. However, Hideyoshi valued foreign trade too much to enforce his edict strictly. Most of the Jesuits remained, to increase the numbers of converts to 300,000 by 1595.

ARRIVAL OF THE SPANISH. In 1591 when Hideyoshi sent a letter to the Spanish governor of the Philippines demanding submission to Japan's suzerainty, Governor de Marianas used this as a pretext for sending an embassy including Spanish missionaries. These missionaries began preaching in violation of Japanese, papal, and Portuguese orders. Finally the pope lifted his restriction to legalize preaching by non-Jesuit priests.

Tokugawa Opposition. Ieyasu Tokugawa first favored Christianity as a means of encouraging Christian traders. However, he came to suspect the missionaries of being a spearhead of armed invasion by the Spanish or Portuguese, and in 1612 he proscribed Christianity. Again, however, the priests clung on, though enforcement of the proscription was often severe.

GROWTH OF EXCLUSION POLICY. The persistence of the Catholic clergy and their native followers increased the shogun's fears, and in 1624, Ieyasu's son ordered the departure of all Spanish from Japan. Finally, in 1636, the third Tokugawa shogun forbade all Japanese to trade abroad on penalty of death. This edict was to a large degree intended to prevent natives from receiving Christian teaching abroad.

SHIMABARA REVOLT. The bloody persecution of the Christians of southern Japan seems to have been one of the major causes of the Shimabara revolt in 1637. The Dutch, determined to save their own trade at any cost, aided in quelling this revolt.

COMPLETE EXCLUSION. After the Shimabara revolt further edicts in 1638 increased the restrictions and penalties. Foreign trade, except with the Dutch and Chinese, was stopped. Foreign religions were suppressed and foreign books forbidden except for those which the Dutch delivered to the shogun.

DUTCH AT DESHIMA. The Dutch, who had not attempted to mingle trade and religion, continued to do business at Hirado. In 1641, however, their operations were forcibly removed to Deshima, where they traded for two centuries under the most humiliating restrictions. During the period of exclusion, the Dutch colony remained almost the sole link between Japan and the outside world.

BIBLIOGRAPHY

Aston, W. G., *A History of Japanese Literature*, 1933.

Bunce, W. K., ed., *Religions in Japan; Buddhism, Shinto, Christianity*, 1955.

Brinkley, F. R., *A History of the Japanese People*, 1915.

Clement, E. W., *A Short History of Japan*, 1936.

Hara, K., *An Introduction to the History of Japan*, 1936.

Kidder, Jonathan E., *Japan Before Buddhism*, 1959.

Latourette, K. S., *The History of Japan*, 1947.

Murdoch, J., *A History of Japan*, 3 vols., 1949.

Reischauer, E. O., *Japan, Past and Present*, 1956.

Reischauer, E. O., and J. K. Fairbank, *East Asia: The Great Tradition*, 1960.

Reischauer, R. K., *Early Japanese History, c40 B.C.-A.D. 1167*, 2 vols., 1937.

Sansom, G. B., *A History of Japan to 1334*, 1958.

Sansom, G. B., *History of Japan from 1334 to 1615*, 1960.

Sansom, G. B., *Japan; a Short Cultural History*, 1952.

Scherer, J. A. B., *The Romance of Old Japan Through the Ages*, 1934.

Takekoshi, Y., *The Economic Aspects of the History of Civilization in Japan*, 1930.

Tsunoda, R., compiler, *Sources of the Japanese Tradition*, 1958.

CHAPTER 3
Early European Interests in Asia

Through most of China's history, China has needed little from the West, but the West has eagerly sought the products of China.

EARLY EUROPEAN CONTACTS

Han Dynasty Trade. The Romans developed an extensive trade in Chinese goods, particularly silk. Overland routes ran from Ch'ang-an in western China through Lop-nor and the Tarim Basin to Antioch. This trade, however, was controlled by the Parthians, who were hostile to Rome. To by-pass Parthia, Rome developed an important water route to western India, where Chinese goods were received by way of land routes through Khotan or by the sea route from south China.

Rise of Arab Empires. In the sixth century A.D., silk worms were brought to Constantinople, and production of silk in Europe and the Near East diminished western dependence on China. Thereafter, the chief trade with eastern Asia was in spices and other luxury goods. This trade fell almost totally into the hands of the Arabs and their converts to Islam after the eighth century. The Arabs continued to dominate the water routes to eastern Asia until the sixteenth century. The land routes were also largely closed to Europeans until the Mongols conquered Asia from the China Seas to Russia.

Early Christian Missionaries. With the rise of the Mongol empire, Europeans became interested in converting the pagan Mongols to Christianity. It was hoped that the Mongols might thus be used as allies against the Moslems. John of Plano Carpini carried a papal letter to the Jenghis Khan in 1246. In 1249 and 1252, France sent embassies led by Andrew of Longomeau and William of Rubruck. These missions failed to obtain either the conversion of the Mongols or the alliance against the Moslems, but they did increase European interest in the Far East.

Marco Polo. In 1264, two Venetians, Nicolo and Maffeo Polo, found their way to the court of Kublai Khan to request commercial privileges. Kublai sent them back to Europe with a request that the pope send 100 educated missionaries to teach the Mongols. In reply, the pope sent only two faint-hearted Dominican friars, who gave up the journey soon after starting. In 1274 the Polo brothers returned to China with Nicolo's son, Marco. On their return to Europe, after spending 17 years in the service of the Khan, Marco wrote Europe's first detailed study of China.

John of Monte Corvino. In 1289, Rome sent John of Monte Corvino to the Khan. John was so successful in his mission that he was created archbishop of Cambaluc in 1328. When the native Ming dynasty ended Mongol power in 1368, however, they wiped out nearly all traces of the Christian and other alien religious groups the Mongols had fostered.

Cessation of Overland Trade. The fall of the Mongols also ended the extensive silk and spice trade between Europe and China and India. Thereafter Europeans had to depend upon the hostile Moslems to furnish these products. The resulting high prices made many Europeans consider searching for new routes to eastern Asia.

THE PORTUGUESE IN ASIA

Prince Henry, the Navigator. The Portuguese under the leadership of Prince Henry the Navigator (1394 - 1460) made the first serious efforts to find a new route to the East. Prince Henry encouraged the development of superior ships, maps, and nautical instruments. Not until after his death, however, did his work bear full fruit. In 1486 the Portuguese rounded the Cape of Good Hope, and 11 years later Vasco da Gama reached Calicut, India. Meanwhile, Columbus, sailing westward to find the Indies, had secured a claim on the Americas. To prevent disputes between Spain and Portugal, Pope Alexander VI divided the world between them along a line ultimately fixed at 370 leagues west of the Azores. This gave Spain most of the New World, but Portugal received the Indies.

Alfonso de Albuquerque.   Alfonso de Albuquerque spearheaded the Portuguese conquests in India and southeastern Asia that broke the Moslem trade monopoly. By force he established trading posts at Gao and elsewhere on the Malabar Coast of India. Malacca was seized on the Malay Peninsula in 1511 to give Portugal control of trade between China and India. The first trading post in China was established peacefully near Canton in 1515, and in the following year diplomacy opened Siam to the Portuguese. Had they maintained discipline among their own subjects, the Portuguese might have gained a strong position in China. But in 1520, just as Thomas Pirez was traveling to the Chinese court to secure a treaty, some Portuguese adventurers seized a Chinese island off Canton, ignoring Chinese authority there. This incident temporarily ended official trade and diplomacy between the two countries, though the Portuguese illegally retained some island posts.

Japanese Trade.   In 1542 three Portuguese seamen were driven by storms to Japan. So well were they received that the Portuguese were soon trading regularly with the Japanese.

Francis Xavier.   It was the Portuguese who carried the Jesuit missionary, Francis Xavier, on his mission around their commercial empire to India, Malacca, Japan, and finally to China, where he died in 1552.

Resumption of Chinese Trade.   Despite official prohibitions, Portuguese traders established a factory at Ningpo. But again their arrogant defiance of Chinese authority brought trouble. In 1546 the Chinese massacred 800 foreigners and destroyed 35 of their ships at Ningpo. A similar event occurred at Chinchow three years later, and only after paying an indemnity were the Portuguese permitted to return.

Macao.   In reward for their aid in suppressing piracy in the region, the Portuguese in 1557 were permitted to lease land at Macao. Although the Chinese claim they did not relinquish sovereignty there, the Portuguese have ever since claimed Macao as their own. Macao was long the greatest Asiatic port under European domination.

SPANISH ENCROACHMENT IN THE EAST INDIES

Philippine Islands.   Only 10 years after the Portuguese seizure of Malacca, a disgruntled Portuguese captain, Magellan, sailed under the Spanish flag around South America and across the Pacific to the Philippine Islands. Spain had no interest in the backward Philippines or even in China, but she did want a share in the Spice Islands, which Magellan claimed lay within Spain's hemisphere according to the papal line of demarcation. Actually both the Spice Islands and the Philippines were in Portugal's sphere, and the Portuguese frustrated for a time all Spanish efforts to encroach in their zone.

Mexican Dollars at Manila.   Not until 1571 did Spain gain a strong position in the East by seizing the Philippine trading center at Manila. While the Portuguese monopoly had kept Spain out of Japan, China, and the Spice Islands, it could not prevent the natives of these lands from trading their goods for Mexican silver dollars with the Spanish at Manila. By generous trading practices, the Spanish encouraged trade to come to them, and the Mexican silver dollar soon became the most accepted coin even in China, where it is still used today. After Philip II, King of Spain, inherited also the Portuguese crown in 1580, Spain for the first time could legally trade in the oriental ports.

Chinese Massacres in the Philippines.   The Manila trading opportunities soon attracted so heavy a migration of Chinese that the Spanish took alarm. In 1603 a large-scale massacre occurred, and in 1639, the Spanish killed two-thirds of the Chinese colony of over 30,000. As a result, China placed strict limitations upon Spanish traders.

DUTCH ADVANCE IN EASTERN ASIA

Although the Dutch did not gain their independence until late in the sixteenth century, they were before that time encroaching upon the Portuguese monopoly of the Asiatic trade.

Dutch East India Company.   In 1602, after seven years of private trading in Asia, the Dutch East India Company was chartered as a semigovernmental joint-stock corporation. By conquest and intrigue, the Dutch East India Company soon acquired bases in the Moluccas. By 1641 the company had so expanded that the Dutch captured Malacca itself to seal their hold upon their new island empire.

Struggle for Chinese Recognition.   Because of Portuguese opposition, the Dutch were forced to found factories on the

Pescadores Islands off the shore of China. When driven from there, they established themselves on Formosa, where they remained until Ming General Koxinga drove them out in 1662. In retaliation, the Dutch aided the Manchu in their struggle against the Ming. In reward, the Dutch East India Company received permission, along with the English, to trade at Amoy. Not until 1729, however, did the Dutch trade regularly with China.

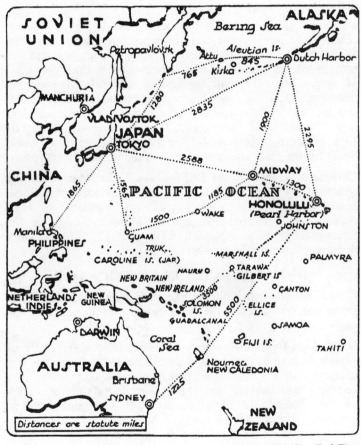

Courtesy of The New York Times

ISLANDS OF THE PACIFIC

Hospitable Reception by Japan.   Better luck attended the Dutch efforts in Japan, where one of their ships was blown by storm in 1600.   Partly because they showed no interest in preaching their religion, the Netherlanders received permission in the following year to establish a factory at Hirado.   Later only the Dutch traders survived Japan's persecution of Christians and the Tokugawa exclusion policy.

Economic Exploitation of the Indies.   The object of Dutch rule in the East Indies was economic exploitation.   Native rulers retained their thrones on the condition that they furnish the East India Company with produce and trade goods as tribute.   In addition, the native rulers were to assure the Dutch a steady supply of island products at prices fixed by the company.   Beyond seeing that peace, order, and production were maintained, the Dutch had little concern for the welfare of their subjects.   Few Dutch came to the East Indies with any intention of staying longer than their contract required.   When they departed, they often left behind a family of half-breed children by temporary native wives.

FRENCH EXPANSION

French East India Company.   French interest in the eastern trade dates from the formation of the French East India Company during the reign of Henry IV; but not until the reign of Louis XIV did the French company become more than a name.   Colbert, Louis' chief minister, advanced the East Indies trade as part of his economic policy for France. The first French factory in India was established at Surat in 1668. However, not until 1674 did the French gain a stronghold at Pondichery.

Missionary Penetration.   French colonial expansion in Asia has often been spearheaded by French Roman Catholic missionaries.   The Jesuit Père Alexander Rhodes was sent by the French to investigate the countries of Indo-China in 1610. Other French Jesuits prepared the way for the unsuccessful early French bids for suzerainty in this area.   In Siam, the French overreached themselves in their zeal and set off a persecution of Christians that in 1688 ended all French influence there.

French Indo-China.   Even in Viet-Nam, where they were

later to establish a protectorate and rule for nearly a century, the French made little headway until the 1800's. In the 17th century, the Portuguese monopolized all trade and diplomatic relations. French trading efforts of 1749-69 failed, and even the early missionaries enjoyed only sporadic success.

RUSSIAN AMBITIONS IN THE EAST

Of all the European countries, Russia was probably best equipped to understand the Far East, for under the Khans Russia had also been part of the Mongol empire.

Eastward Expansion. After Moscow regained its independence in 1480, the Russians began expanding in all directions from Moscow. In the West, their ambition was soon blocked by the European powers, but to the East only the declining Mongols barred the path. During the reign of the first tzar, Ivan IV, Russian power was pushed to the Ob. Much as the American west was won by pioneer settlers, the Russians pushed eastward across Siberia. In 1638 the Amur River was crossed, and by 1652, Cossack raiders began clashing with Chinese forces.

Russian Diplomatic Gains. Russian efforts in 1654 to establish diplomatic and commercial relations with China failed because of Russia's refusal to perform the humiliating kowtow ceremony. After 35 more years of border warfare, peace was restored in 1689 when Russia and China signed the Treaty of Nerchinsk, which defined the border and the terms of trading between Russia and China. This treaty continued in effect with only minor changes until 1858.

TREATY OF KIAKHTA. In the following years, a series of disputes between the two powers over breaches of the treaty caused China to prohibit the trade. In 1720, a diplomatic meeting was made possible by a compromise on the kowtow issue; one of the Chinese emperor's officials kowtowed before the Russian tzar's letter, while the Russian ambassador performed the ceremony before the Chinese ruler. Thus China for the first time recognized a European power on terms approaching equality. The Treaty of Kiakhta (1727) which followed revised the earlier Treaty of Nerchinsk. In addition to clauses regarding the border line and commerce, other important clauses gave the

Russians permission to maintain a church and priests in Peking for the benefit of Russians living in China.

Russo-Chinese Trade. Under the treaty arrangements, an important overland trade developed with its center at the border town of Kiakhta. Russian efforts to enter the sea trade with China met with stubborn refusals from the Chinese government. Finally in 1858, China opened her ports to Russian shipping.

ENGLISH COMMERCIAL AGGRESSION IN EASTERN ASIA

Pioneering of Drake. The first English voyage to eastern Asia was that of Sir Francis Drake in 1577. After visiting California, Drake crossed the Pacific to the Philippines. In the Moluccas he traded stolen Spanish silver for spices before returning to England around South Africa. Drake's feat was repeated six years later by Cavendish, but not until 1591-1594 was the first English trading expedition sent specifically to the East Indies. Only one of the three vessels returned, and for the next few years, the English found plundering the Spanish treasure ships more profitable than independent trading.

English East India Company. In 1601, a group of London merchants received a charter for the East India Company, which was to trade in those parts of the Indies not under European control. This company enjoyed 258 years of continuous expansion in eastern Asia and became the ruler of many times more people than inhabited the British Isles. Profits from some of the early voyages ran over 200 per cent. The first voyages of company ships were exploratory trading missions to the Red Sea, the Persian Gulf, and the East Indies. In 1612 permanent trading posts were set up in India.

Less Successful Commercial Ventures. The pilot of the first Dutch ship to Japan in 1600 had been an Englishman, Will Adams. Adams had become a favorite of the shogun and had gained permission for the English to open a factory and trade in Japan. Because the site for the factory was badly chosen, this venture proved unprofitable, and after ten years the English withdrew from Japan. Diplomacy gave the English a trading post at Patani in Siam, but this venture likewise was unsuccessful. Because of strong Dutch opposition, English efforts, during the 17th century, to share in the lucrative spice trade of the East Indies also proved futile.

Trade with China. The more profitable trade with India kept the English from striking at the Portuguese monopoly of the China trade until 1637. The venture of that year failed, and it was 1699 before regular trade with China and England was inaugurated.

Southeast Asia. With regular trade established between China and India, the British looked with concern at the Dutch control of the Straits of Malacca. In 1786 the British obtained the Island of Penang off the Malay Peninsula from a native prince. Penang became the most important English naval outpost in southeastern Asia until the acquisition of Singapore.

AMERICAN TRADE WITH CHINA

No sooner had the American colonies thrown off British rule than the first Yankee ships entered Canton.

Growth of the Trade. The first American ship to sail to China was the clipper, *Empress of China,* in 1785. It had no difficulty in exchanging its cargo for silk and tea. American traders soon became the chief rivals of the English in China. Although the American clippers were smaller, they were faster than the English ships.

Triangular Trade Route. American trade with China was handicapped by lack of the capital and governmental support enjoyed by British traders. Another serious obstacle was the lack of suitable trade goods until it was discovered that the Chinese would pay high prices for fur. Thereafter a three-cornered trade developed. Clippers carried cargoes of rum, beads, and hardware to the Pacific coast, where they were traded for furs. The furs were exchanged in China for silk, tea, porcelain, and furniture which sold at a good profit in America. Other voyages involved stops at African ports on the route to China.

BIBLIOGRAPHY

Abbott, W. C., *The Expansion of Europe*, 2 vols., 1918.

Backer, J. N. L., *History of Geography and Exploration*, 1932.

Beaglehole, J. C., *The Exploration of the Pacific*, 1932.

Boxer, C. R., *Fidalgos in the Far East, 1550-1770*, 1948.

Butterworth, H., *The Story of Magellan*, 1924.

Dallin, D. J., *The Rise of Russia in Asia*, 1949.

Edwardes, M., *Asia in the European Age, 1498-1955*, 1962.

Gilespie, J. E., *A History of Geographical Discovery*, 1933.

Hall, D. G. E., *A History of South-East Asia*, 1955.

Hudson, G. F., *Europe and China, a Survey . . . from Earliest Times to 1800*, 1931.

Kingsley, G. J., *Vasco da Gama and His Successors, 1460-1580*, 1910.

Latourette, K. S., *Development of China*, 1946.

Latourette, K. S., *A History of the Expansion of Christianity*, 1944.

Lattimore, O., *Inner Asian Frontiers*, 1951.

Lin, Y. T., *Imperial Peking; Seven Centuries of China*, 1961.

Lobanov, A., *Russia and Asia*, 1933.

Merriman, R. B., *The Rise of the Spanish Empire*, 4 vols., 1918-34.

Moule, A. C., *Christians in China Before the Year 1550*, 1930.

Phelan, J. L., *The Hispanization of the Philippines*, 1959.

Prestage, E., *The Portuguese Pioneers*, 1934.

Reischauer, E. O., and J. K. Fairbank, *East Asia: the Great Tradition*, 1960.

Ricci, A., *The Travels of Marco Polo*, 1931.

Vandenbusch, A., *The Dutch East Indies*, 1942.

Wright, A., *Early English Adventurers in the East*, 1917.

CHAPTER 4
East and West Meet in China

INTERNAL DEVELOPMENTS IN MANCHU CHINA
TO 1840

Manchu Government. The Manchus sought to govern China as Chinese rulers, and at the same time to maintain their own identity as Manchus. Chinese officials and Chinese institutions were retained although Manchus headed the chief government offices. The civil service and examination systems were continued with but little disruption.

MANCHU GARRISONS. To maintain their control, garrisons of Manchu troops were stationed in the chief cities. These forces were under the control of Manchu viceroys and were in addition to the regular provincial forces composed of Chinese.

Shun Chih (1644-1662). The first Manchu to sit upon the dragon throne at Peking was Shun Chih, a nine-year-old boy, who succeeded to the Manchu rule prior to the capture of Peking. The 17 years of his reign were spent in rounding out the conquest of China proper and in organizing the government.

K'ang Hsi (1662-1723). Shun Chih's son, who was only eight years old when he began his reign as the K'ang Hsi emperor, became one of the most able Chinese rulers. He excelled as a general, scholar, and administrator. He not only crushed a serious revolt against his throne, but also expanded his empire to include Mongolia, Tibet, and Formosa. K'ang Hsi encouraged the introduction of European science and, for a time, reopened China's ports to world trade. Educated missionaries were welcomed to his court. However, K'ang Hsi viewed a missionary appeal to the pope to solve a theological controversy as a subversion of his own authority, and became hostile to Christianity. Ultimately, he restricted not only missionary activities, but also trade with the West.

Yung Cheng (1723-1735). K'ang Hsi's successor, an able but less tolerant ruler, began a persecution of Christians in China. Moreover, he engaged in costly wars to maintain the conquests of his predecessor.

MAXIMUM TERRITORIAL CLAIMS OF
MANCHU DYNASTY

Ch'ien Lung (1736-1796). The sixty-year reign of Ch'ien Lung saw the greatest extension of China's boundaries. Mongolia and Tibet were brought more completely under Chinese domination, and Sinkiang was added. Burma, Annam, and Nepal acknowledged Chinese suzerainty, along with Korea and the Liuchius. Ch'ien Lung's scholastic interests led him to foster learning as well as to write numerous books himself.

BEGINNING OF DECLINE. Ch'ien Lung's reign saw a great increase in Chinese prosperity and population. But in his later years, Ch'ien Lung permitted the government to slip from his grasp, with the result that political corruption increased and rebellions broke out. His reign marks the zenith and the beginning of the decline of Manchu power, for no able Manchu ruler succeeded him.

Chia Ch'ing (1796-1821) and **Tao Kuang** (1821-1850). The next two reigns were inglorious years of increasing corruption and declining power for the Manchu dynasty. Revolts increased in number and destructiveness. Piracy and brigandage reached dangerous proportions. Foreign relations were marked by arrogant refusal to trade with the foreigners or to accept foreign learning.

Cultural Developments. Under the early great Manchu emperors, the Ming cultural traditions were continued almost unbroken. Little outstanding genius was shown, but much ingenuity was displayed in imitating traditional models. In volume, literary production was enormous. The most original literary products were the numerous novels such as *Ching P'ing Mei (The Golden Lotus)* and *Hung Lou Meng (Dream of the Red Chamber)*.

BEGINNING OF FOREIGN TRADE AT CANTON

Importance of Canton. Since early times, Canton's favorable position made it one of China's most important trading centers. Here the goods of the world were traded for Chinese products. Hindus handled the China trade for centuries before the rise of Islam made the Moslems the chief traders of the Asiatic world.

Arrival of Europeans. In the seventeenth century, the Canton trade became a Portuguese monopoly until the English received permission to establish a factory in 1684. By 1700, Spain, Holland, and France also came to share the Canton trade, but the British carried on by far the largest trade in Canton.

Chinese Supervision. The Manchu government placed Kwangtung and Kwangsi under a governor general who maintained his headquarters at Canton. Due to the important foreign trade there, it was also found expedient to appoint an imperial high commissioner to supervise all relations with the foreigners and to prevent them from seeking direct diplomatic relations with Peking. Later in 1702, a special superintendent of customs, whom the foreigners called the hoppo, was made the sole agent to deal with foreign trade.

Co-hong System. As foreign commerce became too great for one man to handle, the hoppo permitted other Chinese merchants to share in it. These merchants formed a guild, the Co-hong, to avoid bidding against each other for foreign products. The Co-hong was officially chartered to maintain a monopoly of foreign trade.

OPERATION OF THE CO-HONG. This tight monopoly worked so to the advantage of the Chinese that there were many complaints from the foreigners, whose commercial activities were closely restricted. Each foreign merchant fell under the jurisdiction of one of the hong merchants, who would supervise the payments of duties as well as handle the sale of the cargo and the purchase of Chinese produce for the return voyage. Duties were often charged on unsold goods. However, as the Co-hong was the only means of communication with higher Chinese officials, complaints against it were futile. Despite the many objections of the foreigners, the Co-hong system operated with little interruption until 1842.

Restrictions on Foreigners. The Chinese made every effort to prevent the unwanted foreigners from staying in China. Foreign women could not visit Chinese soil. The merchants were permitted to live only in the narrow confines of their factories, and were expected to depart when the monsoon winds shifted to the southeast.

CAUSES OF OPIUM WAR

When peoples of two widely different cultures come into close and continual contact, some conflict is almost inevitable. In the relations between the Chinese and the Europeans, there were a number of important points of difference.

Chinese Sense of Superiority. China throughout her history had been the "Central Kingdom." She was the center of a great economic and cultural orbit and looked upon the surrounding nations as tributary vassals. The European state system in modern times developed the concept of legal equality between all nations, but the Chinese continued to treat all foreigners as politically and culturally inferior.

Anglo-Chinese Diplomacy. At first the British East India Company carried on the Canton trade without diplomatic relations between China and England. The first regular English mission sent to China was the Cathcart embassy of 1787, but the death of Cathcart ended this mission prematurely. In 1793, a second ambassador, Lord Macartney, was received by the Ch'ien Lung emperor without performing the humiliating kowtow, but his mission accomplished nothing.

AMHERST MISSION. In 1816, after Napoleon's defeat, the British sent Lord Amherst as a special ambassador to attempt to improve trade relations. The British hoped to have the trade placed directly under the emperor's protection and to establish an embassy in Peking. When Lord Amherst refused to perform the kowtow or to be bullied into a hasty audience without credentials, the embassy was ordered to leave China.

LORD NAPIER. Despite diplomatic failures and many annoyances, the British East India Company continued to trade in China until its monopoly ended in 1833. At that time England appointed Lord Napier as superintendent of trade in Canton. When he attempted to establish direct relations with the imperial commissioner at Canton, he was rebuffed. He was told not only to communicate through the Co-hong merchants, but also to send his message as a petition from an inferior to a superior. After Lord Napier's death in 1834, his successors tried to carry out a conciliatory policy.

Legal Jurisdiction. Another important source of friction was the difference between the oriental and occidental concepts of justice. European nations in the early nineteenth century still had harsh laws, but they did not operate on "an eye for an eye" basis as did oriental laws. In China, accidental homicide was punishable with death as surely as deliberate murder. Chinese officials, held responsible for obtaining a conviction for every crime, were not always particular who was convicted. The legal differences were aggravated by the fact that Europeans engaging in the China trade were often rough and lawless. The result was a series of crises. In 1780, a French sailor was executed for murder though he had acted in self-defense. In 1784, the Chinese forced the British to turn over for execution a British sailor who had accidentally killed two Chinese women. This event caused the British to send the Cathcart mission.

TERRANOVA AFFAIR. In 1821, Terranova, an Italian sailor on an American ship, became involved in the murder of a Chinese woman. Again, the Chinese forced the surrender of the sailor by the American consul though the man was believed to be innocent. This case increased foreign demand for the right of extraterritoriality (the right to be tried by their own laws and legal methods on Chinese soil).

Co-hong Abuses. By the 1830's, foreign trade had grown to large proportions, yet it was still monopolized by a few Chinese merchants. Not only were the foreigners at the mercy of the Co-hong merchants as to prices, but frequently the Chinese merchants delayed in paying their debts, with the foreigners having no redress.

Opium. Perhaps the chief cause of open conflict between China and Great Britain was the opium trade. After the introduction of opium smoking by European sailors in the seventeenth century, the habit spread rapidly through China with most unfortunate results . An imperial prohibition of opium importation issued in 1729 proved ineffective because the trade was so profitable that foreigners could easily bribe Chinese officials to permit smuggling.

BALANCE OF TRADE. The large demand for opium solved the British problem of finding goods the Chinese would buy. Previously every cargo to China had included silver and gold to help pay for Chinese products. With the spread of the opium habit in China, this balance of trade was reversed in favor of the British. In a few years, so much silver was pouring out of the country that the Chinese economy was badly upset.

EFFORTS AT CONTROL. The British East India Company, which controlled the source of the opium in India, had a natural monopoly which it exploited indirectly, by licensing free-lance British traders to handle the smuggling trade. A second Manchu prohibition in 1799 was no more effective than the first, and by 1833, the opium smuggling trade had reached an annual value of $15 million. Not until 1839 was any serious effort made by the Chinese to stop this demoralizing traffic, and these efforts set off the first shots of the "Opium War."

FIRST ANGLO-CHINESE WAR AND ITS RESULTS

Chinese Justification. From the Chinese viewpoint, opium was the only cause of the conflict with Britain. As a point of fact, the immediate cause of war was the effort by the Chinese to prohibit importation of opium as a moral and economic evil.

Commissioner Lin. To solve the opium problem, some Chinese officials advised legalizing the traffic in order to collect revenues from it. Others who wished it suppressed on moral grounds prevailed, and Lin Tse-hsü, who had proved his ability to stop the opium trade elsewhere, arrived in Canton in March, 1839, with special powers to suppress the traffic. Lin promptly ordered all foreigners to surrender the opium in their possession and to sign bonds not to engage in the trade on penalty of death. By a show of force, Lin compelled the surrender of $6 million worth of opium, which to the surprise of the foreigners was destroyed.

Legal Jurisdiction. Having received the opium, Lin withdrew his troops, announcing cessation of trade until the bonds were given. All but the English agreed; Captain Elliot, British superintendent of trade, was determined not to submit, and ordered the English merchants to leave Canton. For a time thereafter British trade moved into Canton in American and other non-British ships. On July 7, however, some British sailors became involved in a riot that cost one Chinese life, thus stirring up the old problem of legal jurisdiction. When Captain Elliot refused to surrender the British sailors, who had already been punished by English law, Lin cut off British food supplies at Hong Kong and Macao. After weeks of negotiation, firing began between Chinese naval junks and British warships on November 3. The Opium War had broken out.

British Aggressive Action. At this time the British offered their terms for peace, demanding (1) payment for the opium destroyed, (2) proper treatment of British officials in accordance with (western) international law, and (3) cession of an island off the coast of China to provide greater security for British merchants and their trade.

BOMBARDMENT OF CANTON. When these terms were refused, the British blockaded Canton; and when this coercion failed, they bombarded the city in January, 1841. The Canton officials offered terms, but the first treaty drawn up was rejected by both governments. In the following May, the British accepted $6 million ransom for the helpless city.

LEADERSHIP OF SIR HENRY POTTINGER. On the arrival of reinforcements under Sir Henry Pottinger, the British carried the war northward, until Nanking lay at the mercy of British guns. So futile had Chinese resistance been against the small British forces that the Chinese government capitulated and on August 29, 1842, signed the first of a long series of unequal treaties that were to nibble away much of Chinese sovereignty.

Terms of Peace. The Treaty of Nanking opened Canton, Amoy, Foochow, Ningpo, and Shanghai to foreign trade. At these ports, British consuls could be stationed and British merchants could lease land for residential and business uses. Hong Kong was ceded to the British in perpetuity. The Co-hong was abolished and the British were free to trade with any Chinese merchants they chose. China was required to pay an indemnity of $21 million, including $6 million for the confiscated opium, $3 million for overdue Co-hong debts, and the remainder to cover British war costs. Correspondence between British and Chinese officials was thereafter to be expressed in terms of equality. China agreed to a uniform *ad valorem* tariff, not to be changed except by mutual consent. In the supplementary Treaty of the Bogue in the following year, China granted extra-territoriality in criminal cases and included a most-favored-nation clause, which assured Britain any additional privileges China might grant other powers in the future.

Treaty of Wanghia. The new British status induced the other western nations to seek treaty relations. In 1844, Caleb Cushing was sent to open treaty relations between the United States and China. After two months of Chinese delaying tactics, Cushing secured the Treaty of Wanghia on July 3, 1844. This treaty included most of the terms of the two British treaties, but it was superior in its clearer statements and in its extension of extraterritoriality to include civil as well as criminal cases.

French Treaty. The French treaty of 1844 was important primarily for its religious implications. The French assertion of a protectorate over Roman Catholics brought the legalization of Roman Catholicism for foreigners and natives alike, and Roman Catholic property seized in 1724 was restored. As a result of these concessions, all foreign religions were granted limited toleration in 1849.

Growth of Shanghai. Of the five treaty ports only Canton and Shanghai proved to be of great value. Located near the mouth of the great Yangtze Kiang, Shanghai was ideally situated to exploit the resources of that great river valley. As the city had not developed an antiforeign attitude, the foreigners enjoyed full Chinese cooperation in developing the port facilities and in providing adequate space for foreign settlements.

TAIPING REBELLION

One of the indirect results of the increased foreign contacts was the great Taiping Rebellion, which was probably the most destructive rebellion of all times.

Causes of Taiping Rebellion. The Taiping Rebellion was a complicated social phenomena. It was at the same time a revolt of a persecuted minority, an agrarian uprising, an outburst of a new religion, an antidynastic revolution, and a series of bandit and pirate raids. The chief cause, however, was probably the discontent among the peasant class against a corrupt officialdom.

Hung Hsiu-ch'uan. The leader of the rebellion was a village school teacher, Hung Hsiu-ch'uan, who after failing in the civil service examinations, had received in 1833 some Protestant religious tracts. In an illness that followed, Hung had a series of visions for which he found explanation only in the Christian pamphlets. Hung finally concluded that he was the younger brother of Christ, sent with a new Christian revelation to reclaim an erring world. After receiving further religious instruction from an American Baptist missionary, Issacher Roberts, the Chinese prophet developed a large following among the discontented peasants of Kwangsi Province.

Initial Military Action. After being outlawed by the Kwangsi authorities, Hung Hsiu-ch'uan began in 1851 a full-scale rebellion against the Manchu government. With his few thousand followers, he moved north to the Yangtze Kiang, increasing his forces as he marched. The Manchu Banner armies and provincial levies proved useless against the fanatical Taipings. After taking Changsha and Wuchang, the Taiping forces sailed down the Yangtze to Nanking, where they slaughtered 20,000 Manchu to take the city for their capital.

NORTHWARD EXPANSION. While Hung Hsiu-ch'uan remained at Nanking to organize his government and religion, other Taiping armies marched through north China until they met with defeat near Peking at the hands of Mongol tribesmen to whom the Manchu had turned for aid.

Taiping Government. Prior to the seizure of Nanking, Hung had proclaimed himself emperor of the Taiping T'ien Kuo, or heavenly kingdom of great peace. At Nanking other leaders assumed active rule over the Taiping empire, while Hung concentrated on religious studies and writings. Although constant warfare prevented all the theories from being put into practice, the Taiping objective was to create a semicommunistic theocracy. Its chief aims were (1) to destroy the Manchu and set up a native dynasty under Hung, who was ordained by the God Jehovah to rule China and the world, and (2) to carry out the doctrine of the brotherhood of man by a redistribution of wealth and equal division of land. The early effectiveness of the Taiping government is evidenced by the discipline of its armies that made them superior to all Chinese forces opposing them.

Taiping Religion. The Taiping religion was essentially Protestant Christianity with a considerable infusion of Confucian, Buddhist, and Taoist ceremonials. The Taipings had a form of baptism but misunderstood the nature of the Lord's Supper. Their violent opposition to religious images caused them to destroy images and idols wherever they were found in Buddhist temples or Catholic churches. The Ten Commandments were recited on regular state occasions and they worshipped Jesus as the superior celestial elder brother of Hung Hsiu-ch'uan. Like the Moslems they believed that those who died fighting for the faith were promised immediate translation to heaven.

FAILURE OF FOREIGN MISSIONARIES. Of all the millions of Taipings, only Hung and one other had received any formal Christian instruction; consequently doctrinal errors were inevitable. Shocked by Hung's pretensions and errors, the foreign missionaries failed to give the Taipings religious aid. Only Roberts, who had first taught Hung in Canton, made any prolonged attempt to give them further religious instruction. However, he did not go to Nanking until the Taiping doctrines were so thoroughly formulated that his efforts were a tragic failure.

Continuation of Conflict. Despite Hung's preoccupation with religion, the Taiping forces were strong and active. The Manchu forces succeeded in placing Nanking under a partial blockade, but elsewhere the Taiping armies raided Honan, Anhui, and Kiangsi provinces. Some cities changed hands as many as six times in three years, with great destruction each time. The only serious resistance offered to the Taipings was by the "Hunan Braves," a volunteer force led by the retired scholar Tseng Kuo-fan.

TRIADS AT SHANGHAI. Also fighting the Manchu were irregular forces not connected with the Taiping movement. In 1853, Shanghai fell to such a force led by the secret society known as the Triads. The Triads held the foreign section of the city until forced to evacuate by foreign pressure.

Peak of Taiping Power. In June, 1856, under new, vigorous leadership, the Taipings drove the Manchu forces from the Nanking area. Had there been a unified command among the rebels, the imperial cause would have been lost. At this moment, however, dissension arose in the Taiping ranks that resulted in the massacre of some of the ablest leaders. The rebellion might have collapsed then except for the ferocity displayed by the Manchu forces against all even suspected Taipings. Only the interruption of the Arrow War prevented the reconquest of all the rebel territory. This diversion gave the Taiping time to reorganize and regain their strength. In 1860, a new group of Taiping leaders emerged to renew the aggressive.

ARROW WAR AND TREATY REVISION

Continuation of Friction. The signing of the treaties of 1842-1847 did not eliminate all difficulties between the Chinese and the foreigners. The Chinese felt the treaties had granted too many privileges, and constantly evaded the fulfillment of the treaty obligations. The foreigners, not satisfied with the concessions, pressed for more privileges.

CANTON—SITE OF UNREST. The focal point of much of the friction was antiforeign Canton. The antiforeign sentiment was fostered by the mandarins, who used it as a pretext for refusing to comply with treaty provisions to open the city to foreign trade. The Canton High Commissioner of foreign affairs, Yeh, who represented the worst side of the Chinese official class, repeatedly eluded all contact with the foreign diplomats, despite the growing storm.

WESTERN TRANSGRESSION. On their part, the foreigners frequently abused or overstepped their treaty rights. The opium trade, which had been ignored by the treaties, trebled in volume in 15 years, and a new illicit coolie traffic sprang up at Amoy. All treaty nations used their right of extraterritoriality freely, but all except the British failed to accept the responsibilities those rights involved. Pirates, opium smugglers, and coolie traders frequently used the foreign flags to protect their operations, and the convoy blackmail system flourished under the same protection.

Incentive for Armed Conflict. With the accumulation of so many grievances on both sides, only a spark was needed to set off another armed conflict. The British might have hesitated to act alone, but the Chinese provided an ally by arousing the antipathy of France. In 1853, Abbé Chapdelaine, a French Catholic missionary, violated the treaty provisions by opening a mission in Kiangsi Province outside of the treaty port limits. After three years of peaceful preaching, the abbé and his followers were arrested and executed as rebels and violators of the law. Napoleon III of France, seeking glory for his new crown, seized this opportunity to join England in action against China.

LORCHA ARROW INCIDENT. The affair which touched off British action was an outcome of the custom of permitting Chinese ships to use British registry. Pirates and blackmailing convoyers were more likely to respect a foreign flag; consequently, many Chinese shipowners had sought this form of protection for both legitimate and illegitimate activities. In 1856 Commissioner Yeh sent officials aboard the *Lorcha Arrow,* flying the British flag, on grounds that it harbored a pirate. The British flag was insulted and the Chinese crew imprisoned. British demands for release of the crew and for an apology were ignored.

Progress of Arrow War. Upon receiving official sanction from London, the British naval forces seized the forts defending Canton and bombarded the headquarters of Commissioner Yeh. Still no apology came, and when the British withdrew after merely breaching the city wall, Commissioner Yeh reported a brilliant Chinese victory to Peking.

CAPTURE OF YEH. The British reinforcements being sent to China under Lord Elgin were delayed until 1857 by the sepoy uprising in India; consequently only sporadic naval fighting took place until Elgin's arrival. Beginning on Christmas day in 1857, the conflict was renewed by the bombardment and capture of Canton. Commissioner Yeh, who was seized while escaping, died a prisoner the following year in India.

SEIZURE OF THE TAKU FORTS. Next the British and French carried the war to the port nearest Peking. The Taku forts, which the Chinese considered impregnable defenses for the mouth of the Pei Ho, fell such easy prey to the western guns that the Chinese quickly came to terms.

Treaties of Tientsin (1858). At Tientsin, China signed new treaties with the western powers. The United States and Russia, while not engaged in the conflict, had sent their diplomats to share in the fruits of victory. By these treaties, which all shared because of the most-favored-nation clauses, (1) the treaty powers gained the right for their ambassadors to be received in Peking on the basis of state equality without performing the kowtow; (2) foreigners were permitted to trade at a number of additional treaty ports including several up the Yangtze River and in the interior; (3) extraterritoriality was redefined and extended; (4) toleration was granted to Christianity; (5) definite provisions for treaty revisions were made; (6) the opium trade was legalized.

Renewal of War. Immediately, the Chinese recommenced evasion of treaty commitments and delayed the formal ratification by Peking required in the treaties. After the Chinese had made obvious their intentions by heavily fortifying the mouth of the Pei Ho, the Anglo-French forces renewed the attack. A first attempt to go up the river was repelled by the Chinese, but in the following year a joint expeditionary force of 20,000 men took the forts and moved up to Tientsin.

FALL OF PEKING. Now determined to achieve a full victory, Lord Elgin sent Chinese negotiators back to the emperor with an ultimatum, and ordered his forces to move toward Peking. Next, the Chinese reopened negotiations, only to seize treacherously a British emissary, Harry Parks. While Parks himself was unharmed, 18 of his staff were tortured to death. In retaliation for this outrage the British and French destroyed the emperor's summer palace at Peking. The dissolute emperor fled to Jehol, leaving his brother, Prince Kung, to deal with the foreigners.

Peking Conventions (1860). Prince Kung sensibly concluded a new series of agreements, called the Peking Convention, with the foreigners. These agreements (1) assured the foreign ambassadors the right of residence at Peking, (2) added Kowloon to the British base at Hong Kong, (3) opened Tientsin as a treaty port, (4) legalized the coolie traffic, and (5) restored all Catholic properties seized since 1724.

Russian Diplomacy. Russia, after sharing the Anglo-French gains of 1858, pretended friendship for China. While the British and French renewed the attack, the Russians offered advice to the Chinese. After the conclusion of the Peking Convention, however, Russia requested and received her reward from helpless China. In November, 1860, China transferred to Russia the maritime province of Northern Manchuria and granted Russia extensive trading privileges. Britain and France won the war, but Russia won the peace.

BIBLIOGRAPHY

Abend, H., *Treaty Ports*, 1944.

Bau, M. C. J., *The Foreign Relations of China*, 1922.

Beckmann, G. M., *The Modernization of China and Japan*, 1962.

Clark, A. H., *The Clipper Ship Era . . . 1843-1869*, 1910.

Costin, W. C., *Great Britain and China, 1833-1860*, 1937.

Dennett, T., *Americans in Eastern Asia*, 1922 (reprinted 1963).

Dulles, F. R., *The Old China Trade*, 1930.

Dulles, F. R., *China and America*, 1946.

Edwardes, M., *Asia in the European Age, 1489-1955*, 1962.

Fairbank, J. K., *The United States and China*, 1958.

Fairbank, J. K., *Trade and Diplomacy on the China Coast*, 1954.

Feuerwerker, A., *China's Early Industrialization*, 1958.

Gowen, H., and J. H. Hall, *An Outline History of China*, 1926.

Hsieh, P. C., *The Government of China, 1644-1911*, 1925.

Hummel, A. W., *Eminent Chinese of the Ch'ing Period*, 2 vols., 1943.

Kuo, P. C., *A Critical Study of the First Anglo-Chinese War*, 1935.

Latourette, K. S., *Development of China*, 1946.

Latourette, K. S., *The History of the Early Relations Between the United States and China, 1784-1844*, 1917.

Li, C. (tr. by Teng Ssu and J. Ingalls), *The Political History of China 1840-1928*, 1956.

Meadows, T., *The Chinese and Their Rebellions*, 1954.

Morse, H. B., *The International Relations of the Chinese Empire*, Vol. 1, 1913.

Pritchard, E. N., *Anglo-Chinese Relations During the Seventeenth and Eighteenth Centuries*, 1929.

Soothill, W. E., *China and the West*, 1925.

Teng, S., and J. K. Fairbank, *China's Response to the West*, 2 vols., 1954.

Waley, A., *The Opium War Through Chinese Eyes*, 1958.

Willoughby, W. W., *Foreign Rights and Interests in China*, 1927.

CHAPTER 5
Declining China (1860-1894)

After the defeats and humiliating forced treaties of 1858-1860, the Manchu dynasty was weakened and discredited. During the ensuing years, the land was plagued internally with rebellions, brigandage, floods, and pestilence. Externally, China struggled to maintain herself against increased foreign encroachment.

POLITICAL DEVELOPMENTS

Coup d'État of Tz'u Hsi. When the Hsien Feng emperor died in August 1861, the throne passed to his five-year-old son, whose mother was the concubine Yehonala. By Hsien Feng's will, control was vested in three regents, while Yehonala received the title of Tz'u Hsi as junior dowager empress. The clever and dominating Tz'u Hsi quickly joined forces with Prince Kung, brother of the late emperor, to crush the regents. By the end of 1861, she had secured her control of the throne, easily dominating the other two new regents, the senior dowager, Tz'u An, and Prince Kung.

Government under Tz'u Hsi (1861-1873). Tz'u Hsi (Old Buddha) was reactionary, antiforeign, and violently opposed to any western innovations. Court eunuchs increased in power and intrigue, and bribery dominated appointment of officials. The Foreign Office, or Tsungli Yamen, established as a result of the Tientsin Treaties, was the one place in the government where able officials were found. Such able men as Tseng Kuo-fan, Li Hung-chang, and Chang Chih-tung helped to make China's foreign policy as well as to encourage internal reforms.

MAJORITY OF THE T'UNG-CHIH EMPEROR (1783-1875). Although the young emperor officially attained his majority in

1873, he remained under the control of his mother, Tz'u Hsi; hence the two years he ruled until his death in 1875 meant no real change in government.

THE KUANG-HSÜ EMPEROR (1875-1908). When the T'ung-chih emperor died without heirs, Tz'u Hsi secured the selection of her infant nephew as the Kuang-hsü emperor. Despite the opposition of Prince Kung and others, Old Buddha retained control of the throne.

LOSS OF TERRITORY. In the long regency of Tz'u Hsi, China lost her vassal states of Burma and Indo-China to England and France, while her control over Sinkiang and Outer Mongolia was weakened.

Failure of the Kuang-Hsü Emperor. Rule of this reduced China was taken over by the Kuang-hsü emperor in 1889. Until the disastrous Sino-Japanese War, however, he brought no improvement in China's government. The humiliation resulting from the war moved him to collaborate with the liberals at the court to hastily attempt a series of drastic reforms in 1898. When these reforms failed, Tz'u Hsi and the reactionaries returned to power.

INTERNAL DISASTERS

Final Years of the Taiping Rebellion (1860-1865). The treaties of Tientsin (1858-1860) called for the opening of the Yangtze River to trade after the Taiping Rebellion had been crushed. This naturally gave the foreigners an interest in ending the revolt. Regular British and French forces began to cooperate with the Manchu in driving the Taiping from the port areas, and additional aid in supplies was contributed to the Chinese armies.

THE EVER-VICTORIOUS ARMY. In 1860, an American, Frederic Ward, amassed a mixed Filipino and occidental group of mercenaries to aid the imperialists. After achieving several victories, Ward's "Ever-Victorious Army" was incorporated into Tseng Kuo-fan's imperial Chinese forces in 1862. When Ward died in that year, Major Charles Gordon of the British Army took over the command.

VICTORIES OF THE IMPERIALIST FORCES. This mixed force of Chinese armies under Tseng Kuo-fan, Li Hung-chang, and

General Ward, with the aid of several thousand British and French soldiers, sailors, and marines, steadily pressed back the Taiping. In December, 1863, Soochow fell to the imperialists. Hangchow was captured the following March. With the collapse of Changchow in May, 1864, the "Ever-Victorious Army" was disbanded, leaving the final fighting to the regular Chinese forces. Nanking, the Taiping capital, fell in July, 1864, following the suicide of the Taiping emperor, Hung Hsiu-ch'uan. However, it was not until May, 1865, that the last Taiping forces were captured near Amoy.

RESULTS OF THE TAIPING REBELLION. Directly and indirectly, the rebellion cost the lives of about 20 million Chinese. Nine provinces were devastated. The Manchu dynasty was bankrupted by the cost of suppressing the revolution and by losses in tax collections. Since the Taiping leaders professed to be Christians, Chinese officials came to look upon Christianity as a loathsome disease.

Yünnan Rebellion (1860-1873). The Moslems of Yünnan are believed to be descendants of a Moslem army sent by the caliph to aid China in a war in the ninth century. This force is said to have revolted and to have settled in part in Yünnan. By intermarriage it subsequently became Chinese in blood, though remaining militantly Moslem. In 1860, due largely to economic differences over the control of Yünnan's large mineral resources, an uprising of this group occurred. Local Chinese magistrates by instigating a massacre of Moslems stirred up a full-scale rebellion, which under the leadership of Sultan Sulieman (Tu Wen-hsiu) lasted 13 years.

SUPPRESSION OF THE REBELLION. In crushing the revolt, the Chinese were aided by one Moslem faction who sold their services to the Manchu to fight their coreligionists. The combined imperial and Moslem force besieged and took Tali-fu, the rebel's capital, in 1873. Immediately after the victory, the imperial forces carried out a general massacre of Moslems, adding more thousands to the lives already lost.

Sinkiang Revolt. The Sinkiang Revolt contributed much toward the weakening of the Ch'ing Dynasty. This revolt began in 1866 when the tribesmen of Ili in northern Sinkiang set up an independent Moslem state. This was followed by the rising of the Dungari tribes of eastern Sinkiang, who not only gained control of that region but overran Kansu Province and penetrated even into Shensi and Hopei provinces.

TSO TSUNG-T'ANG AND SUPPRESSION OF THE REVOLT. Despite the current drain on China's power, the able imperial general, Tso Tsung-t'ang, built up a strong and disciplined Chinese army which in ten years pushed the rebels out of China proper and regained all Sinkiang except Ili Province. This region had been occupied by the Russians, and was regained by China only through the Treaty of St. Petersburg (1881).

Natural Disasters. In 1877-1878, severe drought, famine, and pestilence took at least ten million lives in the valley of the Yellow River. The rains that failed the north brought floods in the south to devastate several provinces. In 1886, the northern provinces were visited by flood. The Yellow River, China's Sorrow, shifted its mouth a distance of over 100 miles from northern Shantung to Kiangsu Province. Thousands who escaped drowning in the floods died of starvation.

Rise of Brigandage. As a result of the widespread suffering from the rebellions and natural disasters, thousands of starving peasants and coolies were forced to join in robber bands. In China, these bands are usually a sign of bad times.

GROWTH OF ANTI-CHRISTIAN SENTIMENT

Missionary Activities. Christianity acquired legal status in China by the Treaties of Tientsin in 1858. The French and Russian treaties permitted the missionaries to travel into the interior. A disputed clause in the French-Chinese Convention of 1860 granted French Catholic missionaries the right to teach Catholicism and live in the interior. As a result of these various provisions, the French Catholic bishops and priests assumed a semiofficial position of equality with local Chinese officials. The Protestants claimed full rights to build churches and to teach throughout China, and all the missionaries tended to throw the mantle of extraterritoriality over their native converts. The French government asserted a virtual protectorate over the Chinese Roman Catholics. All these claims were disputed and opposed by the Chinese officials who resented the infringement of their own authority.

UNFORTUNATE MISSIONARY PRACTICES. Both Protestant and Catholic missionaries taught their converts that the traditional Chinese religions were pagan and sinful. Ancestor worship, the keystone of Chinese society and religion, was attacked by the missionaries, and converts were forbidden to contribute to the upkeep of village and family temples and shrines or to the cost of the village festivals that had religious significance. These teachings broke up families, interfered with village life and ceremonials, and weakened the bonds of Chinese authority.

Anti-Christian Sentiment. Chinese bureaucrats and scholars encouraged anti-Christian sentiment. The Taiping Rebellion had shown them the menace of Christian doctrines. Lacking the power to drive out the foreign missionaries, they incited the masses to uprisings. False rumors and scurrilous literary attacks stirred up riots and attacks on missionaries throughout China. Churches and mission property were destroyed. Missionaries and converts were killed. France and Britain repeatedly used gunboats to protect missionaries or to exact indemnities. After Lord Clarendon's declaration abandoning the gunboat policy in 1869, attacks on British missions almost ended. At the same time, however, attacks on French missions increased.

TIENTSIN MASSACRE (1870). Anti-French sentiment was strong around Tientsin because of French conduct during the allied occupation of the city in 1860-1861. The Catholic orphanage maintained there became a special source of trouble. The nuns and priests were suspected of practicing evil magic. Stirred to action by agitating officials, the Tientsin mob rioted, destroying much of the church property and killing the French consul, along with 50 foreign and Chinese Christians. Because the Franco-Prussian War weakened France's position, the Peking government settled the affair by sending a mission of apology to Paris and by paying reparations and an indemnity.

CONTINUED MISSIONARY ATTACKS. The war between China and France over Annam increased the anti-Christian and anti-foreign attacks. Serious anti-missionary uprisings occurred in Kwangtung and Szechwan provinces in 1884 and 1886, and in the Yangtze Valley in 1890 and 1891.

FOREIGNERS IN CHINESE SERVICE

The level of Chinese decadence and governmental incapacity is shown by her reliance upon foreigners for important military and civil government posts

Inspectorate of Customs. Because of the difficulties in collecting customs during the Taiping Rebellion, an inspectorate of customs, including French, British, and American representatives, was organized in 1854. Its duties were to collect customs and harbor dues, prevent smuggling and maintain the ports. Under Sir Robert Hart, who from 1863 to 1908 was inspector general, the customs service, staffed largely with foreigners became the most efficient branch of China's government.

DIPLOMATIC RELATIONS

For thousands of years, China had been the central kingdom, maintaining diplomatic relations only with tributary or vassal states. In spite of the defeats and treaties of 1842, 1858, and 1860, Chinese officials refused to recognize western states as equals. The principal objective of the dominant clique of officials under Tz'u Hsi was to resist pressure for change and to evade western demands for equal recognition.

Audience Question (Kowtow). Almost from the first meeting of East and West, western diplomacy had been deeply concerned with the audience question. oT stress her superiority, China had insisted that the foreign diplomats should perform the kowtow. This ceremony, which involved three prostrations before the emperor, acknowledged the tributary status of the state which the kowtowing diplomat represented. The western state system under international law recognized the equality of all states, large or small. Naturally, states like France or Britain would not permit their diplomats to kowtow.

AUDIENCE OF 1873. Until 1873, Chinese officials evaded requests for an audience because of the minority of the T'ung-chih emperor. At his majority, however, arrangements for an audience were concluded whereby the kowtow was to be replaced with three bows. This still did not end the problem, for, by devious methods, the Chinese emperor contrived to subordinate the foreign diplomats.

AUDIENCES OF 1891 AND 1893. Because of the minority of the Kuang-hsü emperor, it was not until 1891 that foreign envoys were again granted an audience. However, it was 1893 before a really satisfactory audience was granted.

American Diplomatic Leadership. Despite her own Civil War, the United States assumed diplomatic leadership in China. Under the guidance of Anson Burlingame, United States envoy (1861-1867), the foreign diplomats pursued a cooperative policy: (1) to hold China to strict treaty observance by united diplomatic action, thus avoiding a gunboat policy; and (2) to maintain by unity a diplomatic stability which would lessen the likelihood of individual powers taking advantage of China's weakness.

Consular Jurisdiction. The principle of extraterritoriality made the foreign consuls the dispensers of justice to their nationals. The British consuls were early furnished jails and constables to administer justice promptly. But the United States failed similarly to support its representatives; hence United States justice in China was notoriously bad through most of the nineteenth century.

MIXED COURTS. In 1864, the Shanghai mixed court was established to handle cases involving both foreigners and Chinese. A deputy of the Chinese magistrate sat with the foreign magistrate to help judge cases involving Chinese in the International Settlements. The Cheefoo Convention of 1876 called for cases to be tried by the law of the magistrate trying the case. This was generally governed by the nationality of the defendant.

CHINESE-WESTERN NEGOTIATIONS (1866 - 1876)

First Chinese Mission to Europe (1866). In order to gain some knowledge of the West, the Chinese government appointed a Commission of Investigation in 1866. The commission reported on material differences between Europe and China, but largely ignored political differences.

Burlingame Mission (1868). After retiring as United States envoy in 1867, Burlingame was named by the Tsungli Yamen to head a mission to the western powers. The object of this move was to ward off the anticipated pressure by the western powers for treaty revision in 1868. Burlingame, however, became over-enthusiastic about his mission. In San Francisco and New York, he rashly declared that China was on the path to westernization and was ready to accept Christianity.

BURLINGAME TREATY (1868). In Washington, Burlingame exceeded his authority by concluding a treaty between the United States and China. Among other things, it provided for (1) encouragement of Chinese emigration to the United States, (2) free access to schools of both countries, (3) reciprocal rights of residence and travel, and (4) freedom for China from interference in her internal development. Of these provisions, only the last was desired by China; nevertheless, China ratified the treaty to demonstrate her faith in Burlingame.

CLARENDON DECLARATION. In Europe, only Britain and Prussia made concessions to China. British Foreign Minister Lord Clarendon declared that Britain would thereafter (1) show restraint in demanding further commercial concessions, and (2) redress wrongs to British subjects only through the Peking government. Bismarck committed the North German Confederation to the general terms of the Clarendon Declaration.

RESULTS OF THE BURLINGAME MISSION. Burlingame's mission helped to relieve the foreign pressure. Britain put off treaty revision for five years, and other powers followed her example. The Sino-American Treaty of 1868 only proved a source of great embarrassment to both powers.

Margary Affair. In 1875 the killing of a British consular agent, Augustus Margary, by antiforeign rioters was seized upon by the British Minister, Sir Francis Wade, as a pretext for forcing settlement of all Anglo-Chinese differences.

CHEEFOO CONVENTION (1876). The resulting convention signed by Wade and Li Hung-chang at Cheefoo in September, 1876, not only settled the Margary affair, but also (1) committed the Chinese government to protect foreign diplomats in China, (2) settled problems of legal jurisdiction in mixed courts, (3) opened three new treaty ports (including Chungking), and (4) made new regulations for internal trade and liken (internal customs) duties. Over half of the articles of the convention required the approval of the other treaty powers, who were unanimous in their objections.

CHINESE EMIGRATION

The Coolie Trade. The Chinese laws prohibiting emigration were almost totally ignored. Migration abroad greatly increased after 1850. Chinese coolies provided cheap labor for gold mines in Australia and California and for railroad building in western United States. The Latin American countries, after the abolition of slavery, substituted Chinese coolies for Negro slaves. The coolie trade involved nearly the same evils that had attended the early African slave trade.

REGULATION OF THE COOLIE TRADE. In 1859, the Canton viceroy officially sanctioned the trade in order to regulate it. All foreign governments, with the exception of Portugal, cooperated with the Chinese officials by licensing coolie depots in Canton and Swatow. In 1875, joint pressure by Britain, France, and Germany induced Portugal to prohibit the coolie trade at Macao.

EMIGRATION CONVENTION OF 1866. France and Britain signed an emigration agreement with China in 1866 which (1) abrogated prohibition of emigration, (2) made kidnaping punishable by death, and (3) permitted emigration only from ports where joint supervision was possible. The Emigration Convention subsequently was approved by the United States, Russia, and Prussia.

Chinese Emigration to the United States. The Burlingame Treaty encouraged the emigration of coolies to the United States. After the Panic of 1873, however, hostility increased against the Chinese, whose low living standard endangered the jobs of occidental workers on the west coast, and mob attacks on Chinese became intense by 1877.

SINO-AMERICAN TREATIES OF 1880. The Burlingame Treaty made it impossible for the United States to prohibit Chinese emigration. However, in 1880, two Sino-American treaties were signed by which (1) the United States was given power to limit or suspend, but not to prohibit Chinese emigration, (2) American citizens and ships were prohibited from opium trading, (3) the most-favored-nation treatment was enlarged, and (4) China agreed to consider proposals extending commercial intercourse.

SUSPENSION OF EMIGRATION. In 1882, the United States Congress passed a bill suspending Chinese emigration for ten years.

Subsequent amendments in 1884 and 1892 strengthened the exclusion of Chinese. In 1894, a new Sino-American treaty prohibited Chinese emigration for an additional ten years.

RUSSIAN-CHINESE DIPLOMACY

Russia and Ili. During the Sinkiang Rebellion, Russia sent troops into the rebelling district of Ili to protect the extensive Russian trade in that region. Although the Chinese were assured that the occupation would end when China could maintain order, the Russians refused to depart.

THE CHUNG-HOU MISSION. The Chinese envoy to Russia, Chung-hou, negotiated the Treaty of Lidaria by which China would have ceded Ili to Russia and granted not only many trade concessions but even a large indemnity. Peking not only repudiated the treaty but condemned Chung-hou to death.

Treaty of St. Petersburg (1881). Both nations feared war, with the result that the Treaty of St. Petersburg was signed in 1881 providing for (1) the return of all but a small part of Ili to China, (2) the payment by China of the costs of Russia's military occupation, and (3) the granting of additional trading rights to Russia, and provision for consulates in Mongolia and Turkestan.

INTERNAL IMPROVEMENTS

Despite its reactionary government, China made some internal progress along both educational and industrial lines in the last decades of the nineteenth century.

Educational Progress. Educational advancement at this period was due largely to foreign influence. In 1862, Tun Wen Kuan, a school of languages for interpreters, was set up under the direction of Sir Robert Hart, inspector general of the customs. The addition of a science department elevated the school to the rank of a college in 1865. Also noteworthy was the Chinese Educational Mission (1871-1887) under the leadership of Yung Wing, a Cantonese graduate of Yale College. The Mission sent 120 Chinese boys to live in New England homes and study in American public schools. In 1881, the boys were recalled by the conservative government, partly because they were becoming too westernized and partly because of growing anti-Chinese sentiments in the United States. Although the students were received in China with suspicion, a large percentage of them eventually attained high office in the Chinese government.

Railways. China was in 1860 the only major country in the world without railroads. The Chinese still depended upon their inadequate system of waterways and highways.

SHANGHAI WOOSUNG LINE (1876). In 1876, an Anglo-American company succeeded, despite Chinese opposition, in constructing a railway line from Shanghai to Woosung. Because of the accidental death of a Chinese, however, the railroad was torn up and the equipment shipped to Formosa.

KAIPING RAILWAY AND COAL MINES. Under the influence of Li Hung-chang, China's first steam navigation company was organized in 1873, and the Kaiping coal mines, 80 miles northeast of Tientsin, were opened to provide coal supplies for the company. By 1882, regular steam locomotives supplanted mules to haul the coal cars from the mines to the nearest canal. By the outbreak of war with Japan Li Hung-chang had brought about the extension of the Kaiping Railway east to Tientsin and northwest to 40 miles beyond Shan-hai-kuan, despite the objections of the Russians, who had designs on Manchuria.

First Telegraph Line (1881). In 1871, an oceanic cable first connected China with London via America. During the negotiations of the Treaty of St. Petersburg, the Chinese learned the value of rapid communication with their ministers abroad. As a result, the Shanghai-Tientsin telegraph line was completed in 1881 and was soon extended to Peking.

Hanyang Iron Works (1890). In the Yangtze Valley, Chang Chih-tung was the leader in the westernization movement much as was Li Hung-chang in the north. In 1890, he opened China's first important iron works at Hangyang near Hankow.

BIBLIOGRAPHY

Bau, M. C. J., *The Foreign Relations of China*, 1932.

Beckmann, G. M., *Imperialism and Revolution in Modern China, 1840-1950*, 1955.

Beckmann, G. M., *The Modernization of China and Japan*, 1962.

Bland, J. O. P., *Li Hung-chang*, 1917.

Cheng, T., *A History of Sino-Russian Relations*, 1957.

Coolidge, M. R., *Chinese Migration*, 1909.

Dallin, D. J., *The Rise of Russia in Asia*, 1949.

Dennett, T., *Americans in Eastern Asia*, 1922.

Dulles, F. R., *China and America*, 1946.

Fairbank, J. K., *The United States and China*, 1958.

Feuerwerker, A., *China's Early Industrialization*, 1958.

Hail, W. S., *Tseng Kuo-fan and the TaiPing Rebellion*, 1927.

Hughes, E. R., *The Invasion of China by the Western World*, 1927.

Latourette, K. S., *A History of Christian Missions in China*, 1929.

Latourette, K. S., *Development of China*, 1946.

Levenson, J. R., *Confucian China and Its Modern Fate*, 1958.

Li, C., *The Political History of China, 1840-1928*, 1956.

McKenzie, R. D., *Oriental Exclusion*, 1928.

Morse, H. G., *The International Relations of the Chinese Empire*, Vol. 2, 1918.

Rowe, D. N., *Modern China: A Brief History*, 1959.

Teng, S., and J. K. Fairbank, *China's Response to the West*, 2 vols., 1954.

Williams, E. T., *China, Yesterday and Today*, 1935.

Willoughby, W. W., *Foreign Rights and Interests in China*, 1927.

Wright, M. C., *The Last Stand of Chinese Conservatism*, 1957.

CHAPTER 6
Modernization of Japan

DECLINE OF THE TOKUGAWA

Relaxation of Tokugawa Power. For 200 years after the adoption of the seclusion policy, Japan enjoyed peace. The shoguns and their courtiers at Yedo lost interest in the arts of war, but the daimyos tended to increase in strength. Despite their greater concern in scholarly pursuits, the samurai retained active interest in their profession of fighting.

Rise of the Middle Class. One result of the seclusion policy and the long period of peace was, as was pointed out in Chapter II, the rise of a mercantile class. The shutting off of the supply of imported goods came at a time when the long peace permitted a rise in general culture and in wealth, which in turn brought increased desires for luxuries. Since luxuries could not be imported, industry and internal trade were so stimulated that the mercantile class was able, by its wealth, to exploit all the other classes — peasant, samurai, and noble, alike. The incomes of the nobility and samurai were limited to the produce of the land that could be extracted from the peasantry. This allowed for very little increased income to purchase luxuries; consequently, the upper classes fell deeply into debt to the mercantile class. Often the only release from these debts was the adoption of the banker's son or of the banker himself. By this route, many wealthy merchant families allied themselves with aristocracy, and the old class distinctions decreased in importance, with the merchants becoming as wealthy and powerful as great daimyos.

Agrarian Discontent. The peasant, caught between the greedy daimyo or samurai and the equally greedy rice broker, was progressively degraded. Hopelessly in debt, he sold his daughter or committed infanticide. Occasionally he rioted in blind fury with his fellows when starvation faced him after his crop failed or his lord and his creditors left no rice to eat.

OPENING OF THE DOOR

Pressure on the Closed Door. In the early decades of the nineteenth century, the steady expansion of the western powers made Japan's isolation policy increasingly difficult to maintain. Russian and American whalers and shippers needed Japanese ports to obtain provisions and make repairs, but the Japanese stubbornly refused to receive foreign ships, and killed or mistreated the seamen who were shipwrecked in Japanese waters.

Early Attempts to Open the Door. As early as 1791, American traders first attempted unsuccessfully to open commercial relations with Japan. In the following years, the Russians used the return of shipwrecked Japanese as a pretext for entering into diplomatic relations, but this and subsequent moves by the Russians and British were rebuffed. In 1837, another advance by American merchants was repulsed by cannon fire. The failure of the first American diplomatic mission under Commodore Biddle in 1846 caused increased pressure in the United States for a stronger delegation to be sent, and since the Japanese continued to abuse shipwrecked Americans, a new mission was finally approved.

Perry Mission. Commodore Perry was commissioned in 1851 to head the new mission. After a thorough study of all available material on Japan and its people, Perry determined to force Japanese respect by assuming all the dignity and pageantry of a medieval bishop. At his insistence, a strong fleet was assigned him. His orders emphasized the peaceful intent of the mission, but also permitted the use of force if necessary.

First Visit to Yedo. Perry arrived in Yedo Bay in July, 1853, with only four ships, but among these were steam vessels, which had never before been seen in Japan. The commodore's stubborn refusal to see any but the highest Japanese officials or to leave for Nagasaki as requested finally induced the shogun to send his representative to receive President Fillmore's letter of accreditation. After the completion of this ceremony, Perry announced his intention to return the following year to negotiate a treaty.

TREATY OF KANAGAWA. Perry's return in February, 1854, was hurried by rumors that a Russian fleet was operating near Japan. The Treaty of Kanagawa, signed March 31, 1854, after weeks of patient negotiation, (1) opened the ports of Shimoda and Hakodate for repair and provisioning of American ships, (2) provided for proper treatment and repatriation of shipwrecked Americans, (3) permitted the appointment of consular representatives if either nation considered it necessary, and (4) promised most-favored-nation treatment for the United States. At the time of ratification, the treaty excited little interest in the United States or in Europe, but in Japan it was an event of great importance, for it ended the two-century-old policy of exclusion. The American treaty was followed by a series of treaties by which Japan granted similar concessions to the British in 1854, the Russians in 1855, and the Dutch in 1856.

IMPERIAL APPROVAL. Nothing could more convincingly have demonstrated the growing weakness of the shogunate than the fact that the shogun not only submitted these treaties to the emperor for approval, but also barely received that approval. Even those at the imperial court who favored ratification desired to keep trade at a minimum.

Townsend Harris. Under provisions of the Treaty of Kanagawa, Townsend Harris, an unusually able man, was sent as the first American consul to Japan. On arriving in Shimoda in August, 1858, Harris found himself most unwanted by the Japanese, who wished neither trade nor foreign consuls. Despite this hostile reception, he gradually won the Japanese confidence and friendship through his extraordinary tact, patience, shrewdness, and honesty. Alone and apparently forgotten by his country (during the eighteen months of his residence in Japan, he received no communication from the United States Department of State), Harris secured an unprecedented audience with the shogun, the first granted a foreigner since 1613. Having won the confidence of the shogun, he patiently instructed the Japanese ruler in the principles of western international relations. Harris' consistent refusal to take advantage of the Japanese won him a place of honor in their history that few foreigners have achieved.

COMMERCIAL TREATY OF 1858. Harris' achievement was the Commercial Treaty of 1858 which (1) opened four more ports to trade (Kanagawa, Nagasaki, Niigata, and Kobe), (2) provided for mutual diplomatic representation, (3) gave to Americans both civil and criminal extraterritoriality, (4) prohibited the opium trade, (5) gave freedom of religion to foreigners, (6) provided for conventional tariffs but gave preference to American products and (7) continued the most-favored-nation treatment. Again, similar treaties with the Dutch, Russians, British, and French quickly followed.

INTERNAL REACTION. The shogun had entertained serious doubts as to whether he could enforce the Harris treaty. Only the news of China's defeat and of the signing of the Treaties of Tientsin had caused him to approve the treaty hurriedly without consulting the emperor. When the emperor subsequently refused to ratify the treaty, the Tokugawa enemies seized the opportunity to support the mikado against the "usurping" shogun. The balance of power was obviously shifting toward the imperial court. Although the emperor ordered that the foreigners be expelled and the exclusion policy be resumed, the shogun was forced by foreign pressure to ignore the order.

RESTORATION OF THE EMPEROR

While the Tokugawa rule was obviously weakening in the nineteenth century, western encroachment produced the crisis which brought its downfall.

Vacillation at Yedo. Had the shogun boldly announced a policy of opening Japan to foreign intercourse in 1853, he might have saved his position. Instead, he requested imperial approval for the treaties on the pretext that conflict should be avoided until Japan could expel the intruder by force. The shogun thus was vulnerable to charges both of double dealing and of direct disobedience of the emperor's orders.

Attacks on Foreigners. Partly from conviction but largely from a desire to embarrass the shogunate, the anti-Tokugawa forces pursued a policy of antiforeignism in the years immediately following the signing of the commercial treaties. The chief leaders of these forces were the Satsuma, Choshu, Hizen, and Tosa clans, often referred to as the Satcho Hito group. Between 1858 and 1865, attacks were made upon Europeans and their employees by "patriotic" supporters of the emperor. These attacks culminated in 1862 in the murder of Richardson, an Englishman, by Satsuma samurai. The British demanded an indemnity from the shogun and the Satsuma daimyo, and the trial and execution of the murderers.

Foreign Aggressive Action. The Richardson incident brought new embarrassment to the shogun. While he refused to enforce a new imperial edict for expulsion of the foreigners, he also rejected offers of foreign assistance. The shogunate agreed to pay the indemnities but admitted its inability to punish the guilty. Thereupon the British assumed the aggressive, bombarded the Satsuma port of Kagoshima in 1863, and largely destroyed the city. This drastic action brought not only payment of the demanded indemnity by the Satsuma but also requests from them for aid in purchasing a European naval vessel for the Satsuma navy.

BOMBARDMENT OF SHIMONOSEKI. It took a similar demonstration to convince the Choshu clan of the futility of their antiforeign policy. Despite American and French retaliation in kind for Choshu attacks upon their ships, the Choshu continued belligerent action. In August, 1864, a joint French, British, Dutch, and American fleet completely destroyed the Choshu coastal defenses. Thereafter the Choshu, like the Satsuma, abandoned their antiforeign attitude and not only accepted the allies' terms, but requested their aid in procuring foreign armaments.

End of Imperial Foreign Opposition. The lessons of Shimonoseki and Kagoshima were soon reflected at the imperial court. When the foreign powers threatened to make a similar demonstration of naval might against Osaka near the imperial court at Kyoto in order to force imperial consent to the commercial treaties, the ratification was secured peaceably in November, 1865. A change of policy was made simple by the death in the following year of both the emperor and the shogun. The new shogun was Keiki, who since 1862 had helped to direct the affairs of the government, and the new emperor was Mitsuhito, who took the reign name of Meiji.

Fall of Shogunate. In October, 1867, the Satcho Hito clans pointed out to Shogun Keiki the dangers to Japan of the continuation of dual government. The following month, Keiki formally resigned his commission as shogun. However, he remained the most powerful feudal lord in Japan and fully expected to receive high office in the new imperial government. His expectations were thwarted by the ejection of the Tokugawa guards by the Satcho Hito group from the emperor's court at Kyoto and the seizure of his fiefs by imperial order. After a brief civil war, the Tokugawa clansmen were defeated, leaving the Satcho Hito clans in complete control of the government.

ORGANIZATION OF THE NEW GOVERNMENT

Imperial Charter Oath (1868). To quiet the general unrest and to pronounce the objectives of the new government, the emperor in 1868 promulgated an imperial oath (Charter Oath) promising (1) public discussion and debate of national problems, (2) application of new political and social principles to benefit all, (3) abolition of feudal institutions and restrictions, (4) employment of the best men and ideas in the world to assist Japan's transformation.

Transfer of Capital. The transfer of the capital from Kyoto to Yedo, renamed Tokyo, accented the break with the past. This change brought the bureaucracy, which was already centered at Yedo, more thoroughly under imperial control. It also brought the court into the stimulating environment of Japan's greatest commercial center.

Government Reorganization. A preliminary reorganization of the government in 1867 divided the chief offices of state among princes of the blood, kuge (court nobles), daimyos, and samurai in order of rank. A deliberative assembly was created, but the real power remained with the Satcho Hito group including Saigo, Kido, Itagaki, and Okuma, who represented the most powerful clans. When a cabinet was created in 1871, these men and Prince Iwakura, a kuge, became members of the first cabinet headed by Sanjo.

Abolition of Feudalism. A decisive step in the movement to abolish feudalism was taken in 1869 when the daimyo of the Satcho Hito clans returned their fiefs to the emperor. All the lesser clans promptly followed suit. In the following year, the emperor abolished the old court and feudal titles. Finally in 1871 an imperial rescript abolished fiefs and disbanded the clans, converting the lands involved into imperial prefectures.

PENSIONING OF THE FEUDAL CLASSES. Since the daimyo and samurai had depended upon the fiefs and clan holdings for a livelihood, the imperial government undertook to compensate them with pensions, which by 1873 consumed one-third of all the land tax receipts. Soon the government decreased the burden by first voluntary and later compulsory commutation of these pensions for fixed sums in cash and bonds. The daimyo often gained by the transaction, for they now had no samurai retainers to support.

SAMURAI DISCONTENT. Many samurai were impoverished by the abolition of feudalism. While the new order allowed them to enter business, they generally lacked the necessary training or capital. The new army was being built up of peasant conscripts, and thus had no room for the proud samurai. This large class of unemployed fighting men represented a serious economic and social problem.

SATSUMA REVOLT (1877). In 1876, the government deprived the samurai of their ancient symbol of rank by prohibiting their wearing swords. This combined with other government actions incited a group of dissatisfied Satsuma leaders to organize a large rebel army of discontented samurai. In the bloody battles that followed, the peasant soldiers of the government conscript force proved their worth. The samurai were crushed with great loss of life. This victory destroyed the prestige of the old-style fighting man and discouraged any further revolts.

Parliamentary Government. The deliberative assembly of the 1868 government proved unsatisfactory; consequently in 1875 the emperor ordered election of local assemblies as popular training in parliamentary methods. In 1881, the emperor promised to summon a national diet in 1890, and Count Ito was sent to study western governments to determine which type would best suit Japan's needs. After visiting America, France, England, and Germany, Ito found a satisfactory model in the constitution of the new German Empire. In preparation for the adoption of a constitution, a Prussian-style cabinet system was adopted, in which the emperor remained absolute but acted upon the advice of his cabinet members. A privy council was also established to handle matters regarding the imperial household and constitutional changes.

Constitution. Under the Japanese Constitution, promulgated on February 11, 1889, the emperor remained the supreme civil, religious, and military head of Japan. The document promised the citizen freedom from arbitrary arrest, protection of property rights, and freedom of religion, speech, and association, but in each instance, made it legally possible for the government to curb these rights. A national court system with public trials was created. Constitutional amendment required permission of the emperor, who acted on the advice of the privy council.

DIET. The Constitution created a Diet with a House of Peers composed of nobility and imperial appointees, and a House of Representatives composed of elected members. The emperor possessed a veto and the right of initiating legislation. Should the Diet refuse to pass a government budget, the one for the previous year carried over automatically.

Rise of Political Parties. Political parties in Japan began in 1881 with the formation by Itagaki of the Liberal party (Jiyuto) to promote constitutional and representative government. In 1882, Count Okuma formed the Progressive party (Kaishinto) for the same purpose. While the Jiyuto appealed to the rural districts and the Kaishinto to the bourgeoisie, the formation of two parties for the same basic purpose illustrates the Japanese tendency to follow leaders rather than principles. By 1883 the government accused the parties of fomenting disorder and ordered them disbanded. The weakness of the political parties tended to make the Diet under the new constitution more an obstructive than a constructive body.

Legal Reforms. There had been much justification for the foreign demand for extraterritoriality. The Japanese legal system was chaotic, individual rights were disregarded, the police were arbitrary and all-powerful, the laws harsh, and prison conditions revolting. The first move toward reform came with the establishing of a criminal law office in 1868. Three years later a judicial department was organized, and in 1882, a new penal code and code of criminal procedure were adopted. The new system separated the judicial from the administrative powers, placing trained lawyers over the former. The reforms were completed in 1889 with the adoption of a code of civil procedure.

END OF EXTRATERRITORIALITY. Japanese desire to eliminate extraterritoriality motivated to a large extent the legal reform. In 1887, Mexico abandoned its consular jurisdiction. An American treaty of 1878 had granted Japan tariff autonomy, and in 1882 an extradition treaty was signed. However, not until 1894 did the United States and Great Britain sign treaties abolishing extraterritoriality and consular jurisdiction. The other nations followed their lead, and in 1899 when the treaties became effective, Japan gained legal jurisdiction over all foreigners on Japanese soil.

ECONOMIC AND CULTURAL CHANGES

The transformation of Japan from a hermit kingdom to a great power was much more than a political change. It was also an economic and cultural revolution.

Economic Changes. The abolition of feudalism, besides ending the fiefs and holdings of daimyo and samurai, opened all careers to all men equally. The daimyos, with their large capital from commuted pensions, tended to join the higher financial circles. The samurai in accordance with their abilities and capital entered all ranks of the middle and agricultural classes. The common man and the middle class were now free to enter many careers formerly closed to them. These newly released energies under government direction made Japan an industrial power in a few decades.

AGRARIAN PROBLEMS. The peasants who in 1872 received legal title to lands formerly held under feudal terms quickly found ownership to be an oppressive burden. To obtain money for Japan's industrialization, the government taxed the land so heavily that many peasant proprietors were reduced to tenants. Furthermore, the great increase in population in the decades following the restoration increased the pressures on the available lands and flooded the cities with cheap labor for the new industry.

GOVERNMENT IN INDUSTRY. The imperial government encouraged the development of needed industries by subsidies, purchase of stock, or by formation of government corporations. At first attention was focused upon providing financial institutions, commodity exchanges, shipping companies, railways, and telegraph lines to facilitate industrial development. After (and to a degree before) the heavy basic industries of mining, steel, and shipbuilding were developed to fill military needs, the light industries such as textiles were built up to produce goods for export. Initially the government entered business directly when private capital proved too timid, but after 1880, the policy was changed to one of indirect protection. Government corporations were gradually turned over to the control of financial leaders. Until her victory over China, Japan's industrialization was achieved largely without foreign loans.

ZAIBATSU. Leading Japan in her industrialization were a few wealthy families collectively known as the Zaibatsu, whose business ability and organization enabled them to gain control over most of the country's wealth. The Mitsui banking family helped finance the Restoration and was richly rewarded by profitable government contracts and monopolies, and ultimately they controlled the new textile industry. The Mitsubishi family, who gained large shipping concessions by shrewd maneuvering during the Formosa incident of 1874-1875, continued to build up Japan's shipping and shipbuilding industry. The Sumitomo family began its fortune by mining copper for the Dutch trade at Deshima. After the Restoration, the Sumitomo profited by turning to heavy industry, munitions, and armaments.

Advancement in Education. As a result of the Charter Oath of 1868, the Japanese education system was revised to copy the best features of the foreign systems. Large numbers of foreign scholars were brought to Japan by the imperial government to help found new schools and universities. Thousands of Japanese who went abroad to study foreign history, science, government, and art, returned to teach in Japan's new schools. The new educational system was kept under close state supervision to achieve uniformity of thought as well as administration. After 1886, four years of primary education were made available at low cost.

Religious Developments. Buddhism had been fostered by the Tokugawa, while Shinto had given religious sanction for the revolt against the shoguns. Shinto was made the state religion in 1868, and Buddhism was disestablished. In the early years of the Restoration, there was some persecution of Buddhists, but after 1872 the religion was again fully legalized, and the Japanese thereafter lived by the two religions. Shinto ceremonies were generally used for marriage, but Buddhist priests officiated for burials. Although as late as 1869 native Christians were ordered exiled, persecutions gradually diminished and Christianity was legalized in 1873. The Constitution of 1889 guaranteed freedom of religion to all as long as the religion did not prejudice peace and order or the duties of the subjects.

BIBLIOGRAPHY

Allen, G. C., *A Short Economic History of Modern Japan*, 1963.

Beckmann, G. M., *The Making of the Meiji Constitution*, 1957.

Bellah, R. N., *Tokugawa Religion*, 1957.

Brown, D. M., *Nationalism in Japan*, 1955.

Craig, A. M., *Choshu in the Meiji Restoration*, 1961.

Dennett, T., *Americans in Eastern Asia*, 1922.

Harris, Townsend, *The Complete Journal of Townsend Harris*, 1959.

Jansen, Marius B., *Sakamoto Ryoma and the Meiji Restoration*, 1961.

Kamikawa, H., ed., *Japan-American Diplomatic Relations in the Meiji-Taisho Era*, 1958.

Latourette, K. S., *The History of Japan*, 1947.

Lockwood, W. W., *The Economic Development of Japan . . . 1868-1938*, 1954.

Norman, E. H., *Japan's Emergence as a Modern State*, 1960.

Reischauer, E. O., *Japan, Past and Present*, 1956.

Reischauer, E. O., *The United States and Japan*, 1957.

Reischauer, R. K., *Japan, Government-Politics*, 1939.

Sansom, G. B., *The Western World and Japan*, 1950.

Schwantes, R. S., *Japanese and Americans*, 1955.

Sheldon, C. D., *The Rise of the Merchant Class in Tokugawa Japan, 1600-1868*, 1958.

Smith, T. C., *The Agrarian Origins of Modern Japan*, 1959.

Takekoshi, Y., *The Economic Aspects of the History of Civilization in Japan*, 1930.

Treat, P. J., *Diplomatic Relations Between the United States and Japan, 1853-1895*, 1932.

Walworth, A., *Black Ships Off Japan: The Story of Commodore Perry's Expedition*, 1946.

Wilson, Robert A., *Genesis of the Meiji Government in Japan, 1868-1871*, 1957.

Yanaga, C., *Japan Since Perry*, 1949.

CHAPTER 7
Struggles for the Lesser Lands

BURMA

Early Hinduized Kingdoms. From early times, Burma was influenced by Indian culture. Hinduized Mon and Pyu kingdoms contended for supremacy until the ninth century. Within two hundred years, however, the Burmese of Pagan had conquered most of Burma. Their Buddhist kingdom was destroyed by Kublai Khan's Mongol hordes in 1287, and Burma thereafter split into warring states. In the sixteenth century, one of these, Toungoo, reunited Burma and then devastated Siam.

European Contacts. D'Albuquerque negotiated a trade treaty between Portugal and Burma following his seizure of Malacca in 1511. Portuguese mercenaries and military advisers aided the Toungoo kings. During the seventeenth century, both the French and English established trading and shipbuilding posts in the Mon areas of south Burma.

Alaungpaya and Burmese Expansion. Although the Toungoo Dynasty fell in 1752 to the Mons of Pegu, a Burmese chieftain, Alaungpaya, managed to reunite the country. Both France and Britain, seeking commercial advantages, opportunistically aided both the Mon rebels and Alaungpaya. As a result, the Europeans were driven from Burma. Alaungpaya pressed an expansionist policy by invading Siam in 1759. Although his death saved Siam, his successors completed its conquest in 1767. Siam soon regained independence, but Burmese expansion into Arakan in 1785 was more lasting.

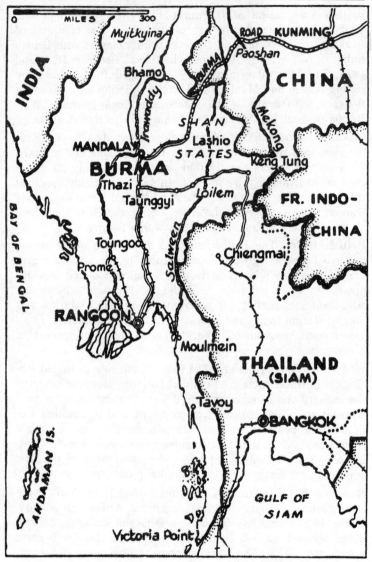

Courtesy of The New York Times

BURMA AND SIAM SHOWING BURMA ROAD

British Annexation of Burma (1824-1885). Burma's successes greatly enlarged the ego of its kings. The conquest of Arakan, moreover, brought frequent border clashes with British India, to which many Arakanese had fled. Between 1819 and 1824, King Bagyidaw arrogantly challenged British India by seizing Assam and Manipur and finally ordering an invasion of Bengal. As a result of the subsequent Anglo-Burmese War, Burma surrendered Arakan and Tenasserim to British India.

CONQUEST COMPLETED. After new wars in 1852 and 1885, the victorious British dethroned the Burmese king and annexed all of Burma. A major motivation was unquestionably the growing Franco-British rivalry in Asia. In 1886, the British pacified the Chinese by recognizing their traditional suzerainty over Burma. It was ten years, however, before the British subdued all the dissident nationalist elements within Burma.

British Rule. The British imposed direct rule upon Burma under a lieutenant governor, responsible to the governor general of India. While an advisory Legislative Council was appointed in 1897, not until 1923 did the Burmese achieve any significant measure of self-government. In 1935, Burma was separated from India, and given a generally representative, semi-autonomous government. World War II, however, prevented a real test.

EFFECT OF BRITISH RULE. The long British rule disrupted traditional Burmese social and cultural patterns. Burmese resented the Indians who received preferred treatment in obtaining government posts and industrial employment, and in addition victimized the peasants by their sharp lending practices. While Burma enjoyed an immense economic development under British rule, the ownership, capital, and management of the new concerns were foreign and the generous profits went abroad.

Burmese Nationalism. A Buddhist revival in the early twentieth century brought the first organized nationalist activity. In the 1920's and 30's Buddhist priests and discontented students agitated against British rule. Political parties became active after 1922. The world depression and nationalist sentiment caused anti-Indian riots in the 1930's. After 1935, political parties increased as the Burmese assumed more responsibility in the government.

FRENCH INDO-CHINA

Pre-French Indo-China. Viet-Nam, which held suzerainty over Cambodia and Laos, was subdivided for administration into Tonkin, Annam, and Cochin-China. Chinese influence predominated in northern Indo-China, while Indian prevailed in the south: hence the name *Indo-China*.

VIET-NAM. Tonkin was directly ruled by China for 1000 years. Even after they won independence in 938 A.D., Vietnamese sent tribute to China, and their political and social patterns remained thoroughly Sinicized. Pushing southward, they destroyed the Hinduized kingdom of Champa, later called Annam, and annexed the southeastern Cambodian provinces which make up Cochin-China. From 1500, Viet-Nam, then Dai Viet, was divided between the Nguyen and Trinh families, although both paid allegiance to the weak Le emperors in Hanoi. After quelling the Tayson Rebellion (1772-1802), the Nguyen leader Gia Long reunited Viet-Nam and established a new dynasty at Hué. Gia Long and successors centralized administration and stimulated a cultural renaissance.

CAMBODIA. Stemming from the Hinduized Khmer kingdom of Funan (3rd-5th centuries), Cambodia (Kambuja) reached its zenith in the early thirteenth century. Its empire stretched from Yünnan to the Gulf of Siam and from southern Burma to the South China Sea. After the disruption of political alignments by the Mongol expansion, the Khmer empire collapsed, with Siam and Laos breaking off as independent kingdoms. The reduced Cambodia thereafter precariously balanced as a buffer between Viet-Nam and Siam.

LAOS. Founded by Lao (Thai) migrants from southern China in the fourteenth century, Laos enjoyed its greatest period in the sixteenth and seventeenth centuries. It subsequently split into four kingdoms, which fell variously under the yoke of their powerful neighbors. In 1833, Viet-Nam annexed all of Laos except Luang Prabang, and even this accepted Vietnamese suzerainty.

French Penetration. In gaining the throne, Gia Long received unofficial French aid, and he later utilized French advisers. His successors, however, fanatically resented efforts of Christian missionaries in Viet-Nam, suspecting them of being agents of foreign governments. Missionary activities and Vietnamese intolerance provoked several incidents, which culminated in a French-Spanish attack on Tourane in 1858. Ostensibly intended to secure fair treatment for the missionaries, this attack enlarged into a French conquest of Cochin-China. From this base, French control gradually spread by a series of campaigns and treaties, including an undeclared war with Viet-Nam's traditional suzerain, China. By 1885, Tonkin, Annam, Laos, and Cambodia were under French "protection." Cochin-China was directly annexed as a colony. The underlying motivation for the French aggression was imperialistic and commercial. Through Indo-China, the French aimed to control the rich trade of southern China. They also moved to counteract the British expansion into Burma and Malaya.

French Rule. In 1887, Cochin-China, Tonkin, Annam, Laos, and Cambodia were joined as the Indochinese Union under a governor general, who had over-all directive power while each of the "states" retained largely autonomous administrations. The royal houses of Annam-Tonkin, Laos, and Cambodia operated native governments paralleling the French officialdom. They possessed very little power, however, and were closely supervised by the French. The communes or villages were self-governed by the native oligarchies. While some Indochinese sat on the various advisory councils, there was in Indo-China, except in the colony of Cochin-China, no provision for responsible native participation in government such as Burma had after 1923. The governor general held and used dictatorial powers through the entire period of French rule.

EFFECTS OF FRENCH RULE. Disillusioned about Indo-China as a gateway to China, the French determined to exploit Indochinese resources. They brought a great economic development in the production of foodstuffs (rice and corn) and forest and plantation crops (especially rubber) and in the mining of coal, tin, zinc, and wolfram. They also introduced some new agricultural products, built roads and railways, improved rivers and canals, set up postal, telephone, and telegraph systems, and established public health and education facilities. For most of these improvements, the average Vietnamese peasant and laborer paid dearly and benefited little. Few Vietnamese shared the French scientific and scholarly institutions in Indo-China, and even by 1939, only about 15 per cent of Indo-China's children received any schooling.

NATIONALIST MOVEMENT. Revolts flared sporadically throughout French rule, but were harshly repressed. Prompt French police action discouraged most political activity. In the 1920's however, several secret revolutionary parties formed, including the Indochinese Communist Party led by Ho Chi Minh. Also influential as nationalist organizations were two new religious sects: the Cao Dai and the Hoa Hao. A series of nationalist uprisings in the early 1930's fostered by both non-Communist and Communist groups brought the most severe French repression. An imperial effort at reform led by the young Emperor Bao Dai for a time brought hope to the royalists, but this too was frustrated by French manipulations. In Cambodia and Laos, there was practically no nationalist activity prior to World War II.

SIAM

Early History. Formed by Thai principalities which had long been under Kambujan dominion, Siam is a cultural offspring of India. In the thirteenth century, strengthened by Thai refugees from South China, the Thai state of Sukhotai wrested independence. It soon fell, however, before another Thai state, which founded Ayuthia in 1350. Ayuthia or Siam quickly subjugated much of the Menam and Mekong valleys and the northern Malay Peninsula. It also destroyed Angkor, capital of Cambodia.

POWER IN SOUTHEAST ASIA. Between 1500 and 1800, Siam was a major power in Southeast Asia, for long periods claiming suzerainty over Laos and Cambodia and much of the Malay Peninsula. Although it was several times devastated by the Burmese, Siam so revived under the Chakkri Dynasty that during the nineteenth century it successfully challenged Viet-Nam for dominion over Cambodia and Laos.

Siamese Independence. The fact that Siam retained its independence through the colony-grabbing era of the late nineteenth century resulted largely from the ability of the Siamese kings to play the French and British against each other. Siam also took some steps toward Westernizing.

EARLY WESTERN CONTACTS. The Portuguese were first to gain trade advantages in Siam, where they also served as military advisers and mercenaries. The Dutch, British, and French traded intermittently during the seventeenth and eighteenth centuries, but strictly on Siamese terms. When French missionary efforts seemed too successful and the French influence too strong at court, a palace revolt ousted all foreigners in 1688 and established a new dynasty.

BRITISH THREAT. The first serious threat to Siam proper came with the British annexation of the Tenasserim coast of Burma in 1826. At the same time, Siam relinquished her interests in several Malayan principalities over which Britain extended a partial protectorate. In 1855, Britain and Siam concluded a treaty providing extraterritoriality and a most-favored-nation agreement along with important trade concessions for Britain. France and the United States quickly moved to conclude similar arrangements.

FRANCO-BRITISH RIVALRY. French conquests sandwiched Siam between British Burma and French Indo-China. Forced by France to relinquish claim to both Cambodia and Laos, Siam was finally carved into spheres of interest by a Franco-British convention of 1896. This did not impair Siamese political control, and both England and France, desiring to preserve Siam as a buffer state, guaranteed her independence. In 1904 and 1907, however, France seized more territory, and in 1909, Britain gained full recognition of her control of Malaya. Siam was thus reduced by one-third, but her remaining territory was compact and largely homogeneous in population.

Modernization of Siam. Under two progressive rulers, Kings Mongkut and Chulalongkorn (1851-1910), Siam countered the threat of Western imperialism by modernizing communications and transportation and introducing Western ideas of education and administration. Chulalongkorn utilized Western advisers of many nationalities and sent young men abroad to study and travel.

Revolution and Constitutional Monarchy. After Chulalongkorn, the Chakkri Dynasty declined in popularity, although his successors continued modernization programs. They moved too slowly to suit the small group of Western-educated young men, and too fast for the entrenched royal administrators. In 1932, the discontent, fanned by financial crisis, erupted into open revolution, which introduced constitutional monarchy. Successive coups entrenched a largely military clique led by Pridi Bhanomyong (Luang Pradit Manudharm) and Pibun (Pibul or Phibun) Songgram, who governed with the aid of a partialiy elective legislature, while the young king was represented by a regent. After 1938, Marshal Pibun became a virtual military dictator.

SIAMESE NATIONALISM. The revolution heightened the growing nationalism and Westernization typical of twentieth-century Siam. As most of the special privileges of Western powers were eliminated, Siam gained in international stature. At this time, Siam's name was changed to Thailand.

INDONESIA (EAST INDIES)

Hindu Kingdoms. Early Indian commercial settlements in Java and Sumatra formed the nucleus of later Hindu kingdoms. Both Buddhism and Brahmanism won acceptance. Social and political structures followed Indian patterns.

RIVAL EMPIRES. In the seventh century, Sri Vishaya of Sumatra built the first important Indonesian empire. It was rivalled by the Sailendras of Java until the two merged in the ninth century. At its peak, Sri Vishaya dominated Sumatra, the Malay Peninsula, and part of Java. Between 1025 and 1090, it was humbled by the Chola rulers of India. As Sri Vishaya declined thereafter, its empire was conquered by the Javanese, who in the thirteenth century built an important kingdom at Singosari.

MAJAPAHIT EMPIRE. In 1292, Singosari fell to Majapahit, which built a great commercial empire. Over its many tributary states, Majapahit imposed a lucrative monopoly, requiring tribute in kind which was traded for the products of India, Indo-China, and China. After 1389, internal dissension combined with the rise of the rival trading empire of Malacca and the spread of Islam to weaken Majapahit. As Java's control relaxed, Siam claimed suzerainty over the Malay Peninsula, and China over the island principalities.

Muslim Conquest. Just as Indian traders had introduced Buddhism and Brahmanism into Indonesia, so they later bore the message of Islam. Having been converted by Arab merchants, Indians carried Islam to Sumatra in the late thirteenth century. After the conversion of the Hindu ruler of Malacca about 1413, the Muslim faith spread rapidly through the island world.

Portuguese Domination. After D'Albuquerque seized Malacca in 1511, the Portuguese established a very profitable trade monopoly over the East Indies, particularly in the Moluccas or Spice Islands. The Portuguese administrators were greedy and cruel, however, and corruption became rampant. After 1595, the monopoly was broken by the Dutch and British, but Portuguese and Spanish ships harassed the Dutch for decades thereafter.

Dutch Expansion. The Dutch had planted posts at strategic points even prior to the chartering of the Dutch East India Company in 1602. The Company took over these posts and in 1619 annexed western Java. By 1685, the Dutch had vanquished all European rivals, captured Malacca (1641), and suppressed several strong native states in Indonesia. As it became obvious that total exploitation required political control, the Dutch empire grew. France and then Britain took over the Indies during the French Revolution and Napoleonic Wars, but the islands were returned to Holland by the Treaty of Vienna in 1815. Dutch control of Indonesia was assured in 1824, at which time Malacca passed to the British.

Dutch Rule. From their capital of Batavia, Java, Dutch officials of the East India Company supervised the native sultans, who continued to govern the people. It was they who enforced Dutch demands for tribute and furnished the armies for the Dutch conquest of the East Indies. Corrupt company rule ended when France overran the Netherlands in 1795. Between then and 1815, administrative changes, particularly under the British Governor Raffles, centralized control in European hands. While the reforms were soon dropped, they weakened the feudal system which was maintained to reduce the cost of economic exploitation.

ROYAL RULE AND THE CULTURE SYSTEM. After 1815, the East Indies were ruled directly by the Dutch crown, which at first attempted liberal reforms. However, the "culture system," introduced after 1830, only exploited the Indonesians as mercilessly as had the Company. Instead of paying taxes, the farmers cultivated one-fifth of their land under government direction and for government profit. Misuse of the system was all too frequent.

Liberal Reforms. In 1867, the Netherlands East Indies ceased to be a royal monopoly. Free enterprise was encouraged, compulsory labor under the culture system was gradually ended, and the judicial system was reformed. While highly centralized, the administration remained in fact largely "indirect."

REPRESENTATIVE GOVERNMENT. During the twentieth century, democratic reforms brought local and then national partially elective advisory councils. In 1922, the East Indies became an integral part of the Netherlands, and 7 years later the People's Council *(Volksraad)* was granted more native members and some actual legislative functions. A general decentralization accompanied the reforms, permitting greater autonomy to the provincial governments in the islands.

EFFECTS OF DUTCH RULE. Dutch imperialism was almost totally economic in motivation and nature. Under Dutch rule, Javanese exports soared, and many new crops were introduced. But the profits went to the Dutch, not the Indonesians. Nevertheless, population increased tenfold on Java and Madura between 1815 and 1942. Indonesian culture, however, sharply declined. Very little effort at mass education was made before 1900, but by 1942, about half of the children received some primary instruction.

INDONESIAN NATIONALIST MOVEMENT. The twentieth century produced an articulate nationalist movement, beginning with educational, trade, and religious organizations. Gradually, political groups formed, some modelled on parent organizations in the Netherlands. The Communist Party attempted revolution in 1922, but was quickly suppressed. As the Netherlands staggered under German pressures early in World War II, the nationalists demanded greater self-government; but the Dutch imprisoned all nationalist leaders and refused even to make any concrete promises.

MALAYA

Checkered History. For centuries, the Hinduized principalities of the Malay Peninsula were dominated by their neighbors. After 1400, however, a Sumatran prince built an independent kingdom at Malacca which became a great commercial center and the suzerain of much of the Malay Peninsula. From here Islam spread rapidly through the archipelago. Malayan control of Malacca ended with the Portuguese seizure of the thriving port in 1511. Malacca passed to the Dutch in 1641 and to the British in 1824.

MALAY SULTANATES. Although Europeans thus controlled Malacca, native sultans continued their traditional rule of Malaya. Malacca's last sultan established a new kingdom, Riau-Johore, over much of southern Malaya. After 1699, Pahang and Johore became independent as did Trengganu and Perak. These sultanates engaged in incessant petty warfare and were in addition subject to recurrent civil disorders. In varying degrees they recognized the suzerainty of Siam. During this period, Bugis from Macassar conquered Selangor and gained power in other states by intermarrying with the ruling families. Minangkabaus of Sumatra also invaded, conquering the region known as Negri Sembilan.

British Penetration. First acquiring Penang, British interest gradually spread over southern Malaya. In 1800, the British gained Province Wellesley, adjacent to Penang. During the French Revolution and the Napoleonic Wars, the British seized Malacca and the Dutch East Indies, but returned them to Holland in 1815. At the instigation of Sir Thomas Stamford Raffles, who dreamed of a great Malay federation under British protection, Britain in 1819 acquired Singapore. Raffles quickly built it into a thriving free port. Shortly thereafter, the Dutch ceded Malacca and in the latter nineteenth century, Perak, Selangor, Negri Sembilan, Pahang, and Johore became British protectorates. When Siam relinquished suzerainty claims over Kelantan, Trengganu, Kedah, and Perlis in 1909, British expansion was complete.

British Administration. In 1826, Malacca, Singapore, Penang, and Province Wellesley were joined in the Straits Settlements under the British India Government. In 1867, the Straits Settlements became a crown colony with a governor and legislative council under the direction of the London Colonial Office. Although civil strife, petty wars, and piracy disrupted the Malay principalities, not until 1873 did the British directly intervene by placing residents or advisers in the Malayan courts. In 1895,

Perak, Selangor, Negri Sembilan, and Pahang joined as the Federated Malayan States, each keeping its native administration under the central authority of a British resident general. Johore and the states relinquished by Siam in 1909 gradually accepted British protection, but remained outside the federation. While native hierarchies administered the states, over-all control was increasingly centralized under British officials.

Effects of British Rule. The British peace permitted great economic development, particularly in rubber cultivation and tin mining. Railroads and roads covered the states. Since Malays remained by preference fishermen, farmers, or craftsmen, so many Chinese and Indians were imported for the new industries that by 1939 they outnumbered the Malays.

NATIONALISM. Never a united nation before World War II the Malays lacked a sense of nationalism except that derived from the Islamic movement. Chinese Malayans, however, were strongly influenced by nationalist movements within China. Among them too grew up a small but solid Communist organization with headquarters in Singapore.

KOREA AND THE SINO-JAPANESE WAR

Ancient History. According to Chinese and Korean legends, Chinese culture was brought to Korea by Kija (Kitze), a Chinese refugee around 1122 B.C. after the fall of the Shang dynasty. Kija's heirs ruled over the northwestern Korean kingdom of Han Chosen until overthrown by Wiman (Weiman), another refugee fleeing before the Han around 194 B.C. Chosen was soon conquered by China and remained a colony for four centuries (105 B.C.-313 A.D.). Under the influence of the Chinese colony centered at Lolang, the Korean tribesmen developed the indigenous kingdoms of Koguryo in the north and Silla, Paekche, and Kaya in the south.

United Silla. With the fall of the Chinese Han empire, Koguryo gradually conquered Lolang. Subsequently, Silla absorbed the Japanese-dominated state of Kaya. During this period of the Three Kingdoms, the Koreans began to adopt Buddhism and Chinese writing and system of government. Finally, with the aid of T'ang China, Silla conquered Paekche and Koguryo. The following period of United Silla (668 A.D.-

935 A.D.) began with an era of cultural flowering, but ended in chaos.

Koryo. The succeeding Koryo (Wang) dynasty (935-1392 A.D.) was characterized by extensive Buddhist influence, a parasitic aristocracy, and a continuing influx of Chinese cultural elements. Koryo fended off invasions by the Khitai and Nuchen tribes, but was overrun by the Mongols who imposed a humiliating vassalage. Under the Yüan, Korea had to assist the Mongols' abortive invasions of Japan.

Yi Dynasty. The Yi rulers who succeeded the Koryo replaced Buddhism with the Chu Hsi school of Confucianism which became the dominating cultural influence. The scholar bureaucrats of the Yi court developed a bitter factionalism that weakened the country especially during such crises as the devastating Japanese invasions under Hideyoshi. Thereafter the Yi closed Korea to the world except for limited trade with their suzerain, China, or with Japan. The aristocratic Confucianist scholars with few exceptions degenerated progressively into sterile, quibbling and vicious factionalists as the court became hopelessly decadent by the nineteenth century.

Western Influences. Despite the isolation of the Hermit Kingdom, western ideas filtered in to influence many scholars. Korean diplomats and traders brought back western books from China. Moreover, Jesuit missionaries in Peking made some converts. A Chinese priest came to Korea in 1795 to die there in 1800 in the first Korean persecutions of Christians. French priests sent to Korea in 1836 and 1845 suffered similar fates. Yet, despite bloody persecutions, Christianity spread and with other western ideas caused new intellectual ferment among dissatisfied scholars.

Foreign Relations. Through most of her history, Korea has looked to China as suzerain power, protector, and cultural tutor. While the Manchu failed to conquer the peninsula, Korea's kings sent regular tribute to Peking and were invested in office by the emperors of China. French protests against the execution of their priests were referred to Peking, but China's influence in Korea weakened as Manchu power declined.

WESTERN PENETRATION. After the Treaties of Tientsin opened north China to trade in 1858, Western powers began attempts to draw Korea from her isolation. In 1866, after anti-Confucianist activities of native Christians set off terrible persecution by the Korean government, the French protested to China but Peking disavowed authority to interfere. The French then made a retaliatory bombardment of Korean forts. In the same year, the American merchant vessel *General Sherman* was burned and its crew killed when it visited Pyongyang for trade. Two American naval expeditions tried unsuccessfully to investigate the incident in the next year. When a larger U. S. expedition was sent in 1871 to negotiate a treaty, it was attacked by Korean forts. After destroying the offending batteries the Americans withdrew. As a result of these incidents, Korea's rulers were further convinced of their superiority.

JAPANESE SUCCESS. Korea's conservative court disapproved the opening of Japan's doors to the West, and emissaries of the new Meiji emperor were rebuffed. When Koreans attacked a Japanese warship, however, the Japanese retaliated with an expeditionary force that extracted a treaty of commerce and friendship in 1876. This Japanese success frightened China, and in 1882, the U. S. concluded a treaty with Chinese assistance. The Japanese and American treaties and those with European powers shortly concluded treated Korea as an independent power.

Internal Affairs. Korea's internal politics were complicated by her foreign affairs. In 1863, a 12-year-old child succeeded to the throne under the regency of his father, who was called the Taiwunkun. The weak boy king, who was married to a girl of the powerful Min family, remained under his father's domination until his strong-willed queen gained control in 1873. This precipitated a long factional strife that weakened the country. The Yi faction led by Taiwunkun was pro-Chinese and opposed Western ideas, while the Min faction led by the queen favored adoption of westernization and friendship with Japan.

POLITICAL TURMOIL. In 1882, the Yi group aided by rioters unsuccessfully attacked both the queen and the Japanese legation. China and Japan alike sent forces to Korea to settle the affair. Japan extracted an agreement which, in addition to providing for an indemnity and punishment of the guilty, gave further trade privileges to the Japanese. To assert their suzerainty, the Chinese imprisoned the Taiwunkun. Increasingly the internal political affairs of Korea were becoming interlinked with the rivalry between China and Japan for Korea.

Chinese Aggressiveness. After the uprising of 1882, China increased her interest in Korea. Yüan Shih-k'ai was sent to Seoul as China's resident minister. China now asserted her special position and gained large controls over Korean trade, customs, and communications. The Min faction had meanwhile come to fear the Japanese and turned to China for support, with the result that the progressive element of the Min, with Japanese aid, seized the king in December 1884. Yüan Shih-k'ai attacked with his forces and drove out the Japanese and their conspirators. By the subsequent treaties, Korea accepted full responsibility for the affair and paid an indemnity. Both China and Japan under the Tientsin Convention of 1885 agreed to withdraw their forces from Korea, and neither was to send troops back into the country in case of disorders without informing the other. Despite the fact that the treaty of Tientsin essentially recognized China and Japan as equals, China continued in control. In 1886, Li Hung-chang threatened to dethrone the Korean king when he sought aid from Russia against China. England, to forestall Russian aggression, occupied Port Hamilton in south Korea for two years.

Opening of the Sino-Japanese War. The Koreans gave the immediate cause for strife. An antiforeign organization known as the Tonghaks led an uprising that the Korean government could not suppress. Upon the Korean ruler's request, Li Hung-chang sent Chinese forces into Korea, and only afterward notified the Japanese. In retaliation, Japan sent large forces also. After the suppression of the rebellion, China refused to recall her forces until Japan had withdrawn hers. Negotiations failed, and Japan opened the conflict without warning by attacking a Chinese troopship on July 25, 1894. Two days later the Korean government, now controlled by Japan, declared war upon China. Not until August 6, did Japan formally declare war.

COURSE OF THE WAR. It is scarcely proper to say that China fought Japan. Only a small fraction of the available Chinese army and navy ever saw action. The war is best described

as one between Li Hung-chang, viceroy of Chili, and Japan.
Even Li's forces were weakened by Chinese corruption, while
the Japanese had a small but well-equipped and efficient military
force and wholehearted national support of the war. The
Chinese consequently were defeated in nearly every encounter.
By November, the Chinese were driven out of Korea and had
lost their main northern fleet. In February and March, Japanese
naval and land forces attacked China proper at Weihaiwei in
Shantung and had invaded Manchuria and Formosa before
Li Hung-chang arrived in Japan to discuss peace terms.

Treaty of Shimonoseki (April 18, 1895). The Treaty of
Shimonoseki concluding the Sino-Japanese War called for
China's cession of Formosa, the Pescadores Islands, and Liaotung Peninsula; the opening of several additional ports to
Japan; and the payment of a large indemnity. Before the two
powers had exchanged ratifications, Russia, France, and Germany intervened to induce Japan to return Liaotung to China
in exchange for an additional indemnity. The Japanese were
greatly annoyed but dared not defy three such powers. After
fighting a successful war with China for domination of Korea,
Japan discovered that in Russia she had an even stronger rival
to contend with on the continent.

THE PHILIPPINES
AND THE SPANISH-AMERICAN WAR

Pre-Spanish Culture. Prior to the Spanish occupation of
the Philippine Archipelago, there existed a moderately high
culture among the natives. At an unknown date, Buddhism
and Hinduism were brought to the islands, but when the Spanish arrived, these religions had been forgotten. Except for
a few Moslems, the population were animists. Early explorers
reported a high percentage of the natives could read and write
in their own dialects. At an early period, the Filipinos learned
to cover the slopes of hills with terraced fields and to construct
extensive irrigation systems. Due to the sparsity of the population and the diversity of the languages, however, no strong
kingdom ever developed.

Spanish Conquest. As we have seen in Chapter III, the
Spanish in 1571 seized the Philippine port of Manila, which
became the capital and the chief commercial port of the Spanish

eastern empire. By 1572, the Spanish conquest was largely complete, although the Moslem Moros of the southern islands and numerous mountain tribes remained unsubdued. Through most of their long rule, the Spanish had intermittently to fight the Moros.

Imperialist Rivalry. Spanish conquest did not secure the island from outside dangers. As early as 1574 the Portuguese almost seized Manila. On two occasions Chinese adventurers menaced the Spanish, and in 1590 the Japanese dictator Hideyoshi threatened invasion. The Dutch between 1600 and 1646 plagued the Spanish and actually held bases on the islands. During the Seven Years' War, the British captured Manila, but returned the city at the end of the struggle.

Spanish Rule. Under Spanish rule, the Philippine government and society were more feudal than that of Spain. The governor general was both the chief administrator and the president of the *audiencia* or supreme court. The only real limitation to his power was the *residencia,* an official investigation at the end of his term of office. Over each province was an *alcalde majore,* who was both administrator and judge. The provinces were divided into *pueblos* over which native officials presided. Unfortunately, the principal offices were bought and sold, while the lesser ones paid such low salaries that they often remained unfilled. Due to the low caliber, if not to the lack, of Spanish officials, the real rulers of the islands were the Spanish friars.

OPPRESSION BY SPANISH FRIARS. So successful was the conquest by the Spanish friars that the Filipinos are the only large population of Asia that accepted Christianity. By 1600, Manila had an archbishop who presided over 400 priests. While the Spanish friars aided to a degree in the Philippine economic advancement, they kept a firm control over their converts. In defiance of church decrees, the Spanish friars monopolized the parishes, although native priests were available, and refused to admit natives into their orders. The best farming lands were held by the friars, who leased them to natives on terms little better than serfdom.

Reform Movements. The opening of the Suez Canal and the establishment of steamship lines increased the economic value of the islands and brought them close to the main lines of commerce. The resultant influx of new ideas stimulated a strong movement to break the economic and political control of the friars. In 1872, however, a revolt at Cavite gave the friars an opportunity to suppress the local reformers. A number of native clergy who had led the reform movement were executed, and Philippine priests were declared incompetent to administer the sacraments.

José Rizal. Increasingly, the wealthy Philippine families sent their sons to Europe for better education. Outstanding among these students was José Rizal, who studied in Spain and Germany after graduating from the University of Manila. Rizal became famous as a nationalist and reformer by organizing a reform party and by writing popular books exposing the abuses of Spanish rule. These activities caused first his exile and ultimately his death. After Rizal's death, his reform movement was replaced by the more militant Katipunan, a revolutionary party led by Andrés Bonifacio.

Revolution. In 1896, after the friars had caused the banishment of hundreds of Filipinos, the Katipunan led an insurrection that continued for months under the leadership of Emilio Aguinaldo. As success for the revolt was not in sight, Aguinaldo in 1897 accepted a Spanish indemnity to retire to Hong Kong where he remained until the outbreak of the Spanish-American War.

Spanish-American War. Prior to the outbreak of war between the United States and Spain, an aggressive and imperialistic-minded commodore, George Dewey, had been sent by an equally aggressive Assistant Secretary of the Navy, Theodore Roosevelt, to take command of the United States Asiatic fleet. Dewey was to prepare the United States fleet to take advantage of any opportunity. On May 1, 1898, after the outbreak of war, Dewey steamed his little force into Manila Bay. Ignoring the dangers of mines and obstructions, he destroyed the unprepared Spanish fleet. Lacking the forces to land and occupy Manila, he contented himself with occupying Cavite while awaiting reinforcements. Having learned of Aguinaldo's prestige, the commodore provided the revolutionists with captured Spanish arms. Aguinaldo, however, proclaimed himself head of an independent Philippine state, which petitioned the foreign powers for recognition. Before Aguinaldo could take Manila, American reinforcements arrived and the city capitulated to the Americans.

UNITED STATES ACQUISITION OF THE PHILIPPINES. The Philippine conquest proved a source of embarrassment to the United States, and it was questionable whether she would retain the islands. Several factors helped to bring about the annexation by the Treaty of Paris: (1) the land acquisitions in China which made it appear necessary for the United States to gain control of bases in the Far East as had the other powers; (2) the probability that Germany would take the islands if the United States did not act (Britain, France, and Japan, moreover, preferred American control); (3) imperialistic tendencies in the United States stimulated by American victories in the war; (4) the Philippine insurrections against United States rule, which led some congressmen to favor annexation of the islands to save American prestige.

American Rule. Until Philippine resistance was quelled, an American military government directed reconstruction. On July 4, 1901, a civil government under William H. Taft took over. Taft was assisted by a mixed Philippine-American Commission to which an elected assembly was added in 1907 to form a bicameral legislature.

PROGRESS TOWARD INDEPENDENCE. Under U.S. President Wilson, the Filipinos progressed rapidly toward self-government. By 1919, they held 94 per cent of all civil service posts. The Jones Act of 1916 promised them independence as soon as they established a stable government. The Islands meanwhile became nearly autonomous with an elective legislature, a responsible cabinet, and a quasi-parliamentary Council of State. A conservative U.S. government in the 1920's, however, vetoed the idea of independence.

COMMONWEALTH STATUS. In 1934, the Tydings-McDuffie Commonwealth and Independence Act made the Philippines a commonwealth and guaranteed independence on July 4, 1946. During the preparatory period, the commonwealth was to set up a democratic government and the Philippine economy was to be made independent of that of the U.S. As provided by the new constitution, presidential and legislative elections were held in 1935.

Effects of U.S. Rule. The U.S. brought cultural, economic, and political advances. Although the friars' control, both economic and religious, was early broken and their lands sold to former tenants, too much land remained held in large estates. Public education was greatly expanded and university enrollment swelled. As late as 1939, however, the literacy rate was only about 50 per cent. Public health and sanitation measures nearly tripled the population. Agricultural production and trade increased phenomenally. Accompanying this was a great increase in transportation and communication facilities and in industrial production, particularly of agricultural goods. Manila became a financial center. Generally, however, the economy was too tied to that of the U.S. and the prosperity was not adequately felt by the small farmers and workers.

NATIONALISM. Unlike other colonial powers, the U.S. encouraged the formation of political parties. Sergio Osmeña, Manuel Quezon, and Manuel Roxas early rose to leadership in the dominant Nacionalista Party *(Partido Nacional Progresista)*.

BIBLIOGRAPHY

Cady, J. F., *A History of Modern Burma*, 1958.
Cady, J. F., *The Roots of French Imperialism in Eastern Asia*, 1954.
Conroy, F. H., *The Japanese Seizure of Korea, 1868-1910*, 1960.
Cowan, C. D., *Nineteenth-Century Malaya: The Origins of British Political Control*, 1961.
Dennett, T., *Americans in Eastern Asia*, 1922.
Hall, D. G. E., *A History of South-East Asia*, 1955.
Hall, D. G. E., *Burma*, 1960.
Herz, M. F., *A Short History of Cambodia*, 1958.
Landon, K. P., *Siam in Transition*, 1939.
Lee, C., *The Politics of Korean Nationalism*, 1963.
Le May, R. S., *The Culture of South-East Asia*, 1954.
Moorhead, F. J., *A History of Malaya and Her Neighbors*, 1957.
Nelson, M. F., *Korea and the Old Orders in Eastern Asia*, 1945.
Thompson, V., *French Indo-China*, 1937.
Vandenbosch, A., *The Dutch East Indies*, 1942.
Vlekke, B. H. M., *Nusantara: A History of Indonesia*, 1960.
Winstedt, R., *The Malays: A Cultural History*, 1950.
Wolff, L., *Little Brown Brother*, 1961.
Woodman, D., *The Making of Burma*, 1962.
Zaide, G. F., *Philippine Political and Cultural History*, 2 vols., 1949.

CHAPTER 8
Road to Revolution in China
(1894-1914)

CONSEQUENCES OF THE SINO-JAPANESE WAR

Chinese Reaction. China's defeat by Japan had little effect upon the Chinese people as a whole because the war had been localized and was viewed as a quarrel between the alien Manchu rulers and the barbarian Japanese. To the Chinese scholar class, who staffed China's bureaucracy, the defeat was a humiliating warning. Many progressive mandarins felt that the governmental decentralization which had prevented all of China's army and navy from entering the struggle must be ended. In Peking, however, the war merely made the Manchu government weaker and more corrupt. The civil service system rapidly decayed as the government increased its revenues by openly selling offices.

REFORMS. As a result of the defeat, Li Hung-chang was dismissed. Yüan Shih-k'ai became head of a new war council created to reorganize China's army and navy. A series of decrees was issued ordering the development of western-style factories and communication systems with Chinese capital. Unfortunately, the provincial officials who were to execute these orders lacked both capital and skill, and relied heavily upon foreign aid.

Foreign Reaction. China's defeat dissipated any lingering respect foreigners had for China's military power. She was now viewed as a melon ripe for cutting, the chief problem being the manner of apportionment.

Methods of Foreign Penetration. The imperialistic powers advanced their interests in China by a variety of methods including the following:

1. Loans to China, often under pressure and under condi-

tions that gave the creditors controls over portions of China's economy.

2. Exclusive economic rights such as railroad or mining concessions, often involving policing rights that could threaten potential military control.

3. Spheres of interest acquired by China's grants of economic priorities or monopolies over large regions; such spheres did not involve change of political authority, but they were steps toward protectorates.

4. Nonalienation agreements by which China promised to one power that she would not alienate or transfer sovereignty of the region in question to any other foreign power.

5. Leaseholds by which portions of Chinese territory were leased to a foreign power for naval bases or similar purposes.

FOREIGN LOANS. China's "friends," Russia, France, and Germany, had forced Japan to retrocede Liaotung to China after the Sino-Japanese War, and when China was unable to pay the heavy indemnity to Japan, Russia offered a loan. France, however, insisted that she should share in the loan; consequently in July, 1895, a Franco-Russian loan of 400 million francs was arranged. In addition, an Anglo-German banking syndicate secured the privilege of making two loans to China in March, 1896, and March, 1898.

RUSSO-CHINESE AGREEMENTS OF 1896. Russia fully exploited Chinese trust resulting from the retrocession of Liaotung. In December, 1895, a Russo-Chinese bank was organized with French capital and Russian initiative. This bank was chartered with the right to collect taxes, coin money, and operate railways. On the occasion of the coronation of the Russian tzar in June, 1896, Li Hung-chang concluded the Li-Lobanov Treaty with Russia, which was to last 15 years and which provided for (1) Russo-Chinese military alliance against Japan, (2) extension of the Trans-Siberian Railroad across Manchuria to Vladivostok under the jurisdiction of the Russo-Chinese bank, (3) extensive mineral, commercial, and industrial concessions in and close to the railway right of way, (4) the railway to be a purely Russo-Chinese concern which would automatically become Chinese property at the end of 80 years, but could be purchased by China after 36 years, and (5) grant to Russia of rights to use certain Chinese ports in the event of war.

GERMAN LEASE OF KIAOCHOW. Germany had intervened to aid China in 1895 because she had designs upon Chinese soil. Her pretext for action came when two German Jesuits were murdered in Shantung in 1897. After Germany landed forces in China and issued ultimatums, China granted to Germany on March 6, 1898, (1) lease of the port of Tsingtao and the lands surrounding Kiaochow Bay as a naval base, (2) a 50-kilometer neutral zone behind the leasehold under German control, (3) railroad and mineral concessions in Shantung province, and (4) a sphere of interest over Shantung.

RUSSIA LEASES PORT ARTHUR. Russia badly needed a warm-water port for her vast northern empire, and Vladivostok was not ice free throughout the year. After being barred from gaining a Korean port by an Anglo-Japanese fleet, Russia secured in March, 1898, a 25-year lease on southern Liaotung Peninsula, including Port Arthur and Dalny (Dairen). In addition, Russia obtained the right to link the Trans-Siberian Railway with the new leasehold.

FRANCE AND KWANGCHOW. France's reward for her aid to China was a series of agreements culminating in April, 1898, which included (1) extensive mineral and railway concessions in Kwangsi and Yünnan, (2) sphere of interest and nonalienation agreements covering Hainan and the Chinese provinces bordering French Indo-China, (3) a 99-year lease on Kwangchow for a naval base, (4) a Chinese agreement to appoint French advisers in a proposed Chinese postal service, and (5) rectification of the Chinese-Tonking border in favor of France.

BRITAIN AND WEIHAIWEI. Her extensive trade already protected by Hong Kong, Britain neither needed nor desired more, but if other countries received concessions, British prestige must be maintained. Consequently, British diplomats by July, 1898 had extracted from China agreements including (1) enlargement of her leasehold on Kowloon Peninsula adjacent to Hong Kong Island, (2) a nonalienation and sphere of interest agreement covering the Yangtze Valley (3) a lease on Weihaiwei for a naval base as long as Russia retained Port Arthur, (4) assurance that British subjects would be appointed inspector general of the Chinese customs while British trade predominated, and (5) rectification of the Chinese-Burmese border in favor of Britain.

End of Territorial Acquisitions. Japan next followed the example of the European powers to demand and receive a non-alienation agreement covering the province of Fukien on the Chinese coast opposite Formosa. Only when Italy requested a leasehold did China summon the courage to refuse and thus end the race for her territory. Some spheres of interest overlapped, but differences between the powers were settled diplomatically. The Siam Convention of 1896, which shared in advance any privileges Great Britain or France would gain in Yünnan or Szechwan provinces, was modified by a supplementary agreement in 1898. A British-German agreement of 1898 defined their spheres of interest. In the following year, Great Britain and Russia chose the Great Wall as the dividing line between their zones.

United States Interests. Throughout its relations with China the United States avoided seeking exclusive privileges but insisted upon most-favored-nation treatment. The acquisition of the Philippines in 1898 made it even less necessary to enter the competition for Chinese territory. The United States, however, did continue her most-favored-nation policy to avoid being excluded from the China trade.

OPEN DOOR POLICY (1899). Because of the Boer War which weakened the British position in China at this crucial moment, Great Britain suggested that the United States should take the lead in inducing the great powers to maintain an open door for all nations' trade into China. The pronouncement of such a policy came as a group of proposals issued by American Secretary of State John Hay to the powers, requesting (1) that they should not interfere with the treaty ports or pre-existing foreign interests within their spheres of interests or leaseholds, (2) that the Chinese tariffs established by treaties should be collected equally on all merchandise of all nations regardless of spheres of interests or leaseholds, and (3) that there should be no discrimination in either spheres of interest or leaseholds in matters of harbor dues or freight rates. The foreign acceptances of Hay proposals were limited by serious reservations, but John Hay nonetheless pronounced them to be favorable, and the Open Door policy was announced as accepted.

HUNDRED DAYS OF REFORM
AND THE REACTION

Chinese Reformers. China's land losses of 1896-1898 gave additional point to the lessons learned by her in the military and moral defeats of 1894-1895, yet her leaders were not united. In Peking, the empress dowager Tz'u Hsi, who had controlled China's policies since 1860, continued to follow the advice of conservatives such as Jung Lu and Yüan Shih-k'ai, who advocated maintenance of the *status quo* with Russian aid. In the south, a group of leaders tended toward revolution or reform. Dr. Sun Yat-sen led a short-lived rebellion in Canton in 1895 and thereafter organized revolutionary groups among Chinese living overseas. Other southern reformers followed more peaceful methods. Weng T'ung-ho, tutor to the young Kuang-hsü emperor, and his disciple K'ang Yu-wei favored friendship with Japan and immediate political and social reforms with the view to gradual adoption of constitutional monarchy. Other important reform leaders were Chang Chih-tung, Liang Ch'i-ch'ao, and Liu Kun-yi.

Reform by Edict. Because of his success in indoctrinating the young emperor with progressive ideas, Weng was dismissed from his position as tutor by the ever-watchful Tz'u Hsi, but not before the emperor had determined on reforms. Between June 11 and September 22, 1898, K'ang Yu-wei, as adviser to the emperor, secured the issuance of a series of sweeping reform decrees that are collectively called the Hundred Days Reform. These decrees were intended to reorganize completely China's government and educational system: numerous sinecures were to be eliminated, the provincial governments were to be more centralized under Peking, new schools were to be created for promoting European learning, western-style production methods were to be encouraged, and a national conscript army was to be created along western lines.

Reaction. Unfortunately the reformers were inexperienced and their decrees had to be carried out largely by unsympathetic conservative officials. Furthermore, the foreign powers continued to embarrass the reform government by demanding still more concessions. Convinced that the reforms would fail unless the opposition leadership were removed, the reformers plotted to eliminate the empress dowager and Jung Lu. However, the plot backfired, and by a *coup d'etat* of September 21, Tz'u Hsi returned to power. The emperor was placed in close confinement for the rest of his life. K'ang Yu-wei and Liang Ch'i-ch'ao escaped, but many reformers were executed.

THE BOXER MOVEMENT

Renewed Resistance to Foreign Aggression. The empress stiffened China's resistance to foreign demands, and it was at this time that Italy was rebuffed. However, the demands of the powers had thoroughly frightened the Chinese, and steps were taken for increasing the army. While the reformers had sought to strengthen China's military potential by centralizing government controls over the military forces, Tz'u Hsi sought the same end by decentralization.

Boxer Reaction Movement. The collapse of the Hundred Days Reform gave the reactionaries full power. Their zeal was intensified by a growing antiforeign movement centered in north China. Many officials tried to channel economic, social, and political discontent against the foreigners. Antiforeign secret societies, promoted by court reactionaries and provincial governors, enrolled their members into local militias to combat foreign aggression. Chief among these societies was the I Ho T'üan or Righteous Harmony Fists popularly termed Boxers. With official connivance, the Boxers began to attack foreigners, and by 1900 numerous Chinese Christians and foreigners had been killed in North China. On June first, 450 marines were added to the detachments guarding the Peking legations. Three days later the Boxers, who believed this was a prelude to foreign invasion, destroyed the Peking-Tientsin Railroad connections. When naval detachments at Tientsin began on June 11 to send reinforcements to Peking under British Admiral Seymour, the Peking court and the Boxers declared war on all foreigners.

Boxer Uprising. When the Seymour expedition was driven back to Tientsin, a larger naval expedition stormed the Taku forts. In retaliation the Chinese attacked the foreign legations at Peking, and the empress on June 24 ordered the extermination of all aliens in China. Fortunately for China, this rash edict was ignored by many provincial officials who opposed the Boxer movement. To localize the conflict, the foreign powers announced they were fighting only the Boxers and were helping China suppress an internal revolt.

UNITED STATES INTERCESSION. The United States, concerned that this might be a prelude to new territorial demands upon China, dispatched to the other powers identical notes stating that the United States policy was (1) the preservation of China's territorial and administrative integrity and (2) the continuance of the Open Door policy in China. This pledge was backed by Great Britain and Germany.

Boxer Protocol (1901). On August 14, the international armies relieved the besieged legations of Peking, and the imperial court fled to Shensi Province. China secured peace on humiliating terms. The Manchu government was required, among other things, to (1) apologize to Japan and Germany for the murder of their diplomats, (2) punish the responsible Chinese officials, (3) suspend Chinese civil service examinations in cities where foreigners were attacked, (4) pay an indemnity of $333 million, (5) destroy the Taku forts and stop armament importations for two years, (6) create a ministry of foreign affairs, and (7) revise the commercial treaties and increase the customs duties to an effective 5 per cent.

MANCHU REFORM PROGRAM (1902-1911)

Conversion of the Empress to Reform. Prior to the Boxer uprising, the empress had frustrated nearly all efforts at reform. After fleeing a second time from Peking to escape the foreigners, however, Tz'u Hsi recognized the necessity for change, and until her death in 1908, fostered the reforms she had previously opposed. Her essential conservatism, however, was evidenced by an edict in 1901 in which she cited precedents for governmental reform in the writings of Confucius.

Reform Program. Among her first reforms, Tz'u Hsi established social equality between Manchu and Chinese by permitting intermarriage. Other important reform measures aimed at improvements in education, the army and navy, the legal system, and the administrative machinery.

EDUCATION. Of fundamental importance were the educational reforms introduced in 1901. Young Manchus were sent abroad to absorb western learning. A Ministry of Education was established. A comprehensive education program, promulgated in 1904, called for establishment in the provinces of western-style education from kindergarten to college and for the founding of an imperial university at Peking. In 1905, the civil service examinations were abolished and study abroad further encouraged. This program was further stimulated by the United States which in 1907 returned part of the Boxer indemnity to support Chinese studying abroad. The education program aimed to achieve a 5 per cent literacy by 1917. Since the reform edicts unfortunately had to be executed by provincial officials who had little understanding of western learning or educational systems, the results were very unequal and generally poor.

ARMY AND NAVY. Prior to 1905, China's military forces consisted of Manchu Banner armies in the chief cities and autonomous Green Flag forces under provincial governors. Both were weakened by corruption, bad leadership, and antiquated armaments. Under Yüan Shih-k'ai a plan was developed to build a modern national conscript army of 36 divisions, but Yüan's dismissal in 1908 virtually ended the program with only 6 divisions equipped and trained. The Chinese navy had been destroyed by the French in the Tonking War. Although the new navy, created by 1894, was considered superior to Japan's, lack of central control permitted the Japanese to destroy the northern fleets in the Sino-Japanese War. In 1907, a Navy Department was created to bring about central control, but again provincial opposition frustrated reforms.

POLITICAL REFORMS. The Reform Edict of 1901 pledged China to a course of adopting the best foreign governmental methods and systems. The Chinese observed that all the great western powers except Russia had constitutions, and Russia had just been defeated in 1904-1905 by the Japanese, who had adopted a constitution. In 1905-1906, a Chinese commission sent abroad to study representative governments chose Japan's oriental adaptation of Germany's constitution as a model, largely because it gave a parliamentary facade without loss of imperial power. Tz'u Hsi chose a policy of slow change. First the principle of constitutional monarchy was to be adopted and the governmental departments were to be revised accordingly. In 1907 an edict called for the formation of provincial assemblies which were to be political schools for representatives to a proposed national assembly of the future and sounding boards of public opinion. All reforms were to come as gifts from the throne which would remain absolute.

NINE-YEAR PLAN. In 1908, the provisional constitution was promulgated together with a comprehensive nine-year program of governmental reform. During the first two years, provincial assemblies would be organized and meet. In 1910, a national assembly would be convened at Peking. After the gradual extension of reforms throughout China, the permanent constitution would be promulgated in 1917, and a national parliament would assemble.

Death of Tz'u Hsi. Only three months after the issuance of the nine-year reform plan, both the Kuang-hsü emperor and the empress dowager died, leaving the throne to the 2½-year-old Pu-yi under the regency of his incompetent but well-meaning father Prince Ch'un. One of the first acts of the regency was to dismiss Yüan Shih-k'ai and thus lose the most capable man in the government.

Meeting of the Assemblies. The change of leaders only briefly delayed the convening of the provincial assemblies in 1909. These bodies, although half elected by restricted suffrage and half appointed, proved to be critical of the government and demanded the speeding up of the reform period. In the following year, the national assembly with one-half its membership elected by the provincial assemblies and the other half appointed by the emperor proved equally intransigent. Demands were made for the early promulgation of the constitution, the establishment of a cabinet, and the convention of parliament by 1913. Only timely concessions prevented the national assembly from impeaching the Manchu Council of State. At this point the Republican Revolution burst out to smother imperial plans.

SUN YAT-SEN AND THE REPUBLICAN MOVEMENT

Failure of the Manchu Reforms. The nine-year program might have started China on the road to modernization, but after the death of Tz'u Hsi, the reform edicts largely remained on paper. Even had all the reforms been carried out, they would not have satisfied the growing group of revolutionists.

Sun Yat-sen. The leader and ideologist of the revolutionists was Dr. Sun Yat-sen. Born near Canton on a small farm, Sun was educated in a mission school in Hawaii and a medical school at Hong Kong. This formal training he augmented with extensive reading in social, political, and military science in libraries all over the world. After his first efforts at revolution in 1895 had resulted in his flight and exile, Sun founded a series of revolutionary societies dedicated to reform. Beginning as an anti-Manchu Nationalist, Sun moved leftward in his political thinking until he became a semisocialistic republican.

T'UNG MENG HUI. In 1905, Sun founded the T'ung Meng Hui (League of Common Alliance) which was to lead the revolution of 1911. The aims of the T'ung Meng Hui were to establish a Chinese republic and to redistribute the land. Sun recognized the infeasibility of immediate radical change and planned to create the new China by three phases: (1) a period of military rule while military conquest from the Manchus was in progress, (2) political tutelage during which the people would be educated to democratic ideals and methods of government, and (3) constitutional government. Only a few Chinese intellectuals were indoctrinated with Sun's ideals when the revolution began, while the mass of the Chinese remained illiterate and apathetic.

Immediate Cause of the Revolution. One part of the Manchu reform program called for widespread construction of railroads with Chinese capital under provincial direction. Provincial corruption and mismanagement finally caused the central government to attempt to nationalize the lines. Claiming that nationalization would place the roads under foreign control, the provincial interests stirred up strikes and riots against the Manchu. This discontent was used by the revolutionists, who worked successfully among the students and the soldiers. A small-scale republican uprising in Canton was suppressed, but on October 10, 1911, an accidental explosion in a revolutionist bomb factory at Hankow led to mutiny among nearby imperial troops. These troops led by Colonel Li Yüan-hung soon gained control of Wuchang and Hankow.

SPREAD OF THE REVOLT. The revolution spread rapidly throughout China despite lack of over-all plans or coordination. The first revolutionary government to be formed was the Reformed Government headed by Li Yüan-hung at Wuchang. Later a military government set up by Cantonese revolutionists at Shanghai under the leadership of Wu T'ing-fang appealed for foreign support. At Peking the leaderless Manchu government was forced to recall Yüan Shih-k'ai to control of the imperial forces under terms that gave him a virtual military dictatorship.

Nanking Government. Sun Yat-sen, who was in the United States at the outbreak of the revolution, delayed his return until he could attempt to arouse sympathy in Europe for the republican cause. After his arrival in China, he was recognized as the only man who could unite the republican factions, and was made president of a provisional government formed at Nanking of the united Hankow and Shanghai factions. Li Yüan-hung, commander in chief of the revolutionary armies, became vicepresident.

Yuan Shih-k'ai. Both the republican and the Manchu governments were in serious financial difficulties. Foreign governments were reluctant to make loans, and the people stopped paying taxes. The man who held the balance of power was Yüan Shih-k'ai. Yüan was Chinese and had little interest in maintaining the Manchu, yet his experience and education was that of an imperial official. He had the best armies in China and dictatorial power. On the other hand, he was in no position to make himself emperor. It was Sun who broke the stalemate by offering to turn over the presidency of the republic to Yüan. After a series of negotiations, terms were reached by which the Manchu emperor was permitted to abdicate with a generous settlement and Sun resigned from the presidency in favor of Yüan. Thus Yüan Shih-k'ai, who controlled the best Chinese army, became president, while Li Yüan-hung with the secondbest army remained vice-president.

INAUGURATION OF REPUBLICAN CHINA

Constitution of 1912. In March, 1912, a provisional constitution was promulgated. A temporary unicameral National Council, representing the provinces, shared the supreme authority with the president, the cabinet, and the judiciary. After ten months the National Council was to be replaced by a bicameral National Assembly.

Difficulties of the New Government. The new republic had little chance for success. The president and the vice-president

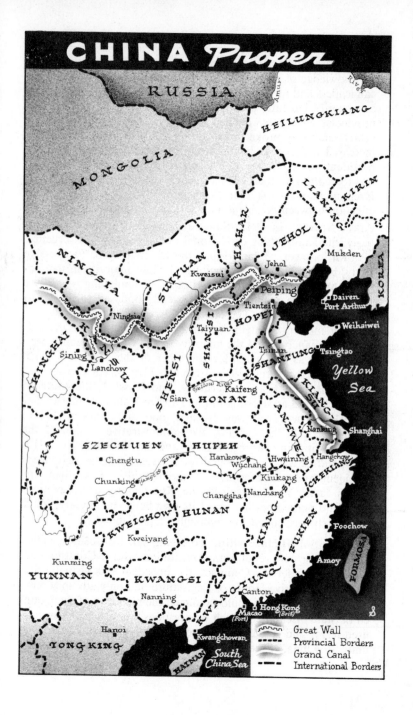

CHINA *Proper*

RUSSIA

Amur River

HEILUNGKIANG

MONGOLIA

LIAONING

KIRIN

NINGSIA

SUIYUAN

CHAHAR

JEHOL

Mukden

Kweisui

Jehol

Peiping

KOREA

Ningsia

KANSU

SHENSI

SHANSI

Taiyuan

Tientsin

HOPEI

Dairen
Port Arthur

Weihaiwei

CHINGHAI

Sining

Lanchow

Tsinan

SHANTUNG

Tsingtao

Yellow
Sea

Sian

Yellow River

Kaifeng

HONAN

KIANGSU

SIKANG

SZECHUEN

Chengtu

HUPEH

ANHWEI

Nanking

Shanghai

Chunking

Yangtze River

Hankow

Wuchang

Hwaining

Hangchow

Kiukang

CHEKIANG

Changsha

Nanchang

KWEICHOW

HUNAN

KIANGSI

FUKIEN

Kweiyang

Foochow

Kunming

YUNNAN

KWANGSI

KWANGTUNG

Amoy

FORMOSA

Nanning

Canton

Hong Kong
(Brit)

Macao
(Port)

Hanoi

TONG KING

Kwangchowan

HAINAN

South
China Sea

	Great Wall
	Provincial Borders
	Grand Canal
	International Borders

were both military leaders and practical politicians with little or no knowledge of constitutional government. The chief republican leaders had received western education and had many political theories but little practical experience. All over China, the provincial governors retained control of local armies. As the central authority broke down during the revolution, brigandage increased and robber bands began to control local areas. The president could neither defeat nor disband these armies and was forced to give them official recognition as republican armies. Even more disastrous for the republic was the growing disaffection between president and National Assembly.

PARTY STRIFE. In 1912, Sun Yat-sen founded a new political party, the Kuomintang or National Peoples' Party. To organize his own followers, Yüan formed the Chinputang or Progressive Party, but the Kuomintang enjoyed a slight majority in the National Assembly. The stronghold of the Kuomintang was in the south where the republicans were greatly opposed to the president's growing power. The president, however, enjoyed not only superior military strength, but also had the backing of the old-school bureaucrats and the majority of the Chinese people, who viewed him as the legitimate successor of the Manchu. When Yüan secured a foreign loan from the Five Power Consortium (Japan, Britain, France, Germany, and Russia), the southern republicans led an uprising in the Yangtze Valley in the summer of 1913. The revolt was crushed, and Sun Yat-sen fled to Japan. Despite the uprising, the administrative section of the new constitution was completed, and on October 10, 1913, Yüan and Li were inaugurated for ten-year terms as permanent president and vice-president of the republic. Less than one month later, Yüan dissolved the Kuomintang as a seditious party and purged parliament of its members. In January, Yüan indefinitely suspended the remnants of parliament.

Presidential Dictatorship. To strengthen his position, Yüan replaced the new republican constitution with a Constitutional Compact. Under the Compact, the president was virtually dictator. The elective House of Legislature had only advisory powers, and the president could nominate the members of the Council of State or cabinet, which was responsible to him. Yüan now used terror and ruthlessness to remove his opponents and bring unity to China. Freedom of press, speech, and assembly was restricted. On the other hand he pleased most Chinese by restoring Confucian practices in the government. Provincial assemblies were abolished, and provincial governments were made subject to central authority. New military governors were appointed over provincial districts to bring about peace and order. By the end of 1914, China was more unified and peaceful than at any time since October 10, 1911.

BIBLIOGRAPHY

Beckmann, G. M., *The Modernization of China and Japan,* 1962.

Bland, J. O. P., and E. Backhouse, *China Under the Empress Dowager,* 1914.

Callis, H. G., *China, Confucian and Communist,* 1959.

Cameron, M. E., *The Reform Movement in China, 1898-1912,* 1931.

Clark, G., *Economic Rivalries in China,* 1932.

Fairbank, J. K., *The United States and China,* 1958.

Feuerwerker, A., *China's Early Industrialization,* 1958.

Griswold, A. W., *The Far Eastern Policy of the United States,* 1939.

Holcombe, A. N., *The Chinese Revolution,* 1930.

Hsu, L., *Sun Yat-sen,* 1933.

Johnson, R. F., *Twilight in the Forbidden City,* 1934.

Joseph, P., *Foreign Diplomacy in China,* 1928.

Latourette, K. S., *Development of China,* 1946.

Linebarger, P. M. W., *Sun Yat-sen and the Chinese Revolution,* 1925.

MacNair, H. F., *China in Revolution,* 1931.

MacNair, H. F., ed., *Modern Chinese History, Selected Readings,* 1923.

Maki, J. M., *Conflict and Tension in the Far East. Key Documents, 1894-1960,* 1961.

Marten, B., *Strange Vigour, Biography of Sun Yat-sen,* 1944.

Morse, H. B., *International Relations of the Chinese Empire,* Vol. 3, 1918.

Powell, R., *The Rise of Chinese Military Power, 1895-1912,* 1955.

Rowe, D. N., *Modern China: A Brief History,* 1959.

Stuart, J. L., *Fifty Years in China,* 1954.

Tan, C., *The Boxer Catastrophe,* 1955.

T'ang, L. L., *The Inner History of the Chinese Revolution,* 1930.

Vinacke, H. M., *Modern Constitutional Development in China,* 1920.

Willoughby, W. S., *Foreign Rights and Interests in China,* 2 vols., 1927.

CHAPTER 9
Russo-Japanese War and Its Aftermath

JAPAN AND RUSSIA (1895 - 1904)

Russian Interests in Manchuria and Korea. After forcibly removing Chinese influence from Korea in 1895, Japan faced a more serious antagonist, Russia. Control of Korea and Manchuria seemed essential to the successful exploitation of Russia's Asiatic empire. Russia had no warm-water port, and to complete the Trans-Siberian Railway on Russian soil would be costly and inconvenient. Manchuria was sparsely populated and rich in resources. Korea had a considerable population but a hopelessly corrupt government. Both seemed fair game to the Russians.

RUSSIAN PENETRATION IN MANCHURIA. Russia, as we have seen, drew China into military alliance and gained a right of way for the Trans-Siberian Railway by the Li Hung-chang-Lobanov agreement of 1896. This advantage they consolidated and extended by the lease of Port Arthur and additional railway concessions in 1898. The Boxer uprising gave Russia an excuse for occupying Manchuria with military forces, which she showed no intention of withdrawing. An agreement with China in 1902 only resulted in Russia's shifting forces from one part of Manchuria to another. In April, 1903, Russia advanced proposals to Peking which, if accepted, would have resulted in a Russian protectorate over Manchuria and Mongolia.

Japanese Penetration in Korea. During and immediately after the Sino-Japanese War, the Japanese were masters of Korea. By a treaty signed during the struggle, Korea agreed to accept Japanese guidance and capital. Under the Japanese minister, Inouye, the Korean government and legal system were revised, and Japanese officials were placed in strategic positions. When

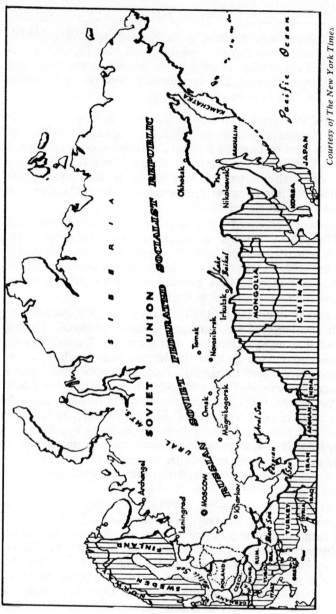

these reforms were opposed by the Korean queen, who led the conservatives, the Japanese minister and the Taiwunkun organized a conspiracy resulting in the murder of the queen and the seizure of the king. Shortly afterward, however, in February, 1896, the king escaped and fled to the Russian legation.

Russian Penetration in Korea. The Korean king now turned to his Russian protectors for guidance. Japanese officials and advisers were replaced by Russians. A timber-cutting concession on the Yalu River was granted to Russia. When Japanese influence was finally ousted, the king left the Russian legation and assumed the title of emperor to assert his independence and his equality with all his neighbors.

YAMAGATA-LOBANOV PROTOCOL (1896). At the same time that Li Hung-chang reached his agreement with Russia in 1896, Japan sent her own emissary, Yamagata, to achieve an understanding with Russia. While China secured a military alliance, Yamagata managed only a protocol by which Japan recognized Russia as an equal partner in Korea.

NISHI-ROSEN PROTOCOL (1898). Russia promptly ignored both spirit and letter of the Yamagata-Lobanov Protocol. Further timber and mining concessions were secured by Russia. Russian advisers were used to train the Korean army, and Japanese-trained forces were disbanded. Russian control over Korean finances was extended. In addition, Russia gained a naval base at Port Arthur, which had been denied to the Japanese in 1895. As a result of both Japanese and Korean hostility, the Russians negotiated with Japan the Nishi-Rosen Protocol by which (1) both recognized Korean independence, (2) both agreed not to assist the Korean army or financial reorganization, and (3) Russia recognized Japanese commercial and industrial interests in Korea.

Anglo-Japanese Alliance (1902). Russian aggression in Manchuria alarmed not only Japan but also England. England had long pursued a policy of keeping the Russian bear in an ice-bound cage, but the bear seemed about to dismember China. Britain had extensive interests in the Yangtze Valley, but did not wish to rule that region directly as she did India. Although the United States had cooperated with the Open Door notes, it was opposed to military alliances. Japan, whose ambitions did not seem to conflict with Britain's, appeared a natural ally against Russia. Germany first suggested a triple alliance against Russia, but failed to follow through. The result was the Anglo-Japanese alliance of 1902 aimed at maintaining the *status quo* in eastern Asia and the integrity of China. Korean independence was acknowledged, but Japan's special interest in Korea and England's in central China were recognized. Both powers agreed to cooperate in the event of disturbances. If either Japan or Britain became involved in war with a third power, the other party would remain neutral unless another power intervened.

RUSSO-FRENCH REPLY. As Russia and France had been allied since 1894, the Anglo-Japanese alliance was obviously aimed at keeping France from aiding Russia in the event of a war. To counteract the new alliance, Russia and France affirmed their solidarity by publicly extending their European alliance to include their Asiatic interests. The Franco-Russian note reaffirmed the two powers' adherence to the Open Door, the *status quo* in eastern Asia, and the integrity of China and Korea.

Prelude to War. Russia showed no intention of observing the Nishi-Rosen Protocol. Attempts to lease a port in southern Korea and to negotiate loans to Korea in return for concessions were frustrated by Japan. On the other hand, Japanese efforts to gain control over Korean commerce, railroads, and port facilities were more successful.

FAILURE OF NEGOTIATIONS. In mid-1903, Japan offered to recognize Russia's sphere of influence over Manchuria if Russia accepted Japan's superiority in Korea. Russia replied by offering Japan only commercial and industrial supremacy in south Korea, while north Korea would be neutralized. Although Japan rejected this reply, Russian war preparations directed by Admiral Alexieff, Russia's new "Viceroy of the Far East," induced the Japanese to make new proposals offering (1) freedom of navigation in the Korean Straits, (2) a neutral zone along the Korean-Manchurian border, (3) railway connection between Korean and Manchurian lines, and (4) recognition of Russian supremacy in Manchuria in return for Russian recognition of Japan's superior position in Korea. This and subsequent proposals were rejected by the Russians, who delayed negotiations until Japanese patience was exhausted. On February 6, 1904, the Japanese minister left St. Petersburg, warning that Japan would resort to action. Two days later, without declaring war, Japanese fleets attacked Russian naval units at Chemulpo and Port Arthur.

RUSSO-JAPANESE WAR

Japanese and Russian Military Power. Since 1895 Japan had been increasing her military might. The Sino-Japanese War and the Boxer indemnities had been used to build up war industries and armaments. By 1904, Japan was prepared for war with a modern fleet and a large well-trained and well-equipped army. Japan also had the advantage of fighting close to her own shores. Russia's war potential was theoretically greater, but could not be readily brought into action. Eastern Siberia and Manchuria were connected with Russia merely by a single-track railroad over 4000 miles long, which had to carry supplies, munitions, and troops. So slow was the process that only at the end of the war did Russia have sufficient forces to achieve any local superiority. The Russian navy was large, but antiquated, weakened by corruption, and widely scattered. Japanese ships, markmanship, and tactical skill proved superior.

Military Campaigns. The war was fought almost entirely on Chinese soil, but China was helpless to do more than recognize Manchuria as a zone of hostilities. Japan early gained control of Korea by defeating Russian forces in a brief but bloody battle on the Yalu River. After eight months of bitter fighting, Port Arthur fell to the Japanese on January 2, 1905. The Russians action took place (February 23 - March 10, 1905). It was a action took place (February 23 - March 10, 1905). It was a costly victory for the Japanese. Had not the December Revolution in Russia frightened the tzar into concluding peace, the tide of war would probably have turned. Russia was only beginning to bring her full force into play, while Japan was fighting further from home and was nearly exhausted.

NAVAL WARFARE. One of the principal reasons for Japan's military victories was her naval superiority. At no time did Russia bring together her naval forces scattered in the Baltic Sea, Port Arthur, Chemulpo, and Vladivostok. Japan had begun the struggle by surprise attacks on Port Arthur, but these failed to weaken the Russians seriously. What surprise failed to do, tactical superiority achieved, and in a series of battles the Port Arthur fleet was largely destroyed. Equally successful attacks on Vladivostok naval units quickly followed. On May 27, 1905, the Russian Baltic fleet, which had sailed around the world, was defeated as a result of tactical blunders and inferior firing power.

Peace of Portsmouth (1905). The Japanese war strategy had been to win a quick victory and a quick peace before Russia could mobilize her full strength. The early victories were spectacular, but not decisive. Japan was financially exhausted, and the foreign powers, even her ally England, would loan no more for fear that Russia would be too severely humbled. The United States hoped for a Japanese victory, and President Theodore Roosevelt recognized that prolongation of strife might result in Japanese defeat. Roosevelt's offer of his services resulted in the meeting of the belligerents at Portsmouth, New Hampshire. Russia was represented by Count Witte and Baron Rosen, while the Japanese emissaries were Takahira and Foreign Minister Komura. Only after considerable negotiation, during which Russia continued to reinforce her Far Eastern armies, was a compromise reached. As signed on September 5, 1905, the Treaty of Portsmouth gave Japan half of Sakhalin Island as a war indemnity. Japan also acquired (1) Russia's Liaotung leasehold together with the Port Arthur-Changchun railway and associated concessions, (2) recognition of her sphere of interest over Korea, and (3) fishing rights in Siberian waters.

RESULTS OF THE WAR

Immediate Results. Japan won a victory that enhanced her prestige abroad and enormously boosted her self-esteem. At the peace conference, however, she failed to gain all she asked for, and the Japanese leaders allowed their people to blame Roosevelt and the United States rather than Japan's military and financial exhaustion. Japan's proven strength caused the renewal of the Anglo-Japanese Treaty in 1905. The new treaty of alliance included India in its scope and recognized Japan's supremacy in Korea. Russia, while internally weakened by revolution, lost little prestige because of general recognition that she might have won had the war continued. Russian influence also remained strong in northern Manchuria.

SINO-JAPANESE ACCORD (1905). Since some portions of the Portsmouth Treaty concerned Chinese interests, Japan negotiated an agreement with China. The Sino-Japanese Accord of

December, 1905, not only secured Chinese acceptance of Japan's war gains, but added concessions. Japan was permitted to construct a railway from Antung to Mukden, new Manchurian towns were opened to Japanese trade, and China agreed not to construct railroads that would compete with Japan's Manchurian lines.

Japanese Protectorate over Korea. Prior to the Russo-Japanese war, Japan had steadily increased her economic stakes in Korea. At the outbreak of the conflict, the Korean ruler tried to save his kingdom by proclaiming neutrality, but Japan promptly landed forces on Korean soil. Although Japan guaranteed Korean territory and independence in a protocol signed in February, 1904, she steadily strengthened her hold on the peninsula. In August, 1904, Japan secured the right to appoint advisers to key ministries, and by early 1905 she had gained partial control over Korean police. In mid-1905, the United States gave official approval of Japan's encroachment by the Taft-Katsura notes, while the new Anglo-Japanese alliance failed to mention Korean independence. Two months after the Treaty of Portsmouth ended Russian competition, a new convention was signed by which Korea gave Japan the right to maintain residents in Korean towns and at court and accepted Japanese control over Korean foreign affairs.

ANNEXATION OF KOREA. Although few protests were heard against the Japanese protectorate over Korea, the Korean emperor looked abroad for salvation. In July, 1907, Korea appealed to the Hague Tribunal for aid. The result was further tightening of the Japanese bonds. The Korean emperor was forced to abdicate in favor of his son, and a new agreement increased the powers of the Japanese. In the same month, a new Russo-Japanese convention settled differences regarding the spheres of interest of those countries and secured Russian acceptance of Japanese political control of Korea in return for most-favored-nation treatment there. In August, 1910, Korea was formally annexed. The Korean royal family was appeased with a financial settlement and Japanese titles of nobility, while the lesser Korean leaders were either bribed or terrorized into acquiescence. The leaderless Korean people could only accept with sullen reluctance. No important protests were heard from abroad.

Manchuria After 1905. The Treaty of Portsmouth gave Japan entrance into Manchuria by the acquisition of Port Arthur and part of Russia's railways and commercial interests. After the war, Japan was too weakened financially to exploit the advantage, and when E. H. Harriman, American railway promoter, suggested an American-Japanese syndicate to exploit the Manchurian concessions, the plan was at first accepted. However, Japanese Foreign Minister Komura objected so strenuously that the agreement was abrogated. Thereafter the Japanese government promoted railway construction by drawing on Japanese and Chinese capital but keeping Japanese control.

AMERICAN INTERESTS IN MANCHURIA. The victory of Japan aroused new American concern for the Open Door and the integrity of China. Partly due to concern for the Philippines' defense, the United States had acquiesced to Japanese control of Korea, but Manchuria was part of China and a different matter. The Harriman railroad promotion scheme created some ill will, but relations were seriously strained by the American oriental exclusion policy. The United States maintained peace (1) by displaying its force in sending the American fleet around the world and (2) by diplomacy. In 1908, notes were exchanged between Secretary of State Root and Japanese Ambassador Takahira by which both countries denied aggressive intentions and both supported the Open Door and the integrity of China. Japan, however, accepted this as giving her a free hand in Manchuria.

KNOX NEUTRALIZATION PROPOSAL (1909). With the aid of the Department of State, Harriman's American railway interests continued to try to gain admission into Manchuria. Preliminary contracts were gained, but before the plan could succeed, Harriman died. Thereafter, Secretary of State Knox advanced in November, 1909, a plan to neutralize politically all Manchurian railroads. By this scheme, China would be loaned money to buy the lines, which would then be operated by an international commission. As Russia and Japan, backed by Britain and France, opposed the plan, it came to nothing. By 1912, American interests were largely eliminated from Manchuria, and Japan and Russia compatibly divided their spheres of interest by a new agreement.

JAPANESE INTERNAL DEVELOPMENTS

Political Parties. Prior to the promulgation of the constitution in 1889, political parties had developed in Japan (see Chapter VI). After the elections of 1890, two parties emerged as the strongest, the Jiyuto or Liberal party and the Kaishinto or Progressive party. The early parties were largely helpless to influence government policies which were controlled by powerful clan leaders under Count Ito. Both parties stood for constitutional government and opposed clan control, but rivalry between their leaders, Okuma and Itagaki, long prevented amalgamation.

Rise of Militarism. When Ito used the Sino-Japanese conflict to end party obstruction in 1894, he soon found he had only handed his power over to the militarists led by Prince Yamagata.

The army was controlled by men of the Choshu clan, while the Satsuma men controlled the navy. Yamagata, a Choshu man, primarily favored the army, but his success during the Chinese war in gaining an imperial order requiring ministers of the army and navy to be in active service strengthened both services. By this move, the army and navy gained the power to overthrow any cabinet or to control the membership of new cabinets.

Failure of Party Politics. The political parties after the war continued unsuccessfully to combat clan rule. In 1898, Okuma and Itagaki amalgamated their parties to form the Kenseito or Constitutional party, but when they secured an opportunity to head a government, they failed. In 1900, Ito attempted to oppose the military factions by forming his own Rikken Seiyukai or Constitution Government party. The Seiyukai with the aid of Okuma's new organization, the Kenseihonto, ousted Yamagata, but did not secure complete control for Ito.

POLITICAL CONNIVANCE. From 1901 to 1912, political parties ceased opposition to the clan government and instead competed for the privilege of allying with it to share the spoils of office. During this period, Katsura, a Yamagata protege, and Prince Sionjii rotated as prime minister, while Yamagata pulled strings behind scenes. The death of the emperor in July, 1912 ended this arrangement.

Renewed Political Strife. In 1912, Katsura rebelled from Yamagata's domination to form his own Doshikai or Unionist party by drawing on members of the older parties. The result was the inability of any party to maintain a majority, and Admiral Yamamoto with Seiyukai support became premier. When Yamamoto's government fell as the result of a naval scandal, eighty-year-old Count Okuma, a staunch party leader, became premier. Okuma stood for peaceful industrial and commercial expansion and reduction of taxes, but the outbreak of the European war in 1914 doomed him to be a war premier until 1916.

BIBLIOGRAPHY

Brown, D. M., *Nationalism in Japan,* 1955.

Carnegie Endowment for International Peace, *Korea: Treaties and Agreements,* 1921.

Clyde, P. H., *International Rivalries in Manchuria,* 1926.

Conroy, H., *The Japanese Seizure of Korea, 1868-1910,* 1960.

Dennett, T., *Roosevelt and the Russo-Japanese War,* 1925.

Grajdanzev, A. J., *Modern Korea,* 1944.

Griswold, A. W., *The Far Eastern Policy of the United States,* 1938.

Iwasaki, U., *The Working Forces in Japanese Politics, 1867-1920,* 1921.

Kamikawa, H., ed., *Japan-American Diplomatic Relations in the Meiji-Taisho Era,* 1958.

Langer, W. L., *Diplomacy of Imperialism, 1890-1902,* 2 vols., 1935.

Lattimore, O., *Manchuria, Cradle of Conflict,* 1932.

Lensen. G. A., *The Russian Push Toward Japan,* 1959.

Lee, C., *The Politics of Korean Nationalism,* 1963.

MacMurray, J. V. A., compiler and ed., *Treaties and Agreements with and Concerning Ching, 1894-1919,* Vol. 1, 1921.

Maki, J. M., *Selected Documents, Far Eastern International Relations, 1689-1951,* 1951.

Norman, E. H., *Japan's Emergence as a Modern State,* 1940.

Okuma, Count S., ed., *Fifty Years of Modern Japan,* 2 vols., 1909.

Reischauer, E. O., *The United States and Japan,* 1957.

Reischauer, R. K., *Japan, Government-Politics,* 1939.

Sands, W. F., *Undiplomatic Memories: The Far East, 1896-1904,* 1930.

Takeuchi, T., *War and Diplomacy in the Japanese Empire,* 1935.

Tewksbery, D. G., *Source Materials on Korean Politics and Ideologies,* Vol. 2, 1950.

Treat, P. J., *Diplomatic Relations Between the U.S. and Japan, 1895-1905,* 1938.

Yanaga, C., *Japan Since Perry,* 1949.

Yarmolinski, A., ed., *The Memoirs of Counte Witte,* 1921.

CHAPTER 10
World War I and Its Aftermath

In terms of fighting, World War I was primarily a European affair, yet it could not fail to have repercussions in Eastern Asia. European imperialism had reached a stalemate because of the approximate balance between the powers. With Germany land-locked in Europe, her possessions in Asia became fair prey for the one imperialistic power free to move, Japan, who had the added pretext of alliance with England.

JAPANESE PARTICIPATION AND DIPLOMATIC NEGOTIATIONS

Entrance into War. The terms of the Anglo-Japanese alliance did not require Japan's entrance into the war, and Britain definitely declined Japan's offer of aid. But Japan was determined to seize Germany's holdings in the Far East, and on August 15 sent an ultimatum to Germany to hand over within eight days her Kiaochow Bay leasehold together with her warships in Chinese waters.

WAR IN EASTERN ASIA. Hoping to avoid Japanese penetration, China considered both the possibilities of the retrocession of Kiaochow by Germany or a declaration of war upon Germany. When both plans were sharply vetoed by Japan, China attempted to limit the conflict by setting up a war zone around Kiaochow Bay. However, Japanese and British forces proceeded with careful preparations for the seige of Tsingtao, the German stronghold at Kiaochow. In November the small German garrison surrendered. With little reason the Japanese callously invaded Chinese soil beyond the zone of hostilities and treated non-belligerent Chinese as conquered people. The entire 250 miles of the German Tsingtao-Tsinan Railway was seized despite the fact that it was owned by private Chinese and German capital.

WAR IN THE PACIFIC. The Japanese failed to capture Germany's Tsingtao squadron which fled to the Caroline Islands. A British-Japanese fleet was dispatched to seize these German-owned islands and to capture the German commerce raiders. By the end of 1914, the German islands north of the equator had been seized by the Japanese, while those south of the equator, including New Guinea, had been taken by Australians and New Zealanders. Not until December, 1916, however, was the last German commerce raider cleared from Pacific waters.

The Twenty-one Demands.

After the capitulation of Tsingtao, China sought to rid her soil of Japanese troops by abolishing the war zone. Japan claimed this was an unfriendly act and used it as pretext for advancing upon China a group of demands which had been prepared months before. The Twenty-One Demands, which were delivered to Yüan Shih-k'ai on Japanese War Department stationery, consisted of five groups. Group I required advance Chinese assent to any settlement reached between Japan and Germany regarding German holdings in China. The Japanese also would be granted extensive concessions in Shantung, which would become a Japanese sphere of interest covered by a nonalienation agreement. Group II would increase Japan's economic and political hold on Mongolia and Manchuria and extend the Port Arthur lease to 99 years. Group III was designed to give Japan a monopoly over China's important Yangtze mining, coal, and iron industries. Group IV committed China not to cede or lease more ports or coastal territory to other powers. Group V was a general catchall which would (a) give Japan sole right to advise China on political, financial, and military matters; (b) require China to purchase most of her military supplies from Japan; (c) grant Japan extensive railroad concessions; (d) grant to Japanese rights to own Chinese land for schools, hospitals, and temples, and permit Japanese special missionary rights; and (e) give Japan prior investment rights in Fukien Province.

SINO-JAPANESE TREATIES OF 1915. Although the Japanese had requested secrecy, China permitted the demands to be publicized in hope of gaining foreign aid. Japan first denied the demands had been made, but later admitted to them while minimizing their importance. Of the powers that would aid China, only the United States was not at war, but President Wilson was content merely to remind Japan of the Root-Takahira commitments. With no foreign aid forthcoming, China procrastinated until forced to yield to reduced demands by a Japanese ultimatum delivered May 7, 1915. The result was a series of agreements between Japan and China by which China accepted the first four demands plus that part of Group V dealing with the use of Japanese capital in Fukien. In return, Japan agreed to restore the Kiaochow leasehold to China after the war. Kiaochow was to become a commercial port in which Japan retained a concession. In addition, Japan secured concessions relating to Manchuria and Mongolia and the extension of the Port Arthur leasehold. Consideration of the rest of the demands of Group V was postponed.

Treaties of 1917-1918. To consolidate her gains in China and the Pacific, Japan moved quickly. The Allies were seriously menaced by German submarines, and in return for the aid of Japanese destroyers in the Mediterranean, France, Britain, Italy, and Russia agreed to support Japan's war gains in the future peace conference. To mollify China, Japan put on a front of friendship. The northern militarists controlling the Peking government constantly needed money and were appeased by a series of loans in 1917-1918 which helped them to consolidate their power. This in turn increased Japan's stake and political influence in north China. After the Russian revolution, Japan used the threat of Communism to extract a new agreement from China calling for joint military cooperation against the Reds. This arrangement practically placed Chinese armies under Japanese control.

Lansing-Ishii Notes. After the United States became an ally of Japan by declaring war upon Germany, Japan was quick to seize the opportunity to obtain American acquiescence to her gains in China. Viscount Ishii, head of a Japanese war mission to Washington, cleverly maneuvered an exchange of notes with Secretary of State Lansing by which (1) the United States and Japan reaffirmed their support of the Open Door and the integrity of China, but (2) the United States recognized Japan's special relations with China on the basis of territorial propinquity. While the American Department of State considered this a victory for the Open Door policy, the Japanese viewed it as a triumph for Japan's special position in China.

CHINA DURING THE WAR

China at the Outbreak of War. In August, 1914, the presidential dictatorship of Yüan Shih-k'ai seemed secure. It was legalized not only by Yüan's commission from the Manchu to form the new republican government, but also by the new Constitutional Charter. Parliamentary opposition had proven inefficient, and the new parliament was under presidential control. The bureaucracy found it easy to transfer its allegiance to Yüan as the center of authority, and the general population did not care. The president still controlled the armies of north China, and at least partially controlled the war lords. The government's financial needs had been partly met with consortium loans, and a stable government could resume tax collections. In the hope that peace might be maintained in the Far East, Yüan declared China neutral after the outbreak of the European war on August 1, 1914.

Revival of Empire. Yüan's training and experience made him prefer a monarchy to a republic. These sympathies were fortified by the propaganda of a Chinese monarchist society, the Chou-an-kui, and by the recommendations of his American adviser, Dr. F. J. Goodnow. After gestures to satisfy public opinion, including the calling of a special convention which voted for the move, Yüan announced he would assume the title of emperor on January 1, 1916. The foreign powers were unanimous in their disapproval, although Japan had first offered support in return for concessions which Yüan refused to grant. Internal Chinese opposition was demonstrated by a revolt which broke out in Yünnan in December, 1915, and quickly spread. Yüan found it necessary first to postpone and finally in March, 1916, to abandon the restoration of the monarchy.

Return to Republic. Yüan was forced to accept cabinet government and might have been compelled to resign all power had his sudden death not saved him from complete disgrace. Vice-president Li Yüan-hung peacefully succeeded Yüan but was unable to control the revived republic. Before the death of Yüan, the National Parliament of 1913 reassembled in Shanghai and was called to Peking by the new president. Military factions were appeased by the appointment of General Tuan Ch'i-jui as premier and the election of General Feng Kuo-chang as vice-president. Conflict between premier and president was inevitable, for Li held republican sympathies but lacked political ability, while Tuan opposed representative government and was politically competent. The revived Parliament proved capable only of heckling and obstructing Tuan's government.

FACTIONALISM. Several distinct factions were emerging on the political horizon. Behind them all were the tuchuns or war lords who controlled parts of China by virtue of their personal armies. In the south at Canton, Dr. Sun Yat-sen and his reconstituted Kuomintang were supported by the war lords of four southern provinces. The Fengtien clique, dominated by Chang Tso-lin, ruled over most of Manchuria from its Mukden headquarters. The Chili clique was headed by Marshal Ts'ao Kun, General Wu P'ei-fu, and Feng Yü-hsiang, the "Christian general." Supporting Premier Tuan Ch'i-jui was the Anfu Club founded by Hsü Shu-ts'eng.

INVOLVEMENT IN EUROPEAN WAR AND MANCHU REACTION. The issue that again destroyed parliamentary government was the problem of war with Germany. When a French ship carrying Chinese laborers to the European war zone was torpedoed, China broke relations with Germany in March, 1917. Germany's contemptuous attitude caused Premier Tuan to insist upon a declaration of war. Parliament, rightly fearing that war might result in a military dictatorship under Tuan, demanded his dismissal before declaring war. After the whole cabinet except Tuan and the Minister of Education had resigned, President Li replaced Tuan with Wu T'ing-fang on May 23. When Tuan, backed by the Anfu Club, threatened revolt, Li called upon General Chang Hsun for assistance. Chang Hsun, who was a loyal supporter of the Manchu dynasty, demanded dismissal of Parliament, and the harried president was forced to accede, although he also ordered new elections. Chang Hsun, moving too rapidly, overplayed his hand. On July 1, 1917, he placed the former emperor, Pu-yi, back on the throne at Peking.

Declaration of War. Resentment at this restoration of the Manchu dynasty was widespread. Tuan led the republican armies back into Peking, driving Chang back into refuge in the foreign legation. The discredited President Li resigned, and Tuan re-established himself as premier, while Feng Kuo-chang moved up as president. The new government, dominated by pro-

Japanese militarists, declared war on Germany on August 14, 1917, in hope of gaining itself international prestige and financial assistance. The chief contribution of China to the Allied war effort, aside from furnishing raw materials and foodstuffs, was the recruiting of 190,000 Chinese for labor on the western front.

Effects of the Peace Treaties. Tuan appeared content to rule China as premier, and when Feng's term as president ended in 1918, Parliament elected one of Tuan's tools to succeed him. Tuan also attempted to negotiate a union between the Anfu-held north and Sun's Canton group. The failure to win back Shantung at Versailles wrecked Tuan's power before unity could be achieved. Known to be pro-Japanese, Tuan was accused of submitting to Japanese dictation. When thousands of students paraded and rioted in Peking and merchants boycotted Japanese products, the irate Japanese withdrew their financial aid. The most unpopular pro-Japanese ministers were forced to flee, although Tuan remained premier until forced out by a coalition of tuchuns headed by Wu P'ei-fu in July, 1920.

THE INTERNATIONAL CONFERENCES

Conflicting Issues at Versailles. Japanese and Chinese interests at the peace conference were almost totally at odds. Japan demanded outright cession of the German holdings in Shantung and was strongly supported by secret wartime treaties with Britain, Italy, France, Australia, and New Zealand, who also were hoping to share in the division of the German empire. In addition, Japanese claims were fortified by her treaties of 1915 and 1918 with China. China, requesting the return of Shantung, the sacred birthplace of Confucius, was supported by President Wilson. Japan shrewdly advanced a demand for acceptance by the conference of the principle of racial equality. This was unacceptable to most western powers, and the necessity for rejecting it forced Wilson to yield on the Shantung question. Wilson also looked to his proposed League of Nations to heal such open wounds as the Shantung problem by future negotiations.

CHINA'S GAINS. Because of the sharp popular reaction to China's diplomatic defeat at Versailles, the Tuan government negotiated a separate peace with Germany. However, membership in the new League of Nations was achieved by signing the Allied treaty with Austria. By the peace treaties, China secured (1) end of the "unequal treaties" with the central powers, (2) remission of further Boxer indemnity payments to Germany, (3) abolition of Germany's concessions at Tientsin and Hankow, and (4) cessation of extraterritoriality privileges for Hungary, Austria, and Germany. These materials gains were small, yet they were a start towards regaining for China a position of equality among the nations. Equally important was the spontaneous outburst of national consciousness that followed the Versailles conference.

Washington Arms Conference. The Harding administration, although rejecting participation in the League of Nations, found international cooperation a necessity. The American problem was to secure the Open Door and the integrity of China and to safeguard American interests in the Pacific, at the same time that armaments were drastically reduced. To attempt this, the Washington Conference was called in the fall of 1921 to discuss disarmament and problems of the Pacific.

PROBLEMS OF THE CONFERENCE. Among the difficulties facing the nine powers (Great Britain, France, Japan, China, Italy, Belgium, Portugal, the Netherlands, and the United States) were (1) the Anglo-Japanese alliance which, with Russia neutralized by revolution, was viewed as a menace by the United States; (2) the naval armament race then in progress, which required consideration of fortification of Pacific island bases and the achievement of an equitable balance of naval power; and (3) the Open Door and the integrity of China, which included reconsideration of the Shantung issue which Japan considered a closed case. In addition, there was the fear that the influence of Soviet Russia might spread to China as a result of Chinese disillusionment over Versailles.

FOUR-POWER PACIFIC TREATY. The United States, with the aid of pressure from Canada and other dominions, persuaded Britain and Japan to end their treaty of alliance in favor of a broader Pacific treaty including France and the United States. By this new pact, the powers guaranteed to respect each other's Pacific possessions and to discuss jointly any Pacific problems or aggressive actions.

FIVE-POWER NAVAL TREATY. In opening the conference, Secretary of State Hughes proposed drastic arms reductions on a capital ship ratio of 5:5:3:1.75:1.75, for Great Britain, United

States, Japan, France, and Italy respectively. Japan resented her inferior ratio, but consented to accept it if the powers agreed not to further fortify their eastern Pacific possessions. Ultimately these principles were adopted with some modifications, including the provision that the treaty could be terminated by any signatory on two years notice. In the end, Japan gained most, for her capital ship ratio was sufficient to assure her predominance in Far Eastern waters. Britain lost the right to fortify only those possessions that she could not have readily defended anyway, while the United States received as large a fleet allotment as American taxpayers would support.

AGREEMENTS CONCERNING CHINA. Any consideration of China's problems also vitally concerned Russia, yet the new Soviet Republic was not invited to participate in the conference. With regard to China, the conference desired to (1) strengthen the Peking government, (2) secure the Open Door, (3) placate Chinese fears of further foreign aggression, if possible by returning Shantung, (4) provide some plan for future elimination of extraterritoriality. The measures taken to strengthen the Peking government financially and increase its prestige involved increase in Chinese tariff duties to an effective 5 per cent *ad valorem* and abolishment of foreign postoffices and radio stations on Chinese soil. In addition, Britain agreed to negotiate for the return of Weihaiwei to China.

SINO-JAPANESE TREATY. The Shantung question was not taken up by the Conference but was settled by the separate Sino-Japanese Treaty of 1922 by which Shantung was returned to China, but the Japanese retained control of the Tsingtao-Tsinan Railway. In addition, Japan withdrew Group V of the Twenty-One Demands which had previously been postponed. Japan refused to reconsider the clauses of the earlier treaties concerning Manchuria.

NINE-POWER OPEN DOOR TREATY. Most important of the treaties concerning China was the Nine-Power Pact by which all the signatories agreed to (1) respect the Open Door, (2) guarantee the sovereignty and territorial integrity of China, (3) refrain from seeking special privileges in China, (4) aid China in developing a stable government, (5) refrain from making treaties with one another that would impair any of the foregoing. By subsequent agreements, the signatories invited other powers to join the pact and agreed to discuss frankly any disagreements that might arise regarding it.

Significance of the Treaties. The Versailles and Washington treaties attempted to solve the world's problems around the conference table. They might have succeeded had all countries fully cooperated both at the conferences and after. But as we have seen, China and the United States found it desirable to reject the Versailles Treaty. Japan went to the Washington Conference reluctantly and emerged dissatisfied not only with her inferior capital ship ratio, but also with what she considered unwarranted interference with her affairs in eastern Asia. Japan was also outraged by the refusal of the powers to admit the principle of racial equality. As a result, Japan ignored the agreements, fortified her Pacific possessions, and armed herself as thoroughly as her economy would permit. In China, the Peking government, which the powers tried to strengthen, was merely the tool of the war lords and soon fell to the Kuomintang.

SOVIET RUSSIA AND SIBERIAN INTERVENTION

Russian Revolution. The collapse of the Russian tzarist regime as a result of the revolution created a host of new problems for the Allied powers during the war. The liberal Kerensky government cooperated with the western powers, but the Red government succeeding it drew Russia out of the war by the treaty of Brest-Litovsk. Only after a long struggle, however, did the Reds gain control over all Russia. A Far Eastern Council of People's Commissars was formed by the Reds as a buffer state to deal with the western powers and rule eastern Siberia, but throughout Siberia, local pockets of resistance to Bolshevik rule persisted. In addition, some 50,000 Czech soldiers who had deserted the Austrian armies to fight for the Allies were caught by the revolution while being transported across Siberia to Vladivostok. When the Reds appeared to be double dealing, the Czechs seized control of much of the Trans-Siberian Railroad and assisted the local White Russian forces.

Kolchak Regime. Among the White Russian leaders who influenced Far Eastern affairs was Admiral Kolchak. This tzarist official first secured an appointment as Minister of War of a liberal regime centered at Omsk, and in November, 1918, seized control of that government to establish himself as military dictator. His object was to move westward to gain control of all Russia, but his brutally reactionary policies alienated all supporters. Despite Allied aid, his government collapsed in January, 1920.

SUCCESSORS OF KOLCHAK. Semenov, a vicious Cossack leader, next proclaimed himself dictator, but his tyranny only stirred up more support for the Soviet forces and further disgusted the Allies, as did the actions of Kalmikov and Rozanov, other would-be successors of Kolchak. By the summer of 1920, all the main reactionary forces were defeated by the Soviets, and the Far Eastern People's Commissar Council was converted into the Far Eastern Republic with the approval of Moscow. In 1922, the Republic was incorporated into the Soviet Union.

Allied Intervention. As early as 1917, the United States was requested by Kerensky to send railway experts to operate the Trans-Siberian Railway. After the Treaty of Brest-Litovsk, Japan proposed active intervention in Siberia. The plight of 50,000 Czechs furnished a pretext for Allied intervention in July, 1918. Disavowing any desire to control the political destinies of the Russians, the Allies agreed to send not over 10,000 men each. The French and British hoped to use intervention to help the White Russians to overthrow the Reds and return Russia to war against Germany, and, incidentally, to secure the honoring of the Russian war debts repudiated by the Bolsheviks. Britain, moreover, was concerned with preventing the spread of Communism. In addition to these motives, Japan hoped to gain control of eastern Siberia.

DISCORD AND WITHDRAWAL. Despite American protests, the Japanese ignored the intervention agreement by sending 70,000 men into Siberia and by pushing far beyond the prescribed zones. Disagreements as to motives and methods created friction among the Allied forces. To this was added dissatisfaction with the conduct of the White Russian leaders. The rescue of the Czechs and the end of the war in Europe ended the need for the occupation, and all the Allied forces except Japan's departed from Russian soil in 1920. The Japanese lingered on under various pretexts until the pressure of the United States and the Washington Conference, together with the unpopularity of the occupation in Japan, forced further withdrawal in 1922. However, not until Japan and Russia signed an agreement in 1925 regarding outstanding disputes did Japan finally evacuate northern Sakhalin Island.

Mongolia and Tibet. The Chinese revolution of 1911 was followed by a revision in the status of China's remaining subject peoples in central Asia. The Mongolians and Tibetans under Manchu rule had been at least partly protected from Chinese exploitation, but when the Manchu were overthrown these peoples became restless. In 1913, a conference of Chinese, Tibetan, and British officials divided Tibet into an Outer Tibet which would remain under Chinese suzerainty but would become autonomous, and an Inner Tibet which would be directly controlled by the Chinese. Although China rejected the agreement, Britain recognized it and considered the case closed.

SINO-RUSSIAN AGREEMENTS. The problem of Mongolia concerned not only China, but also Japan and Russia, who were seeking to include it in their spheres of interest. In 1913 and 1915, Sino-Russian agreements recognized Outer Mongolia as an autonomous part of China. Both countries agreed not to interfere with internal politics in Mongolia though China controlled its foreign relations. Japan's wartime treaties with China gave her concessions in Inner Mongolia, which was recognized Chinese territory. Following the Red Revolution, China regained direct control of Outer Mongolia at the request of Mongolians who feared the Siberian hostilities. Disputes between Chinese and Mongolians followed, and a Russian-sponsored People's Revolutionary Government established in 1921 received recognition from Moscow despite Chinese protests. In 1924, a Sino-Russian pact again recognized Outer Mongolia as an autonomous part of China, and the Soviets agreed to evacuate their forces.

CHINESE EASTERN RAILWAY. Another problem settled by the Sino-Russian Convention of 1924 was the ownership of the Chinese Eastern Railway. This line was previously under the control of the Russo-Asiatic Bank which the Soviet government had nationalized in 1918. French investors who had a heavy stake in the railroad organized a new bank which the Peking government authorized to operate the line under the jurisdiction of a Chinese-appointed board of management. By the settlement of 1924, the Russians effectively regained control of the operation of the line and to a large degree of its management.

BIBLIOGRAPHY

Bau, M. J., *The Foreign Relations of China*, 1922.

Bau, M. J., *The Open Door Doctrine in Relation to China*, 1923.

Beckmann, G. M., *The Modernization of China and Japan*, 1962.

Buell, R. L., *Washington Conference*, 1922.

Bywater H. C., *Sea Power in the Pacific*, 1921.

Dennis, A. L. P., *The Anglo-Japanese Alliance*, 1923.

Fahs, C. B., *Government of Japan*, 1940.

Fairbank, J. K., *The United States and China*, 1958.

Feis, H., *The Road to Pearl Harbor*, 1950.

Godsall, W. L., *The International Aspects of the Shantung Question*, 1923.

Graves, W. S., *America's Siberian Adventure, 1918-1920*, 1931.

La Fargue, T. E., *China and the World War*, 1937.

Latourette, K. S., *Development of China*, 1946.

Lockwood, W. W., *The Economic Development of Japan: Growth and Structural Change, 1868-1938*, 1954.

MacNair, H. F., *China in Revolution*, 1931.

Maki, J. M., *Conflict and Tension in the Far East, Key Documents, 1894-1960*, 1961.

Millard, T. F., *Democracy and the Eastern Question*, 1919.

Norman, E. H., *Japan's Emergence as a Modern State*, 1940.

Pollard, R. T., *China's Foreign Relations, 1917-1931*, 1933.

Reinsch, P. S., *An American Diplomat in China*, 1922.

Reischauer, E. O., *Japan, Past and Present*, 1956.

Schuman, F. L., *American Policy Toward Russia Since 1917*, 1928.

Seiji Hishida, *Japan Among the Great Powers*, 1940.

Takeuchi, T., *War and Diplomacy in the Japanese Empire*, 1935.

Unterberger, B., *America's Siberian Expedition, 1918-1920*, 1956.

Willoughby, W. W., *Foreign Rights and Interests in China*, 2 vols., 1927.

Yanaga, C., *Japan Since Perry*, 1949.

CHAPTER 11
China and Japan Between Wars

THE TUCHUN ERA

Tuchunate in China. The ten-year period from 1917 to 1927 in China is usually described as the tuchunate period. During this era rival tuchuns, or war lords, struggled for power and for control of the Peking government. As we saw in Chapter X, the Chinese defeat at Versailles resulted in the fall of Tuan Ch'i-jui's pro-Japanese Anfu government and the rise of Wu P'ei-fu of the Chili clique with the aid of Chang Tso-lin, tuchun of Manchuria, and Feng Yü-hsiang, the Christian general who controlled Inner Mongolia. Chang assumed the premiership, which he used to his own advantage until Wu turned upon him and with the aid of Feng drove him back into Manchuria. Next, after recalling Li Yüan-hung to the presidency, Wu made an attempt to unite China. When this failed, Marshal Ts'ao Kun, tuchun of Chili, placed himself in the president's chair with the aid of Feng, and Wu was pushed into the background.

CONTINUED STRIFE. Chang Tso-lin meanwhile had strengthened himself by an alliance with the remnants of the Anfu faction, and early in 1924 reopened war, winning his way back into Peking with the assistance of the turncoat General Feng and Tuan Ch'i-jui, who emerged from retirement. The office of president was now abolished, and Tuan was made head of the government as Provisional Chief Executive. From 1925 to 1927, chaos ruled at Peking. In 1925, a split between Feng and Chang temporarily drove the latter back to Manchuria, which he ruled independently with the blessings of Japan. Feng, with financial aid from Russia, retained control of Peking, where Tuan remained nominal head of the government. Further south, Wu P'ei-fu was regaining power and beginning to drive northward. In the Canton regime, Dr. Sun's reorganized Kuomintang was becoming more effective.

END OF TUCHUNATE. In 1926, Chang Tso-lin united forces again with Wu P'ei-fu to end the Christian general's hold on Peking. Tuan fled, leaving China without even the semblance of unity or central administration. Before Wu could regain control in the north, he was defeated by the Kuomintang armies, who were beginning their march to victory. Chang was left in control of Peking, until he too was forced out by the advancing forces of Chiang K'ai-shek, who had the aid of Feng Yü-hsiang, now a proponent of the nationalist cause.

REVIVAL OF THE KUOMINTANG

Dr. Sun Turns to Russia. During the first years after the war Sun Yat-sen led a precarious existence. Sun's Canton administration claimed to be the true government of China, but the foreign powers continued to recognize the shadowy Peking government. Sun actually enjoyed only such power as the southern tuchuns chose to give him. In 1920, he reorganized his Kuomintang party, and in 1921, a special parliament formally elected him president. By 1922, he was again in exile at Shanghai, and was convinced that outside aid was necessary to save China. Russia, having proclaimed itself the enemy of imperialism, seemed the best chance. Conversations between Sun and Adolf Joffe, a Russian emissary, resulted in an agreement by which Russia offered to advise China in her struggle to achieve unity and independence, but agreed that China was not yet ready for Communism and the Soviet system.

REORGANIZATION OF THE KUOMINTANG. After Sun returned to Canton in 1923, he was joined by Michael Borodin, sent as political adviser from Moscow. Following Borodin's suggestions, Sun completely reorganized the Kuomintang along the lines of the Russian Communist party. To broaden the foundation of the party, local party groups were organized into cells to provide party indoctrination, discipline, and administration at the ground level. The local groups were linked together in district and provincial organizations. The whole structure was capped by the National Party Congress which was to meet annually. While the Congress was to control policy, actual administration was in the hands of a Central Executive Committee, which controlled all party activities. The Central Committee in turn appointed a standing Supervisory Committee which directed the government between meetings of Congress. Dr. Sun was made lifetime president of the party with veto powers over the party congress and the decisive vote in the Central Executive Committee. In a registration of party members only those who accepted Kuomintang ideals and discipline were enrolled, but Communists were included.

Party Ideals. The ideals of the reorganized Kuomintang were essentially those of Dr. Sun as publicized in his writings and lectures, which included the following:

1. *Plans for National Reconstruction,* an unfinished three-volume work that included the subjects "Psychological Reconstruction," "Material Reconstruction," and "Social Reconstruction."

2. *The San Min Chu I* or *Three Principles of the People.* These principles, first adapted from Lincoln's "of the people, by the people, and for the people," were elaborated in a series of lectures later published in book form.

3. *The Party Manifesto,* issued by the party congress of 1924. This outlined the party history and program and became the party bible.

4. *The Fundamentals of National Reconstruction* was an outline of the party program drawn up by Sun in 1924.

5. *The Will* of Dr. Sun, published after his death in 1925.

SAN MIN CHU I. Basic in Sun's program were his Three Principles of the People: the people's sovereignty (democracy), nationalism, and the people's livelihood. Sun considered it the government's duty to help the people provide for their four necessities: food, clothing, shelter, and means of travel. Though not a Communist, Sun was influenced by socialist thought. He advocated state redistribution of the land to provide equal ownership for all; unearned increment on land should be confiscated by taxation. His second principle, the people's sovereignty, or democrcay, involved the duty of the government to train the people to exercise their powers of election, recall, initiative, and referendum. Sun's third principle, nationalism, required that the government should (1) train the racial minorities towards self-determination and self-government, (2) resist foreign aggression, and (3) revise the foreign treaties to regain China's equality and independence among the nations.

PROGRAM OF RECONSTRUCTION. The program of national reconstruction was to be advanced in three successive periods: (1) government under military control while external obstacles to unity were removed by war; (2) political tutelage under Kuomintang direction when order was restored within a province to train the people for local self-government in each hsien or county and to teach and help them to exploit the local resources and promote industry and commerce to provide for their livelihood; (3) constitutional government to begin in each province when all the hsiens had achieved self-government; elected provincial governors, however, would remain subject to the direction of the central government. With the beginning of the third period, the central government would form a five-power government consisting of executive, legislative, judicial, examination, and control Yuans. After one-half the provinces reached the constitutional period, a constitution, drawn up by the legislative Yuan, was to be promulgated.

National Congress of 1924. The first Kuomintang Congress, which met at Canton in January, 1924, accepted the organization and program of Sun and Borodin. A party constitution was adopted and a party manifesto was drawn up. Earlier a national army had been established and the Whampoa Military Academy founded under Chiang K'ai-shek to train its officers. This new force received its baptism of fire in November, 1924, when it put down an uprising of Cantonese merchants who were alarmed by Sun's radicalism and communist alliance.

Death and Deification of Sun. In 1925, the temporary unification of north China under a coalition of Feng Yü-hsiang, Tuan Ch'i-jui, and Chang Tso-lin brought about the last attempt peacefully to unite all China. Sun entered into discussions with the northern leaders in January, 1925, only to find agreement impossible. On March 12, 1925, Sun died in the northern capital, signing in his last moments his *Will,* urging the continuation of his struggle for unity, the fulfillment of the three Principles of the People, and cooperation with Russia. Alive, Sun Yat-sen had been a poor administrator and politician, but dead, his faults were forgotten. Almost overnight, he became a national hero, a second Confucius, and a patron saint of the Chinese Revolution. The Kuomintang placed his body in an impressive monument at Nanking that serves as a national shrine for Communists and Kuomintang party members alike.

RISE OF CHIANG K'AI-SHEK

Struggle for Leadership. Since no party member could claim an undisputed right to succeed Dr. Sun as party leader, a struggle ensued. Chief contenders for power were Borodin, who controlled the Communists; Wang Ch'ing-wei, close friend of Dr. Sun and leader of the noncommunist left-wing faction; and Chiang K'ai-shek, who was commander in chief of the Kuomintang armies and who feared and mistrusted the Communists. The three were held together by a common desire to unite China, but when Borodin was absent in the north, Chiang seized the opportunity to oust Wang. Thereafter, Chiang became Chairman of the Standing Committee of the Central Executive Committee, while Borodin remained as adviser. This reduced the party conflict to one between the Communists and the right-wing militarists.

March to the North. In mid-1926, the great military campaign to reunite China was begun. Ahead of the military advance moved a secret army of agitators and propagandists who worked so effectively that whole provinces fell to Chiang with scarcely a struggle. Hankow was taken in October, and by spring 1927 the Kuomintang held most of China south of the Yangtze. In the north, General Feng and the war lord of Shensi province declared for the Nationalists.

Party Conflict. While Chiang was occupied in leading his armies, Borodin organized a movement to oust him from power. In November, 1926, the Canton government moved to Hankow, where it was rejoined by Wang Ch'ing-wei. The remarkable victories brought a flood of popular support to the Communist-dominated peasant and labor unions. Encouraged by the Communists, workers seized control of the British concessions at Hankow. In March, 1927, Communist-led troops attacked foreigners and their properties in Nanking to embarrass Chiang in the eyes of the foreigners. In the same month, when the left-wing faction at Hankow called a meeting of the Central Executive Committee, Chiang refused to attend, and was expelled from the party and replaced as chairman by Wang Ch'ing-wei.

EXPULSION OF THE COMMUNISTS. Chiang next turned to the right wing for support. After entering into an alliance with the wealthy merchants and bankers of Shanghai, he set up his own government at Nanking. Meanwhile, Chang Tso-lin raided the Russian embassy at Peking, where papers were discovered revealing the Communist plan to sovietize China under Borodin's direction. As a result of these disclosures, even Wang Ch'ing-wei repudiated Borodin, who was forced to flee to Russia. By August, 1927, Chiang's rightist faction enjoyed a strong position, but Chiang was unable to reach an agreement with the left-wing faction led by Wang Ch'ing-wei and T. V. Soong. In an effort to encourage party unity, Chiang resigned his military command and retired to the foreign concession at Shanghai. Even in retirement, however, Chiang's influence remained strong and hindered party peace. A middle-class government organized at Nanking in September quickly collapsed of internal dissension, while a successor at Canton failed due to war-lord opposition.

March to Peking. In December, 1927, Chiang married Mei-ling Soong, sister of both T. V. Soong and Madam Sun Yat-sen, and formally allied himself to Wang Ch'ing-wei and Soong. In the spring of 1928, Chiang again assumed command of the Kuomintang armies and moved his forces northward. Marshal Chang, who ruled all Manchuria with Japanese aid, was no match for the combined Nationalist armies. To save their stake in north China, the Japanese attempted to block Chiang with Japanese forces. After a brief clash at Tsinan in May, the Japanese were forced by public opinion to withdraw, and the Kuomintang forces occupied Peking. While fleeing on the Japanese-controlled South Manchurian Railroad, Marshal Chang was killed by a bomb explosion of dubious origin. When Chang Tso-lin's son and successor, Chang Hsueh-liang, the "Young Marshal," announced his allegiance to the Kuomintang, China for the first time since the death of Yüan Shih-k'ai was united under one government. Nanking now became the national capital and the name of Peking (Northern Capital) was changed to Peiping (Northern Peace).

Organic Law of 1928. The conquest of north China and the resulting recognition of the Nanking government by Japan and the western powers in 1928 completed the military phase of the revolution and began the period of political tutelage. This change was marked by the promulgation of the First Organic

Law which was to serve as a provisional constitution. The new law provided for Kuomintang dictatorship over China similar to the party rule in Russia. The party made and administered the law. Party power was to be exercised by the Party Congress through the Central Executive Committee and its Standing Committee. Chiang remained both head of the party and commander in chief of the Nationalist armies.

Nationalist Disunity. The chief weakness of the Nanking government was its lack of power to eliminate the tuchuns, who still controlled large areas. Chiang's Nanking government directly ruled only the Yangtze provinces. In January, 1929, a conference called to discuss plans for reducing the private armies was followed by a revolt by the war lords of Kwangsi. After this was put down in 1930, Feng deserted the Kuomintang and was driven by the Nationalists with the aid of Chang Hsueh-liang into Mongolia. Thereafter, Chiang concentrated his power against the Communists.

CHINA'S FOREIGN RELATIONS

Diplomatic Gains. Despite China's obvious internal weakness in the 1920's, gains were made toward removing her semi-colonial status. As we have seen, the postwar treaties ended the Austrian and German concessions, Boxer indemnities, and extraterritoriality. The Sino-Russian treaty of 1924 canceled the remaining Boxer indemnity, in addition to arranging for the dual control of the Chinese Eastern Railway and returning Outer Mongolia to Chinese sovereignty. The Kuomintang's march to Hankow was followed by Britain's return of her concessions in Hankow, Kiukiang, Chinkiang, and Amoy in 1927 and 1928. Conflicts between Chinese and the foreigners resulted in the addition of Chinese to the Shanghai Municipal Council in 1926 and 1930.

Tariffs and Extraterritoriality. By 1929, China had almost completely regained her tariff autonomy with only Japan ignoring the new 25 per cent import taxes. New treaties were concluded with some lesser western powers in 1929 and 1930, giving China completely equal status. Portugal abandoned her extraterritorial status, while Belgium, Denmark, and Italy agreed to abolish theirs when the majority of powers followed suit.

LIBERALISM VERSUS MILITARISM IN JAPAN

Rise of Liberalism. Japan went into World War I for imperialistic purposes under a liberal premier, Count Okuma. Under him the infamous Twenty-One Demands were delivered to China. In foreign policy, Japan's political leaders differed on methods, but not on objectives. As for internal politics, there were sincere efforts made by Japanese liberals to achieve more democratic government. The emphasis on democracy in World War I propaganda bolstered their endeavors. Partly to align Japan with this propaganda, a commoner, Mr. Hara, the Seiyukai party head, was made premier in 1918. However, the same Mr. Hara dissolved the Japanese diet in 1920 on the grounds that a universal suffrage bill had been introduced. Hara honestly desired to rid the government of military influences, but in 1921 he became the first victim of a long series of assassinations by Japanese militarists and Nationalists. Despite Hara's death, liberalism enjoyed several victories. The Washington Conference agreements were ratified, the Siberian and Shantung expeditions were recalled, universal manhood suffrage was achieved in 1925, civilians gained increasing influence in the bureaucracy, and interest in politics increased.

Tanaka Memorial. The Seiyukai party was split by Hara's death. From 1922 to 1924, nonparty governments ruled. In 1924, Viscount Kato, head of the Kenseikai party, became premier by forming a coalition cabinet with the Seiyukai. When the coalition broke up the following year, Kato retained control with a Kenseikai cabinet. Meanwhile, Baron Tanaka, a militarist popular with the aggressive young army officers, became head of the Seiyukai. Under his leadership, the party advocated a positive foreign policy. After Tanaka became premier in April, 1927, he presented to the emperor a secret memorial outlining a plan for Japan's aggressive imperialism in eastern Asia. The plan called for (1) acquisition and economic development of Manchuria and Mongolia as a prelude to (2) conquest of China, after which (3) the conquest of all Asia would easily follow. Tanaka recognized that to control China, Japan would have to crush the United States.

POSITIVE POLICY IN ACTION. The first application of Tanaka's positive policy was seen in the shift of Japanese troops from

Manchuria to Shantung during the Kuomintang march to the north in 1927. However, in 1928, Tanaka was forced by world-wide as well as Japanese public opinion to end his efforts to block Chiang K'ai-shek's advance to Peking. The circumstances of Chang Tso-lin's death after this incident further embarrassed Tanaka.

PARIS PEACE PACT. Despite the implications of the positive policy, Japan became a signatory of the Kellogg-Briand Treaty for the Renunciation of War, or the Paris Peace Pact. The Tanaka government accepted the pact with the reservation that the phrase above the signatures, "in the names of their respective peoples," indicated that the Japanese emperor signed on "behalf of the people." However, this reservation was not written into the treaty, and the incident was used by the new Minseito or Democratic party to attack Tanaka's government. It was this, added to the repercussions from the assassination of Chang Tso-lin, that overthrew Tanaka's cabinet in July, 1929.

Shidehara Policy. Opposed to Tanaka's aggressive foreign policy were large numbers of Japanese liberals who found leadership in Baron Shidehara. Shidehara, who controlled Japan's foreign policy as foreign minister from 1924 to 1927 and from 1929 to 1931, was allied to the big business interests. His policy was to achieve economic predominance in Asia by peaceful penetration. China's sovereignty and territorial integrity would be respected. Cooperation with China would be encouraged at the same time that Japan's interests were promoted. Shidehara also preferred world-wide cooperation through such agencies as the League of Nations and the Washington and London Conferences.

INTERNATIONAL COOPERATION. In 1929, Shidehara returned to the Foreign Office in a cabinet headed by Hamaguchi, the Minseito party president. Hamaguchi's government desired to promote business and foreign trade, to increase Japan's industrial efficiency, to improve the welfare of the workers, and to pursue a peaceful foreign policy, particularly in China. In 1930, Shidehara represented Japan at the London Armament Conference. When Japan was forced to accept an increased naval ratio short of her demands, the Seiyukai and the militarists organized a violent propaganda attack on Hamaguchi that culminated in the assassination of the premier. A second Minseito government headed by Wakatsuki continued to oppose the militarists until the army forced a cabinet crisis by creating the Manchurian incident late in 1931.

ECONOMIC TRENDS IN JAPAN

Postwar Problems. During World War I, Japan was free to move into world markets temporarily vacated by the European powers. To meet these new demands and the Allies' requests for munitions and shipping, Japan greatly increased her industrial capacity. With the armistice, the favorable balance of trade ended, and much of this capacity became idle. In postwar years, Japan was faced with declining exports, inflation, and rapidly rising food costs that contributed to the growing labor unrest.

POPULATION INCREASE. Prior to the Meiji Restoration, Japan's population had been stable at about 30 million. The industrialization of Japan that followed the restoration encouraged a large population. By 1920, the population was 56 million, and by 1930 it was 64 million. Since the agricultural lands were already heavily exploited, much of this increase flooded into the cities. At the end of the war there were 230 cities over 10,000 population, while only seven years later the number had more than doubled. The problem of providing for a population increasing at the rate of 700,000 yearly was foremost in the minds of Japanese statesmen. Emigration provided no answer. The United States and several other countries callously barred Japanese immigration, while the Japanese were even reluctant to move into vacant lands in their own home island of Hokkaido.

Struggle for Survival. Like England, Japan no longer produced enough food for her mounting population. Food had to be imported in increasing quantities. To buy food, Japan had to export manufactured products, but she had also to import iron, coal, and many other raw materials necessary for industry. To maintain this cycle and provide for an increasing population, Japan had constantly to open new markets for her goods. This was the driving force behind the policies of all Japan's political parties. Most Japanese viewed China and Manchuria as sources for raw materials, markets for Japanese manufacturers, and outlets for Japan's surplus population.

Western Influences. Throughout the early decades of the twentieth century, western culture continued profoundly to influence Japan. The rise of liberalism is but one of the many facets of this trend. The new wealthy families that emerged from World War I especially took to western-style clothing, food, literature, entertainments, and conduct. American baseball became almost as popular in Osaka as in Brooklyn, and large numbers of Japanese youths took to active participation in western sports. Women enjoyed increasing freedom and education, as the increased costs of living gave them importance as breadwinners. Japanese education remained largely under close state supervision.

BIBLIOGRAPHY

Borton, H., *Japan's Modern Century*, 1955.
Borton, H., *Japan Since 1931*, 1940.
Chen, H. S., *Landlord and Peasant in China*, 1936.
Chiang, W., *The Chinese Student Movement*, 1948.
Clark, G., *Economic Rivalries in China*, 1932.
Fahs, C. B., *Government of Japan*, 1940.
Feis, H., *The Road to Pearl Harbor*, 1950.
Griswold, A. W., *The Far Eastern Policy of the United States*, 1939.
Houn, F., *Central Government of China, 1912-1928*, 1957.
Hu, S., *The Chinese Renaissance*, 1934.
Hsu, L., *Sun Yat-sen*, 1933.
Linebarger, P. M. A., *The Political Doctrines of Sun Yat-sen*, 1937.
Latourette, K. S., *Development of China*, 1946.
Lockwood, W. W., *The Economic Development of Japan*, 1954.
Maki, J. M., *Conflict and Tension in the Far East, Key Documents, 1894-1960*, 1961.
Mallory, W. H., *China, Land of Famine*, 1926.
Moulton, H. G., *Japan, an Economic and Financial Appraisal*, 1931.
Quigley, H. S., *Japanese Government and Politics*, 1932.
Reischauer, E. O., *Japan, Past and Present*, 1956.
Scalapino, R., *Democracy and the Party Movement in Prewar Japan*, 1953.
Sun Yat-sen, *San Min Chu I*, 1929.
Takeuchi, T., *War and Diplomacy in the Japanese Empire*, 1935.
T'ang, L. L., *The Inner History of the Chinese Revolution*, 193C
Yanaga, C., *Japan Since Perry*, 1949.
Wang, T. C., *The Youth Movement in China*, 1927.

CHAPTER 12
Undeclared War — 1931-1941

THE MANCHURIAN CRISIS

Manchuria (1931). By 1931, Manchuria's 400,000 square miles had for 40 years been the object of a struggle between Japan, Russia, and China. The Manchu dynasty endeavored to keep Chinese out of this unexploited hinterland, but after 1911, hordes of Chinese flooded in to settle. In 1931, 90 per cent of the 30 million population were Chinese, with Mongolians, Koreans, Japanese, and Russians following in order of importance. China thus held Manchuria not only by legal rights of sovereignty but also by virtue of occupation of the soil. Russia's sphere centered around the Chinese Eastern Railroad, while Japan's interests included the South Manchurian Railway and the valuable Liaotung leasehold including Port Arthur and Dairen. By virtue of the 1905 and 1915 treaties with China, Japan also had numerous additional privileges in Manchuria.

The Changs in Manchuria. Chang Tso-lin, who, as we have seen, figured prominently during the tuchunate era in China, was born a Chinese peasant. He had gained power prior to the Russo-Japanese War as a Manchurian bandit leader. After aiding Japan against Russia, he joined forces with the Chinese government as a regular army officer. Following the revolution, he became tuchun of Fengtien Province. By 1918 he controlled the three eastern provinces of Manchuria, which he ruled almost as an independent autocrat until his death in 1928, following the Kuomintang victories. Although opposed to any alien rule over Manchuria, Chang cleverly used the Japanese to maintain his own position. Chang Hsueh-liang, who succeeded his father in 1928, openly opposed both Japan and Russia and joined the Kuomintang, receiving confirmation of his own control of Manchuria from the Nanking government.

Kuomintang Advances. After the Young Marshal's alignment with Nanking, a Kuomintang propaganda campaign was begun in Manchuria, stressing nationalism and attacking treaties and foreign imperialism. With Kuomintang support, Chang worked to increase the economic strength of the northern provinces and to link them more closely to China's economy.

RAILROAD POLITICS. Japan insisted that in 1905 China had agreed not to construct any Manchurian railroads that would

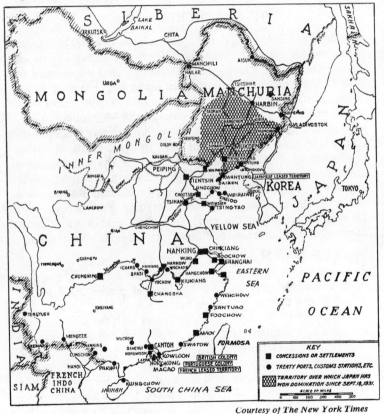

Courtesy of The New York Times

FOREIGN ZONES OF OPERATIONS IN CHINA
FEBRUARY, 1932

compete with Japanese-owned lines. China denied the claim and proceeded to construct lines paralleling Japan's except that they carried inland produce to Chinese-controlled ports and away from Japan's Port Arthur and Dairen. In addition, the Chinese lowered rates on their lines and repudiated some of the railroad loan contracts concluded with Japan in 1918 by the Anfu clique.

INCREASED FRICTION. Outstanding among the 300-odd "incidents" which increased friction between Japan and China were the Wanpaoshan and Nakamura affairs of June, 1931. The first involved the illegal digging of irrigation ditches by Koreans on land leased from Chinese. After some bloodless strife, the ditches were completed under Japanese police protection. Distorted accounts in Japanese and Korean newspapers provoked bloody anti-Chinese riots in both countries. The Nakamura incident concerned the arrest and execution by Chinese of a Japanese major for espionage in the interior of Manchuria. This was widely publicized in Japan as an insult to the Japanese army.

The Manchurian Incident. On September 18, 1931, a bomb explosion caused minor damage to the South Manchurian Railway. By morning, Japanese troops had occupied Mukden, and the Kwantung Army had begun its drive to occupy Manchuria, virtually completing the conquest with the seizure of Harbin on February 5, 1932. Chang Hseuh-liang, having no large force in Manchuria, retreated without serious resistance.

ESTABLISHMENT OF MANCHUKUO. To consolidate their military gains, the Japanese stimulated with money and bayonets a local "independence" movement. On March 1, 1932, the independence of the new state of Manchukuo under the regency of Henry Pu Yi, last emperor of China, was declared and promptly recognized by Japan. While the Manchukuo government had a veneer of pro-Japanese Mongols, Manchus, and Chinese, their Japanese advisers actually controlled policy. The mass of Chinese were unsympathetic with the new government.

Shanghai. An upsurge of Chinese nationalism following the seizure of Manchuria caused rigid boycotting of Japanese goods and services. In January, 1932, a mob attack on five Japanese Buddhist priests provided a pretext for large-scale Japanese military operations against Chinese troops in Shanghai and the nearby fortifications of Woosung. The Chinese Nineteenth Route Army surprised the world by resisting stubbornly until March 3.

INTERNATIONAL REACTION TO MANCHUKUO

China Appeals to the League. Unable to resist Japan, China appealed to the League of Nations on September 21, 1931. Japan issued countercharges, argued self-defense, and proclaimed its peaceful motives, while her Kwantung Army completed the seizure of Manchuria. An American representative attended the League discussions, but without power to act. England was still too resentful of the Chinese anti-British attacks and boycotts of the late 1920's to aid China, while France refused to risk the enmity of Japan.

LYTTON COMMISSION. In December, 1931, the League appointed a commission of inquiry headed by the British Earl of Lytton. The Lytton Commission report in October, 1932, not only condemned Japan as an aggressor, but also recommended that Manchukuo should not be given diplomatic recognition by any nation. However, recognizing that the powers would not fight for China, the commission also recommended that Manchukuo remain under Chinese sovereignty but be given an autonomous government that would safeguard Japan's special rights. This was satisfactory to neither Japan nor China. When the League adopted the Lytton report by unanimous vote, Japan withdrew from the League of Nations in March, 1933.

Stimson Doctrine. After appealing to China and Japan on the basis of their commitments under the Kellogg Peace Pact and other agreements, United States Secretary of State Stimson in January, 1932, issued the notes known as the Stimson Doctrine, stating the official American stand regarding Japanese aggression. The United States would not recognize any treaty, agreement, or situation that impaired the rights of the United States or was brought about by means contrary to the agreements of the Kellogg Peace Pact. The American stand was implemented by retention of the main United States fleets in the Pacific and by additions to its land forces in Shanghai.

Tangku Truce. Despite international protests, Japan resolutely advanced her conquests, adding Jehol Province to Manchukuo in early 1933. After Japanese forces invaded the Peiping region, a truce, marking the end of the first phase of the Sino-Japanese War, was signed at Tangku on May 31, 1933, calling for creation of a demilitarized zone in north China to be policed by a Japanese-controlled Peace Preservation Corps.

MANCHUKUO

Manchukuo Government. On March 1, 1934, Henry Pu Yi was installed as the Emperor Kangte of Manchukuo. According to the constitution then promulgated, the emperor exercised his sovereign rights through five councils. The real ruler of Manchukuo, however, was the commander in chief of the Japanese Kwantung Army, who was also named Japanese ambassador to the Manchukuo court, governor of the Kwantung Territory, and commander in chief of all Manchukuo's forces. The chief officers of state were Chinese, but Japanese with subordinate titles retained control. From the start, certain important government offices, such as those heading finance, education, commercial affairs, and information, were monopolized by Japanese. Through the short history of Manchukuo, the number of Japanese holding government positions steadily increased.

ECONOMIC DEVELOPMENT. As a result of Manchukuo's full recognition of all the rights and privileges the Chinese had previously granted Japan in the area, the Japanese directly controlled much of the wealth and resources. They worked steadily to integrate Manchukuo fully into the Japanese economic system. New railways, roads, ports, power plants, and factories were built, mines were opened, and oil shale deposits developed. When private capital failed to satisfy the ambitions of the Kwantung Army leaders, large government corporations such as the Manchurian Industrial Development Company were organized.

TRANSPORTATION AND COMMUNICATION. In 1931 Japan already controlled most of the Manchurian railways. After the creation of the new state all Manchurian lines except the Russian-controlled Chinese Eastern Railway were integrated into one network under the South Manchurian Railway, which also controlled highways, harbors, and various other interests. In 1935, after two years of negotiations, the Russians evinced their willingness to retire from Manchuria by selling their Chinese Eastern line to Japan. Manchurian communications were similarly merged into the government-controlled Manchurian Telegraphy and Telephone Corporation.

EFFECTS OF JAPANESE CONTROL. Most of Manchurian trade had been with China, and that trade was lost after 1931. Despite tremendous Japanese investments, benefits were slow to accrue. The imposition of law and order did much more to improve the welfare of the Manchurian peasant in the long run. The standard of living for the Chinese was sufficiently high to attract large-scale immigration from Nationalist China. To the discredit of the Japanese is their elimination of higher education for all except their own favorites, and still worse their deliberate encouragement of the use of opium.

Japanese in Mongolia. After the conquest of Jehol in 1933, the Mongols of the other provinces of Inner Mongolia were encouraged to look upon the Japanese as protectors against the Chinese. In 1935 China was compelled to agree to the demilitarization of that region and to prohibit Chinese migration there. When Japan endeavored to press further into Outer Mongolia, she met with Russian forces in a series of border skirmishes that helped convince Japan to sign the Anti-Comintern Pact with Italy and Germany in 1936.

North China. Immediately south of Manchukuo, in the provinces of Shansi, Hopei, and Shantung which were controlled by the anti-Japanese Chang Hsueh-liang, Japan sought to create a buffer region of Chinese territory to protect their puppet state from Kuomintang China. Despite the Tangku Truce, Japanese steadily pressed into this region. A wide-scale propaganda campaign which tried to stir up an autonomy movement was countered by China's granting greater local self-government to the region. Japan tried to prevent the powers from giving aid to China by proclaiming a Japanese Monroe Doctrine, but China denied Japan's right to control the destinies of eastern Asia. As a result of negotiations, however, the Ho-Umetsu Agreement was reached in 1935, by which the Nanking government agreed to withdraw its forces from the demilitarized region and promised to end anti-Japanese propaganda and boycotts.

NATIONALIST CHINA

Nationalists versus Communists. It was China's tragedy to face the aggressor while disunited. The 1927 purge of Communists changed the political orientation of the Kuomintang sharply to the right and placed the propertied interests in control. The purge did not, however, remove the Communists entirely. In November, 1931, during the Manchurian incident, Mao Tsetung and Chu Teh established a soviet government in Kiangsi, which by 1932 controlled perhaps one-sixth of China. Chiang considered the Communists a greater enemy than the Japanese. While appeasing the latter, he organized six large-scale campaigns against the Reds. These, together with an intensive propaganda campaign and the promise of social and economic changes, brought a degree of success. The Communists were driven out of the Kiangsi region, but they then marched 6000 miles on a circuitous route to Shensi, where in 1936 Mao Tse-tung proclaimed a Chinese People's Soviet Republic.

COMMUNIST COMPROMISE OFFER. Safe in their Shensi retreat, the Communists carried out a large-scale economic and social reorganization within the territory they controlled. By 1936, however, the menace of the Nazis had caused Russia and the Communist International to adopt a party line calling for cooperation with the democracies and with the enemies of fascism. Following this line, Mao sought to join with the Kuomintang against Japan by offering a compromise program that included (1) resistance against Japan, (2) reorganization of China's fiscal and tax structure, (3) development of trade and industry, (4) improvement of the educational facilities, and of the working and living conditions of the people, and (5) cooperation with friendly foreign powers. These terms were rejected.

SIAN EPISODE. Despite popular demands for resistance to Japan, Chiang ordered Chang Hsueh-liang to wipe out the Communists. However, Chang failed to carry out these orders. When Chiang K'ai-shek, while at a conference in Sian, ordered the arrest of Chang, the latter's supporters kidnaped Chiang. Although the generalissimo refused to fight the Japanese or to talk terms, his life was saved by the Communists, who believed he was the only man who could lead the nation against Japan. Finally Chiang was released and Chang was arrested, tried, and sentenced to imprisonment, but thereafter pardoned. Although Chiang had promised nothing, a temporary agreement with the Communists followed by which (1) Nanking officially sanctioned Red rule over the Shensi region, (2) the Communist army joined the Nationalist forces, and (3) the Communists agreed to relax their socialization program.

Economic Developments. A cooperative movement, begun around 1922, achieved official recognition in 1934 by special government legislation encouraging the formation of various cooperative societies. In 1938, the movement received additional impetus with the formation of the Chinese Industrial Cooperatives (Indusco) by Reivi Alley and T. V. Soong. Indusco especially aimed at the rehabilitation of workers dislocated by the war. The cooperatives helped prevent China's economy from collapsing after the Japanese invasion.

The New Life Movement. An important factor in the Kuomintang success in driving the Communists out of the Kiangsi region was the inauguration of the New Life Movement in 1934. This movement aimed at spiritual regeneration of China by reviving Confucian principles of morality and public behavior. New Life Movement Association members not only carried on propaganda campaigns against improper conduct but also organized agencies to eliminate illiteracy, teach personal hygiene, and improve agricultural methods.

MILITARISM IN JAPAN

Growth of Anti-Democratic Societies. After World War I, new ultranationalistic societies were formed. The objectives varied, but almost invariably they advocated Kodo (the Imperial Way) and various combinations of racial and cultural superiority, aggressive imperialism, and hostility to "western" doctrines such as liberalism, democracy, capitalism, and individualism. While the thought behind these Japanese ideologies was often fuzzy, in general they advocated a state socialism that would abolish representative government and private capitalistic monopolies. The chief difference between these various "patriotic" societies lay in the particular class or clique they believed should control Japan behind the divine impersonal symbol of the emperor.

GOVERNMENT BY ASSASSINATION. At first Japanese political parties, seldom very strong or popular, were largely led by aristocrats. When in 1920 Hara, a commoner, became premier, he was assassinated by an ultranationalist. In 1930, another commoner, Premier Hamaguchi, was assassinated, and thereafter political murders became frequent in Japan. The death of Hamaguchi left no strong leader of the Minseito party to support Shidehara, with the result that the armed forces gained control of Japan's foreign policy, and the Manchurian incident began. To secure complete political control, a group of ultranationalist young army and navy officers perpetrated a series of assassinations that ended with the death of Premier Inukai. While the assassins failed in their purpose, they further discredited party government by showing its weakness.

Military Coup of 1936.   After Inukai's death, the ultranationalists and militarists intensified their propaganda. When they lost the 1936 elections to the Minseito party, however, they reverted to terrorism. A group of lower ranking officers led 1400 soldiers to seize the public buildings in the heart of Tokyo and attempt to assassinate the entire cabinet and the Genro Saionji. While several of their intended victims were killed, Saionji and Premier Okada escaped. Again, although the plotters failed in their purpose, and although the army was temporarily discredited, political parties lost further prestige. The guilty officers, in this and previous murders, were widely publicized as patriots, although they were in some cases executed.

Victory of the Military.   While the militarists and fascists lost the elections of 1937, the enlargement of Sino-Japanese strife assured their eventual political ascendancy. A Munitions Mobilization Law of September, 1937, greatly increased the government's control of Japan's economy. An Imperial Headquarters was formed in the following month to place the military command on a wartime basis, while early in 1938 a National Mobilization Bill placed the entire country on a war footing. The resultant military dictatorship had no single man or even small group of men at its head. Instead, it was a dictatorship of the army officers of Japan, who were constantly striving among themselves for control of the army and the government; but ultimately, all sought to make Japan supreme in eastern Asia.

MILITARY DICTATORSHIP. When the dissolution of political parties in 1940 did not end opposition to the dictatorship, the militarists organized the "New National Structure Movement" to extend military control not only over the resources of Japan but also over the private lives of its people. To propagate their doctrines, the Imperial Rule Assistance Association (IRRA) was established with the chief government officials as its leaders. The Association was designed to regiment through its local councils practically every aspect of life. All other patriotic societies were in effect merged with the IRRA.

Economic Developments. The decade prior to Pearl Harbor was one of rapid economic change in Japan. After the beginning of world-wide depression in 1929, Japan's markets for silk, her principal export, collapsed, yet textile production in general increased. Metal, machinery, and chemical production was greatly expanded. Industry became more diversified, and as industrial efficiency increased and the value of the yen went down, Japan became a serious competitor in world markets with all types of manufactured goods. Despite an increase in exports, however, Japan had to buy more abroad than she sold, and the continued demands of war in China increased this disparity. After 1930, there was a strong tendency toward rationalization of industry by merger and formation of cartels. Previously over half of Japan's industrial population worked in shops employing five or fewer workers. The rationalization trend was sponsored by the "Law for Regulating Associations Manufacturing Exportable Goods," which was enforced by the Bureau for the Rationalization of Industry.

Agrarian Problems. Despite progress in industrialization, Japan remained predominantly agricultural. However, industrialization was largely achieved at the expense of the peasant. Never prosperous, the Japanese farmer was further impoverished by the depression following World War I, and he never shared in what little prosperity Japan enjoyed. The government stabilization program prevented the rise of prices of farm products during years of bad crops, but failed to hold up prices during years of good crops. The organization of rural cooperatives was considered one answer to the agrarian problem. In 1930, the government established a five-year plan to encourage the cooperative movement. To help provide rural credit, the government periodically advanced money to banks and cooperative societies for loans to farmers. Despite these measures, rural distress continued and food production decreased. Other reasons for the decrease were the drafting of men for the army, increased labor demands of industry, decreased supplies of fertilizer, and other dislocations due to the war.

Social Trends. The industrial and agrarian developments of the 1920's and 1930's caused an increase in peasant and labor union strength. This union movement was always frowned upon by a government that was dominated either by the Zaibatzu or the militarists. After reaching the peak of its strength around 1936, unionism declined rapidly as the fascist-minded government gradually tightened the controls upon Japan's man power to meet the needs of war. The General Mobilization Law of 1938 gave the government control over wages and working hours. In 1940 the labor unions were dissolved and their members enrolled in the government-sponsored League for Service to the State. While the workers thus lost their bargaining power, there was during the same period an increase in social security legislation such as compulsory government insurance covering medical attention, hospitalization, old age, retirement, and death. Augmenting the government plans were numerous Mutual Aid Societies that provided similar benefits.

THOUGHT CONTROL. Intensified nationalism in Japan brought increased restraint of speech, press, and thought. The military totalitarians gained control of education in 1938 with the appointment of Baron Sadao Araki, former war minister, to the Education Ministry. To militarize education, military training was introduced to all schools in 1938, discipline became more rigid, Kodo and nationalism were stressed, and individualism was discouraged. Emperor worship within the schools was emphasized both to counteract foreign religious influences and to stimulate patriotism. In 1940 a Religious Organization Law gave the education minister extensive powers over all religious sects. Throughout the 1930's, press, radio, and movie censorship, never absent in Japan, grew increasingly more rigid, particularly after 1937.

SINO-JAPANESE WAR (1937-1941)

Resumption of Hostilities. After the Japanese militarists' defeat in the elections of 1936 and 1937, it appeared that only foreign involvement could bring about the desired military dictatorship. In China, Chiang was rapidly building up military potential and seemed on the verge of uniting with the Communists against Japan. Great Britain and the United States were becoming increasingly hostile to Japanese militarism. Russian defenses in Mongolia and Siberia had been tested and proved dangerously strong, and Japan had joined Germany and Italy in the Anti-Comintern Pact. In July, 1937, the Japanese troops at Peiping, augmented far beyond treaty provisions, claimed to have been attacked during maneuvers by Chinese troops. Refusing to treat the affair as a local incident, the Japanese armies quickly pushed out to win the entire Peiping-Tientsin area and to occupy Suiyuan province by the end of August. In Shansi, however, they were stopped by the Communist Eighth Route Army, recently incorporated into the Nationalist forces.

OCCUPATION OF NANKING. In August, 1937, the Japanese claimed another "incident" as pretext for an attack on Shanghai. Again without declaring war, a Japanese fleet bombarded the city and landed large numbers of troops. Avoiding the foreign settlements, the Japanese with superior arms steadily pushed back the Chinese defenders. Chiang slowed the march, but did not attempt a last-ditch stand. After the fall of Shanghai in November, the Japanese pressed upriver to occupy Nanking the following month. By this time, the defeated Chinese defenders were demoralized and might have been captured or wiped out had not the victorious Japanese forces indulged in an orgy of raping, looting, and destruction. As a result, Chiang found time to reorganize his forces in an orderly retreat.

RETREAT TO CHUNGKING. Before the fall of Nanking, the Nationalist capital was moved to Hankow. By October the capital had to be moved still further to Chungking as the Japanese pushed up the Yangtze to seize Hankow. Meanwhile, the great port of Canton was lost to the invader. Thus by the end of 1938, the Japanese could penetrate the interior of China from the south, center, and north. They held the most important ports, cities, and industrial centers, and controlled most of the important railroads. On the other hand, they had failed to defeat decisively the Nationalist forces which were now defending rugged territory where bombers and tanks were less effective. The capture of Nanking was a hollow victory, only arousing greater Chinese resistance. Millions of Chinese scientists, professors, students, workers, and peasants marched into the interior, carrying dismantled machines and all manner of equipment, books, and personal belongings to re-establish factories and schools in the Chungking area.

MILITARY STALEMATE. After 1938, the Japanese made few gains. By 1940, they had won a corridor as far up the Yangtze as Ichang and had enlarged their control of the coast. Hainan Island fell in 1939. Yet at no time did the Japanese gain control of the entire coast except in north China, and despite vigorous efforts, they never succeeded in gaining full control of the Canton-Hankow or the Hankow-Peking railroads. In November, 1939, a major Chinese victory held back the Japanese at Changsha, and in the following year the Japanese were driven out of Kwangsi Province. After Hankow, the Chinese resorted to guerilla warfare to make Japan's hold on her conquered territory precarious. In this mode of fighting, the Communists led the way. Large Chinese forces, with the aid of the Chinese peasants, found it possible to operate over long periods behind the Japanese lines.

The New Order in East Asia. In 1938, the Japanese government announced its intention to create a New Order in Eastern Asia that would include China, Manchukuo, and Japan. China could share in this order by exchanging her raw materials for Japanese manufactures, but first she must cleanse her government of anti-Japanese elements. When the Kuomintang failed to make peace on these terms, the Japanese organized a Chinese puppet government that would. In 1937, Wu P'ei-fu was approached to head a new government, but died before its formation. Finally, for reasons not completely known, Wang Ch'ingwei, former friend of Sun Yat-sen and rival of Chiang K'ai-shek, accepted the dubious honor of heading a Japanese-dominated government at Nanking. Wang attempted to carry on Sun Yatsen's ideals with an imitation Kuomintang under Japanese jurisdiction, but found himself a helpless tool of Tokyo. He had the good fortune of dying in 1944 before the defeat of Japan.

United States Reaction. The United States government was officially neutral, but in fact aided China by failing to invoke the neutrality acts of 1935 and 1937 on the grounds that no war had been declared. In a speech in October, 1937, Roosevelt suggested an international quarantine of the aggressors, but public opinion did not favor action. In November, 1937, the United States joined 18 other nations at the Brussels Conference in denouncing Japan as an aggressor and treaty breaker. In the following month, Japanese aircraft deliberately bombed and sank several American ships on the Yangtze, including the gunboat *Panay*. Still the American public refused to be aroused, and their government demanded and received reparations and apologies.

AID TO CHINA. When Japan announced her "New Order" in 1938, the United States strongly warned Tokyo that no unilateral abrogation of the Open Door would be accepted. In July, 1939, Washington gave the required six months' notice of its intention to end the American-Japanese commercial treaty that had been in effect since 1911. This gave the United States freedom to restrict or end trade with Japan. While no embargo was declared, and shipments of scrap iron and gasoline were merely restricted, China was given more direct aid in the form of loans. In December, 1938, the Export-Import Bank advanced $25 million to finance Chinese purchases in America, and an equal sum was added in 1940. America's reply to Japan's joining in a triple alliance with Germany and Italy was to extend China an additional $100 million in credits and to warn Japan that no combination of powers would stop this aid.

PRELUDE TO PEARL HARBOR. The year before Pearl Harbor was one of futile diplomatic maneuvering between the United States and Japan. After the fall of France, Tokyo, with German aid, gained control of Indo-China. From there Japan asserted her will upon Siam by bribes and pressure. Vichy was induced to cede portions of Laos and Cambodia to Siam. After Japan's occupation of Indo-China, Washington further restricted trade with Japan, and ordered retired General Douglas MacArthur to active command of United States forces in the Philippines. Roosevelt and Churchill met off Newfoundland and issued the Atlantic Charter, and General Tojo was named premier of Japan. In October, 1941, Saburo Kurusu, who had signed the triple alliance for Japan, joined Ambassador Nomura in negotiations at Washington. Japan's peace offer would have required the ending of United States restrictions on trade with Japan and blanket approval of a Japanese-dictated peace with China, while Japan would remove her troops from southern Indo-China and agree to keep her forces out of the rest of southeastern Asia. The United States countered with an offer of a nonaggression and reciprocal trade treaty with commercial concessions, if Japan would withdraw from the regions she had won since 1931. When no agreement could be reached, Roosevelt appealed personally to the Japanese emperor for peace. On the following morning, Pearl Harbor and other American naval and army installations were heavily bombed by Japanese carrier-borne planes.

Japan's Relations with Europe. Despite Russia's sale of her Manchurian railroad interests to Japan, frequent border incidents occurred. In 1938 these reached major proportions in a ten-day battle involving planes and tanks. Less than a year later, an even larger battle occurred involving several divisions. Russia proved her strength on these occasions, and when she offered a settlement after the beginning of the war in Europe (September, 1939), Japan readily accepted. Early in 1941, after learning of the contemplated German attack on Russia, Japan signed a neutrality pact with Russia, paying for the privilege by abandoning her mineral concessions in Russian Sakhalın. Before the fall of France, Franco-Japanese relations had been embittered by the arms traffic from Indo-China to Nationalist China. In retaliation, Japan occupied Hainan Island and other Chinese territories in the French sphere of interest. In September, 1940, Japan concluded the triple alliance in Berlin, by which Japan recognized Germany and Italy as the arbiters of European destinies in return for their recognition of Japan's ambitions for a "new order" in east Asia. Great Britain, involved in a European struggle, was also harassed by Japan in Asia. The British Tientsin concession was blockaded on petty pretexts in retaliation for Britain's permitting aid to reach China over the Burma road and through Hong Kong. Churchill reluctantly closed the Burma road in July, 1940, but after Japan's occupation of Indo-China, reopened it and strengthened British east Asiatic garrisons. In 1941, Britain and the Dominions abrogated their commercial treaties with Tokyo.

BIBLIOGRAPHY

Bisson, T. A., *Japan in China*, 1938.
Borton, H., *Japan Since 1931*, 1940.
Byas, H., *Government by Assassination*, 1942.
Chiang, K'ai-shek, *Resistance and Reconstruction . . . 1937-1943*, 1943.
Colegrove, K. W., *Militarism in Japan*, 1936
Dalin, D. J., *Soviet Russia and the Far East*, 1948.
Fahs, C. B., *Government of Japan*, 1940.
Fairbank, J. K., *The United States and China*, 1958.
Feis, H., *The Road to Pearl Harbor*, 1950.
Lory, H., *Japan's Military Masters*, 1947.
Hudson, G. F., *The Far East in World Politics*, 1939.
Johnson, C. A., *Peasant Nationalism and Communist Power . . . 1937-1945*, 1952.
Jones, F. C., *Japan's New Order in East Asia . . . 1937-1945*, 1954.
Lockwood, W. W., *The Economic Development of Japan . . . 1868-1938*, 1954.
Maki, John M., *Conflict and Tension in the Far East, Key Documents, 1894-1960*, 1961.
Maxon, Y. C., *Control of Japanese Foreign Policy . . . 1930-1945*, 1957
Quigley, H. S., *The Far Eastern War, 1937-1941*, 1942.
Reischauer, E. O., *Japan, Past and Present*, 1956.
Scalapino, R. A., *Democracy and the Party Movement in Pre-War Japan*, 1953.
Shigemitsu, M., *Japan and Her Destiny*, 1958.
Snow, E., *Red Star Over China*, 1944.
Taylor, G. E., *The Struggle for North China*, 1940.
Yanaga, C., *Japan Since Perry*, 1949.

CHAPTER 13
World War II

RETREAT

Pearl Harbor. The strong possibility of a Russian defeat in Europe by the fall of 1941 influenced the Japanese attitude toward the United States. When General Tojo became premier in October, he spoke of "peace with justice," but Japanese newspapers anticipated war. In November Churchill declared Britain's solidarity with the United States in the event of war with Japan. When Kurusu arrived in Washington on November 15, for peace discussions, a Japanese fleet was at sea prepared for war. Although the military command at Hawaii was notified on November 24 and 27 of the possibility of a surprise attack and the imminence of war, inadequate defenses were provided. On December 7, a Japanese naval squadron reached striking distance without being discovered. Despite the fact that a small Japanese submarine was sunk off Pearl Harbor at 7:00 A.M., and a radar operator detected planes approaching, no alert was sounded. Within a few hours of the initial attack at 7:48 A.M., Japanese air power had destroyed or temporarily put out of action 95 per cent of the naval and air power in Hawaii, and killed or wounded over 4000 men. The cost to Japan was about 100 aircraft and five small submarines.

War in Southeast Asia. As was anticipated, the United States and Great Britain declared war on December 8. By the attack on Pearl Harbor, the Japanese immobilized American naval power while their own forces invaded Guam, the Philippines, Malaya, and the East Indies. Japan hoped to become so firmly intrenched there that America, deeply involved in the European war, would make peace on favorable terms. In a four-months offensive, Japan achieved incredible victories. Guam fell December 13, and Wake followed 10 days later. Despite a heroic delaying campaign, American forces surrendered the Philippines on April 9, after the American commander, General MacArthur, was evacuated to Australia by orders of President Roosevelt.

RETREAT OF BRITAIN. British possessions fared no better. Hong Kong, also attacked on December 7, surrendered on Christmas Day. Britain's Far Eastern fleet was crippled by the loss of the battleships *Prince of Wales* and the *Repulse* on December 10. A quickly successful invasion of Siam was followed by a Japanese march down the Malay Peninsula to Singapore. That presumably impregnable sea base, having no defenses against land attack, surrendered with 75,000 troops in February. In Burma, inadequate and scattered forces were handicapped by an active Burmese fifth column. Rangoon fell March 10. Despite the leadership of the British General Alexander and the American Lieutenant General Stilwell, the Allied forces, weak both in

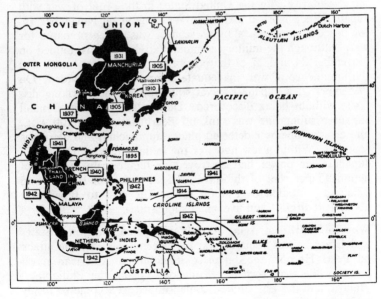

Courtesy of The New York Times

EXPANSION OF JAPAN'S EMPIRE TO DECEMBER, 1943

equipment and in numbers, continued their retreat. By mid-1942, the Burma road was cut and nearly all the country was lost.

INVASION OF THE INDIES. While Malaya was being taken, the Netherlands East Indies were also attacked. With inadequate sea, air, and ground defenses, the Allies again could hope only to delay the Japanese advance. Although almost half the Japanese invasion fleet was sunk, the East Indies were largely in Japanese hands by the end of March. In April, the Japanese prepared for further thrusts at Port Moresby in New Guinea. However, in the Battle of the Coral Seas, an American carrier squadron inflicted such serious losses on the Japanese fleet that Japan's advance in the south was halted.

Renewed Attack on China. China declared war upon the Axis powers immediately after Pearl Harbor, thus finally creating a legal state of war against Japan after ten years of "incidents." In the same month, Japan launched a large-scale attempt to take Changsha and so gain complete control of the Hankow-Canton Railroad. Changsha was reduced to rubble, but the Chinese held on to win a major victory while her allies were almost everywhere on the retreat.

ALLIED ADVANCE

Island Hopping. The Battle of the Coral Seas marked the end of the Allied retreat. One month later, this fact was brought home to the Japanese by the disastrous defeat of their invasion fleet en route to Midway Island. On August 7, 1942, the Allied Pacific offensive began with the invasion of Guadalcanal. Six months of bitter land, sea, and air fighting were required to win this much needed base, but thereafter the Allied pace accelerated into a fantastic island-hopping campaign. Allied army units enlarged their hold on New Guinea in mid-1943. United States marines captured strategic islands in the Gilberts during the fall, while navy and air attacks ate away Japanese air and sea power in the south. Attu and Kiska, islands in the Aleutians seized by Japan, were retaken in May and August, 1943. By early 1944, Allied power had grown overwhelming. Kwajalein in the Marshalls fell, and Truk, Japan's main naval base in the South Pacific, was heavily bombed. In June, July, and August, Guam, Saipan, and Tinian of the Caroline group of islands were seized in a bloody campaign. General MacArthur renewed the attack in the south during the same period. Hollandia in Netherlands New Guinea was taken in April, 1944, and the seizure of Peleliu in the Palaus opened the way for the invasion of the Philippines.

Return to the Philippines. On October 20, a quarter million Allied troops were landed on Leyte in the center of the Philippines. Efforts to repulse the invasion cost Japan most of her remaining fleet. During the Leyte campaign, Mindoro and Marinduque were invaded. On January 9, 1945, American forces landed near Manila, and by mid-February Luzon was securely held, although pockets of Japanese continued resistance for many months.

Attacks on Japan. Immediately following the surrender of Corregidor, last Japanese strong point in the Philippines, Iwo Jima, one of the Bonin Islands within striking distance of Japan, was taken in one of the bloodiest of the Pacific battles. In the following invasion of Okinawa, the bitter fighting of Iwo Jima was repeated on a larger scale, with the added terror of the kamikazes, Japanese suicide bombers. Three weeks after the collapse of the Japanese defense of Okinawa, the Allied fleets shelled Japanese defenses on the home islands of Honshu and Hokkaido, including the Tokyo area.

AIR WAR AGAINST JAPAN. As early as August, 1942, air attacks on Japan had been inaugurated by General Doolittle's carrier-launched raid. Only in mid-1944, however, when the American B 29's began operating, did large-scale raids on the home islands begin. In July, 1945, carrier-based aircraft added their weight to that of the superfortresses. To the usual destruction of concussion-type bombs were added the devastating effects of incendiary bombs that converted Japan's wood and paper cities into seas of fire.

War on the Continent. For the first two years of the war, little man power or assistance was available for the China-Burma-India (C.B.I.) theater of operations. When demands for immediate self-government were not granted, India, under Gandhi's leadership, embarked on a campaign of civil disobedience and nonresistance to Japan. The loss of the Burma road cut off the supply of Chinese man power. Despite these handicaps, the Allies attempted in December, 1942, an offensive that floundered in the monsoon rains.

Burma Campaign. In the following year, General Stilwell trained a Chinese army in India with new American equipment. These Chinese, strengthened by American veterans of the Pacific campaigns, renewed the offensive early in 1944. Meanwhile, the new Ledo road was constructed west of the old Burma road to renew communications with China. By early 1945, the Japanese were driven back sufficiently to effect a junction between the Burma and Ledo roads. The opening of these roads greatly increased the volume of war materials reaching China, where Chinese forces were being reorganized and re-equipped. By the end of the war, the Japanese had been largely eliminated from Burma.

China. While the United Nations advanced in Burma and the Pacific during 1944, they were forced to retreat in China. On several fronts, the Chinese were pushed back. American airfields were lost, and the air and land connections with Burma and India were endangered. By August, 1945, however, the reorganized Chinese armies with American air support were driving back the Japanese, although Chiang's fear of the Communists prevented full utilization of the Nationalist armies.

INTERNAL DEVELOPMENTS IN JAPAN

Cabinet Changes. Two months prior to Pearl Harbor, the cabinet headed by the court noble Konoye resigned in favor of Premier General Hideki Tojo. Without becoming an absolute dictator, Tojo gained greater control over Japan than any man since the shogunate. Despite the long-standing feud between the militarists and the Zaibatsu, the economic necessities of total war at length forced Tojo to utilize big businessmen in cabinet positions. To achieve greater centralization of power, Tojo in 1943 served simultaneously as premier, war minister, munitions minister, and president of the Imperial Rule Assistance Association. Japan's losses in the air attack on Truk Island in February, 1944, impelled Tojo to reshuffle his cabinet and high command and take personal command of the general staff.

Fall of Tojo. Having assumed so much responsibility, Tojo naturally received the blame for Japanese defeats. Finally after the loss of Saipan, Kuniaki Koiso was named premier. The best efforts of Koiso proved inadequate. In April, 1945, when defeat was obvious after the loss of Iwo Jima and Russia's annulment of her neutrality treaty with Japan, the elder statesman Suzuki formed a new cabinet, representing not only the militarists but the bureaucrats and businessmen as well.

Economic Problems. By 1941, Japan was already weakened by ten years of intermittent war in China. Only a high degree of central control kept the economy from complete collapse. Even in peacetime, Japan's industrial potential was largely controlled by a few concerns known as the Zaibatsu. Between 1941 and 1945, a series of acts even further centralized controls over war industries, bringing many under the direct supervision of the Ministry of Munitions. However, Zaibatsu opposition prevented complete rationalization of industry. Despite governmental efforts, production declined as the allied blockade cut off raw materials and food. Allied air attacks greatly hastened this economic decline by wiping out numerous industries and by rendering one-third of Japan's urban population homeless and slaughtering 333,000 civilians.

Social Effects. Life for the average Japanese, none too satisfactory even prior to Pearl Harbor, grew far worse. Inflation raised prices of available goods, and strict rationing was imposed on food and clothing. To control inflation, a forced savings plan was adopted, and taxes were raised. Food supplies remained inadequate despite subsidies and other inducements to production. A labor shortage both in industry and in agriculture forced the government to conscript not only men but finally women and children over 12 for labor. Higher education, except in science and technology, almost ceased.

INTERNAL DEVELOPMENTS IN CHINA

Occupied China. Japan ruled over 200 million Chinese through her unhappy puppet Wang Ch'ing-wei. Failing in an attempt to gain the willing cooperation of her subjects by abandoning extraterritoriality and signing a treaty of alliance with the puppet government, Japan asserted large controls over the Chinese economy through the Central and North China Development Companies. Through these tools, Chinese mineral resources were exploited. To provide labor for mines, railroads, factories, and agriculture, large-scale conscription was resorted to. Education was brought under close control, and Japanese language and cultural studies were promoted. The Japanese found, however, that their efforts in every field were frequently sabotaged by patriotic Chinese. Communist and Kuomintang guerrilla bands with popular support made communications and production precarious.

Politics in Nationalist China. The Kuomintang had made some progress toward achieving local representative government prior to the flight to Chungking, but thereafter it became increasingly reactionary. The representative Peoples Political Council, initially convened in 1938, continued throughout the war to furnish some voice for popular dissatisfaction, but the opponents to governmental policy were closely watched by an efficient secret police and frequently placed in concentration camps or executed. Despite such government coercion, the liberals and left-wing elements united in 1944 to form the China Democratic League, and demanded an end of Kuomintang dictatorship and police-state methods. In the face of a united opposition, Chiang's cabinet was reshuffled, but no real reforms were effected.

Nationalist-Communist Rivalries. A sore spot with China's allies, as well as with the left-wing nationalists was the failure of the Chinese Nationalist and Communist forces to unite against their common foe. Following the Sian episode, the Communists had officially abolished their Chinese Soviet government and Red Army and promised cooperation with the Kuomintang government and army. By 1938, however, it was obvious that this was only a gesture. Not only had the government not dissolved, it had actually extended its territory by guerrilla activities at the cost of both the Kuomintang and the Japanese. For his part, Chiang appears to have demanded complete submission rather than cooperation from the Communists whom he believed as dangerous as the Japanese. Chiang's use of scarce war materials against the Communists rather than the Japanese brought him into conflict with General Stilwell, Vice-President Wallace, Donald Nelson, and General Patrick Hurley, sent successively by President Roosevelt, to attempt to end this fratricidal conflict. Chiang insisted that Mao's forces should lay down their arms in return for partial representation in the national government, while the Communists demanded a real coalition government and adoption of broad social and agrarian reforms. Negotiations broke down early in 1945.

Communist China. While the Nationalist government was weakened by economic strangulation, by the alienation of the intellectual and business classes, and by internal conflicts and confusion, the Communists increased their territory, winning greater popular support and strengthening their organization. During the war years, Mao Tse-tung emerged as the unquestioned party leader and party theoretician. Early in 1940, he published his adaptation of Stalinist theories to the Chinese situation in his *On the New Democracy.* This document advanced the theory that in un-industrialized China, the "bourgeoisie democratic" or capitalist stage of the class revolution should be merged with the succeeding socialist revolution under a joint dictatorship of all revolutionary classes. Thus, a coalition government including intellectuals, peasants, labor, and some small business elements would be formed under Communist Party direction to operate a mixed economy of state-owned private and cooperative enterprises in the first stage of the Chinese revolution. During this stage, which Mao called the "New Democracy," large banks and big businesses and industry would be nationalized and the lands of big landlords would be confiscated and redistributed to peasants. In 1943, the Chinese Communist Party adopted the principle of one-third of the government positions to party members and two-thirds to non-party. This presented a façade of cooperation with middle parties, which won the cooperation of many intellectuals and businessmen while not relaxing the effective dictatorship of the party. Compatible with the "New Democracy," land redistribution and socialization programs were restricted temporarily to avoid alienating the property-owning classes whose cooperation was sought.

Free China's Economy. Since most of China's industries were in Japanese-occupied areas, China found it necessary to obtain munitions and equipment from an agricultural region with little industry. Under the auspices of the National Resources Commission, to which large powers were granted, a remarkable number of industries were established in Free China. To provide industrial manpower, a mobilization act was passed empowering the government to regulate the movement and conditions of labor. To meet the food needs of a population swelled by 50 million refugees from the Japanese zone, the Kuomintang pressed land reclamation and encouraged increased food production by such inducements as teaching new methods of farming and providing better seed. Government regulations failed to stop China's soaring inflation, and price controls only encouraged a flourishing black market.

DIPLOMACY AND THE END OF THE WAR

International Conferences. During the long conflict, the Allied leaders held a series of conferences that helped to correlate their activities and objectives in the Pacific area. In August, 1943, Churchill, Roosevelt, and T. V. Soong met at Quebec to plan for increased collaboration with Russia and increased aid for China. In October of the same year, at the conference of foreign ministers in Moscow, Britain, Russia, and the United States declared their solidarity in demanding the unconditional surrender of the Axis powers, and in planning a postwar organization of the United Nations. China subsequently concurred in these declarations. At a meeting between Churchill, Chiang, and Roosevelt at Cairo in November, 1943, it was agreed that after her unconditional surrender, Japan would be deprived of her conquests since 1894, and Korea would be given her independence. Further plans for the proposed United Nations Organization were made at the Dumbarton Oaks and Yalta conferences.

YALTA. At the Yalta conference between Stalin, Churchill, and Roosevelt in Russia in February, 1945, plans were made for the final destruction of both Nazi Germany and Japan. Russia agreed to declare war upon Japan three months after the capitulation of Germany, but in return received the right to occupy the northern half of Korea pending the establishment of Korean independence. In addition, Russia was to receive the southern half of Sakhalin Island and the Kurile Islands as permanent territorial acquisitions from Japan. In Manchuria, Stalin gained many of the privileges held by the tzars prior to 1904, including control over certain Manchurian railroads and the ports of Port Arthur and Dairen. These privileges were confirmed by China in the Sino-Russian treaty of August 14, 1945.

POTSDAM. Despite the death of President Roosevelt, the San Francisco conference opened on schedule on April 25, to draw up the charter for the United Nations. Four days after the opening of the conference, Germany surrendered unconditionally. In the following July, President Truman took his place in the Big Three at the Potsdam conference, where an ultimatum was signed by the major allied powers promising utter destruction to Japan if she did not surrender unconditionally.

The Atomic Bomb. Although Allied sea and air power alone had made inevitable Japan's defeat, the Japanese Premier Suzuki did not immediately accept the Allied terms. On August 6, however, a single atomic bomb nearly destroyed the city of Hiroshima, killing 78,000 people and maiming countless others. Before Japan could recover from this disaster, Russia declared war on August 8, and began driving the Japanese from Manchuria. On the following day, another atomic bomb destroyed much of Nagasaki with its naval base, killing another 40,000.

Capitulation of Japan. Considering Japan's commitment to a fanatical last-ditch stand and the ferocity with which Japanese soldiers had fought against hopeless odds at Iwo Jima and elsewhere, there were grave doubts as to whether Japan could be taken without enormous cost in life for the invaders. Consequently, when the Japanese offered to surrender on the Potsdam terms only on the provision that the prerogatives of the emperor would not be jeopardized, the Allies agreed. Moreover, it was generally believed that the emperor alone could induce the Japanese to accept peace without further struggle. Except for isolated pockets, Japanese resistance ended with an imperial proclamation on August 14. The occupation of Japan began on August 30, although not until September 1, 1945, did Supreme Allied Commander General MacArthur receive the formal surrender of Japan aboard the *USS Missouri* in Tokyo Bay. One week later, Tokyo viewed the first parade of Allied power.

BIBLIOGRAPHY

Benedict, R., *The Chrysanthemum and the Sword,* 1946.

Bisson, T. A., *America's Far Eastern Policy,* 1945.

Bisson, T. A., *Japan's War Economy,* 1945.

Butow, Robert, *Tojo and the Coming of the War,* 1961.

Chiang, K'ai-shek, *Resistance and Reconstruction . . . 1937-1943,* 1943.

Cohen, J. B., *Japan's Economy in War and Reconstruction,* 1949.

Department of State, Far Eastern Series 30, *The United States Relations With China,* 1949.

Fairbank, J. K., *The United States and China,* 1958.

Feis, Herbert, *Japan Subdued,* 1961.

Gordon, D. C., and R. Dangerfield, *The Hidden Weapon: the Study of Economic Warfare,* 1947.

James, David H., *The Rise and Fall of the Japanese Empire,* 1951.

Johnson, C. A., *Peasant Nationalism and Communist Power . . . 1937-1945,* 1962.

Jones, F. C., *Japan's New Order in East Asia: Its Rise and Fall, 1937-1945,* 1954.

Kato, M., *The Lost War; a Japanese Reporter's Inside Story,* 1946.

Lattimore, O., *The Making of Modern China,* 1944.

Maki, H. L., *Japanese Militarism,* 1945.

Maxon, Y. C., *Control of Japanese Foreign Policy, a Study of Civil-Military Rivalry, 1930-1945,* 1957.

Morton, L., *The War in the Pacific, Strategy and Command: The First Two Years,* 1962.

Rossinger, L. K., *China's Wartime Policies, 1937-1944,* 1944.

Rowe, D. N., *China Among the Powers,* 1945.

Shigemitsu, Mamoru, *Japan and Her Destiny,* 1958.

Shug, R., and H. A. De Weerd, *World War II,* 1946.

Stein, G., *The Challenge of Red China,* 1945.

U. S. Strategic Bombing Survey, *Japan's Struggle to End the War,* 1946.

Yanaga, C., *Japan Since Perry,* 1949.

CHAPTER 14
The New Japan

POWER POLITICS

Postwar Power Patterns. The world has become so politically and economically complicated that the defeat of a major power presents almost insoluble problems. After the war, the whole pattern of power was radically altered, with the United States and Soviet Russia standing alone as great powers. By international agreements and by conquest, Russia had gained partial control of Manchuria, half of Korea, and all of Sakhalin Island, while the United States occupied the Japanese home islands, the remainder of Korea, and most of Japan's Pacific islands. The influence Nationalist China might have exerted was negated by war with the Chinese Communists.

The Economic Vacuum. Prior to the war, Japan had exported manufactured goods to eastern Asia and had, in turn, imported raw materials in great volume. Deprived of Japan's industrial potential, the economic recovery of eastern Asia would have been difficult even without the loss of China's productivity. With neither a stable economic nor political foundation on which to build, eastern Asia faced reconstruction problems of baffling complexity.

U.S. MILITARY OCCUPATION

Terms of Surrender. The Potsdam Proclamation called upon the Japanese to (1) eliminate the influence of those responsible for Japan's aggression, (2) limit her sovereignty to the home islands, (3) demobilize and demilitarize, (4) punish her war criminals, (5) develop democratic and responsible government, and (6) establish freedom of speech, thought, religion, assembly, press, and other basic human rights. Japan was to retain industries necessary to maintain her economy, but not those that could serve to rearm. Given access to necessary raw materials, Japan was to rebuild foreign trade. Although the prerogatives of the emperor as sovereign ruler were not to be prejudiced, both the emperor and the Japanese government were to be subject to the Supreme Allied Commander. The peaceful occupation of Japan by the Allies followed with speed and efficiency and exhibited a remarkable passivity on the part of the Japanese.

Machinery and Policy of Occupation. In theory, the occupation was an Allied venture. An eleven-nation Far Eastern Advisory Commission (FEC) was established in Washington to formulate occupation policy for the Supreme Commander for the Allied Powers (SCAP), who was under the direction of a committee representing the United States War, Navy, and State Departments. An Allied Council for Japan, established to satisfy Russia with delegates of the U.S., Soviet Russia, China, and the British Commonwealth, had only consultative and advisory powers and was made useless by sharp conflict of views between the Russian and American delegates. In the end, the dominating personality of General MacArthur as SCAP, plus the unique nature of his position, made him the almost absolute ruler of Japan. SCAP policies were essentially those laid down in the terms of surrender. So total was the defeat of Japan, moreover, that the occupation force soon found its task less a problem of holding Japan down than of putting her on the road to reconstruction.

Demilitarization. Demobilization was carried out quickly and efficiently. The Japanese general staffs and navy and war ministries were dissolved, and civil as well as military aviation was banned. The problem of reducing Japan's industrial capacity and providing for reparations was complicated by the obvious need of industrial capacity for a self-supporting economy. Drastic reductions were recommended in steel, iron, chemical, aluminum, oil refining, copper, nickel, and rubber plants, and sharp curtailment of her merchant marine and railroad rolling stock. Actual removal was delayed, however, pending decisions as to the distribution of reparations. A survey made in 1948 concluded that the removals should not exceed 17 per cent of the value of the plants so that Japan might maintain a living standard equal to that of 1930-34. The civil war in China and the cold war between Russia and the United States, however, emphasized the strategic value of Japan's industrial potential. Consequently, only minor plant dismantling occurred to provide limited reparations to China, the Philippines, and the Asiatic portions of the British and Dutch empires.

DISSOLUTION OF THE ZAIBATSU. While a decision was difficult on industrial disarmament, Japan's economic demobilization proceeded rapidly. In November, 1945, SCAP ordered the dissolution of the largest industrial combines in order to weaken Japan's war potential and to provide a wider base for ownership and economic activity. Later, the Yasuda plan for voluntary disbanding of business combinations was adopted. Unfortunately, however, the dissolution of the great cartels only handicapped Japan in competing in world markets without stripping the Zaibatsu families of their enormous wealth.

Land Reform. To eliminate the old problem of land tenancy, SCAP in late 1946 pressed a land reform bill through a reluctant Japanese Diet. This law provided for the sale of land to three million of the 3.8 million tenant families. Absentee owners had to sell their lands at fixed prices payable in money that quickly lost much of its value in the inflation. The new owners conversely gained by buying land on very liberal terms. While the land reform was not universally satisfactory, in its total impact on both the society and the economy it probably will be remembered as one of the occupation's outstanding achievements.

Economic Rehabilitation. By 1948, the realities of the Cold War, the failure of the Japanese economy to recover, and the continuing large costs of the occupation convinced the United States to revise its economic policies for Japan. Goals were redirected toward recovery to the point of self-sufficiency based on the 1930-34 average. This called for increases of 300 per cent in mining and manufacturing, 900 per cent in exports, and 200 per cent in national income. To achieve these levels, many earlier occupation policies had to be revised. Among these was the policy of dissolving the great business combinations which were found necessary if Japan's industry was to be strengthened.

War Crime Trials and the Purge. Among the earliest acts of the occupation was the arrest and trial of those accused of war crimes. As a result of these trials by the International Tribunal for the Far East, by tribunals in Japan and the Philippines, and by the Russians in Manchuria, about 5,000 men, including Tojo, were tried. This action by the victorious powers did little to convince the Japanese of the justice of the trials and tended to make martyrs of those executed or imprisoned. Moreover, the wholesale purge from positions of responsibility of hundreds of thousands considered guilty of contributing to Japan's war and expansionist efforts decimated the ranks of Japanese government, business, industry, and education, as well as military personnel. Later, as the outlines of the Cold War emerged, this policy was reversed, especially after General Ridgway succeeded General MacArthur in April, 1951. By the end of the occupation, virtually all those purged, except the worst war criminals, had been "unpurged" and made eligible for responsible positions.

Democratization. Another problem of the occupation was to teach the fundamentals of democratic government to a people accustomed to semi-feudal leadership. One important step was the elimination of Shintoism. The emperor personally announced that he was not a living god and that the Japanese were not a superior race. To encourage them to teach democracy, the press and radio were given great freedom, but MacArthur found it necessary to coerce many conservative editors into accepting their new mission. To remove restriction on personal liberty, secret police organizations were abolished. The problems of reorienting Japanese education toward democracy involved printing 100 million rewritten textbooks, reindoctrinating and carefully screening 417,000 teachers, decentralizing school administration, and reorganizing the curriculum. To reduce the power of the antidemocratic bureaucracy, a new public service law was enacted, introducing the merit system.

CONSTITUTION OF 1946. The Japanese constitution of 1946 was another step in the democratization process. It recognized that sovereignty resides in the people and reduced the emperor to a powerless symbol, who could act only with the advice and approval of his cabinet. The cabinet was responsible to a bicameral legislature. The freedoms of the Bill of Rights were guaranteed without ambiguity. The constitution is unique in war, threats, or force to settle disputes with other nations. that it denies to Japan the right of belligerency or the use of

Revival of Politics. Under the occupation, Japanese politics resumed the prewar tendency to follow personalities rather than issues. New parties formed and reformed, with varying unstable coalitions among them. In general, however, conservatives dominated, though some prominent conservative leaders like Hatoyama Ichiro were temporarily ousted from active politics by the purge. When they won the 1946 elections, Hatoyama's successor Yoshida Shigura became premier. It was Yoshida's coalition cabinet which approved the constitution promulgated that November. The next year, however, an economic crisis forced new elections that gave the Socialists a chance briefly to form a cabinet with Democratic Party support. Lacking a sufficient majority, the Socialists were unable to effect their plans for nationalization and extensive economic controls. In 1948, internal conflict destroyed their coalition.

STABILITY UNDER YOSHIDA. With a reformed party, Yoshida returned to the premiership, which he retained through five cabinet reshuffles until 1954. Under Yoshida's firm and courageous leadership the U.S. occupation ended and, despite strong internal opposition, Japan concluded the first security treaty with the U.S. and began her own rearmament.

COMMUNIST ACTIVITIES. One unwanted result of the democratization was the resurgence of Communist activities. Many Communists gained freedom in the general amnesty granted political prisoners at the beginning of the occupation; others returned from exile in China and elsewhere. Moreover, for the first time, the Communist Party was legalized in Japan. Led by Nozaka and well-supplied with funds, the Communist Party soon became a potent force. Efforts among workers and peasants proved so successful that half of the organized labor force was under Communist control by 1948. Violent tactics in labor disputes brought repressive measures, however, and lost much popular support. In 1950, Nozaka and other leaders were replaced, and a new militant revolutionary approach was adopted. The wave of riots and demonstrations that followed forced the Japanese government and SCAP to stern measures that pushed the party underground.

SOVEREIGN JAPAN

Korean War. The outbreak of the Korean War in June, 1950, marked a clear turning point in Japanese history. Suddenly

Japan became a vital link in the free world security. As a major procurement center for United Nations forces in Korea, Japan ultimately received orders amounting to over four billion dollars. Moreover, Communist aggression in Korea made more clear the need to make Japan a strong, independent nation capable of defending herself.

Japanese Peace Treaty. The division of the world into two hostile spheres made slim the chances of a universally acceptable peace treaty. General MacArthur had wanted an early treaty, and the U.S. State Department by 1950 had won over most non-Communist nations to the need for concluding peace. However, Russia obstructed every effort and even endeavored to intimidate Japan by directing against her certain clauses of the 1950 Sino-Russian Treaty. After the invasion of Korea, the U.S. moved ahead resolutely. In September, 1951, forty-eight nations signed a treaty with Japan at San Francisco. Burma, India, and Yugoslavia refused to attend, but signed separate treaties later. Of the fifty-two nations at the conference, only Russia, Poland, and Czechoslovakia rejected the treaty.

TREATY TERMS. By this pact, Japan (1) renounced claims to Sakhalin, the Kuriles, Formosa, and her former League of Nations mandates; (2) agreed to place the Ryukyu and Bonin Islands under a U.N. trusteeship administered by the United States; and (3) recognized the independence of Korea. Japan received the right to defend herself and to conclude agreements for stationing foreign forces in Japan. Relations with China were to be resolved by separate agreement. No reparations were called for, but Japan agreed to make her skills and industry available to war-devastated lands for rehabilitation. Japan's remaining assets abroad were transferred to the International Red Cross for distribution among prisoners who had suffered hardships in Japanese camps. Australian and New Zealand fears of a revived Japan were reduced by a mutual defense pact concluded at this time between those nations and the United States. Philippine disappointment at failing to receive large reparations delayed ratification by their legislature until 1954. Meanwhile, the San Francisco Treaty came into force on April 28, 1952, marking the re-emergence of Japan as a sovereign nation.

Japanese Security. A security pact in 1952 gave the U.S. the right to maintain land, air, and sea forces in Japan. The pact also stipulated that Japan was gradually to assume responsibility for her own defense against both direct and indirect aggression. Under this provision, the Japanese converted the National Police Reserve into a Self-Defense Force. In 1954, a U.S.-Japanese Mutual Defense Assistance Agreement provided for U.S. aid in equipping a Japanese army of 275,000 with supplementary naval and air forces. While many Japanese Conservatives worried that the agreements did not provide sufficient guarantees for Japan's security, the Socialists and Communists agitated long and noisily against both the presence of U.S. forces and any increases in Japan's own defense forces. As a result, Japan was so slow in building up her forces that by early 1964 she still had not reached the level agreed upon ten years earlier. A new U.S.-Japanese Security Treaty in 1960, which made Japan a full-fledged ally of the U.S., had rough sledding in the Japanese Diet before it was finally approved.

JAPANESE-AMERICAN FRICTION. Although the United States in 1960 for the first time clearly guaranteed to defend Japan in the event of foreign attack, the continuing American use of Japanese bases was widely resented. The atomic bombs dropped on Hiroshima and Nagasaki left a legacy of hostility to war and a popular rejection of nuclear weapons. These attitudes are thoroughly exploited by leftists. The accidental killing of a Japanese woman on an American firing range in 1957 provided fodder for anti-U.S. propagandists despite the fact that the U.S. Supreme Court returned the American soldier to Japan where he was convicted of manslaughter but given a suspended sentence. In their campaign against the 1960 Security Treaty, the leftists pulled out all stops. Rioting demonstrators repeatedly broke into the Diet building and disrupted proceedings. Their violent tactics failed to prevent the passage of the agreement, but they did force the government to cancel a planned visit of President Eisenhower. Although this violence frightened many Japanese out of the leftist camps, in mid-1963, leftists were again parading, this time against the visits of American nuclear submarines to Japanese harbors.

Party Politics. Following the restoration of civil and political rights in 1952, Hatoyama returned to the political arena to challenge Yoshida's right to Liberal Party leadership. Yoshida stabilized his position by calling new elections which he won on a program calling for rearmament and pro-American policies. In 1953, however, Hatoyama joined forces with the opposition Progressive Party leader Shigemitsu to form the Japan Democratic Party. By a coalition with the right-wing Socialists, Hatoyama won the premiership in December, 1954, with Shigemitsu as foreign minister. Their foreign policy aimed to restore friendly relations with Russia and China, while maintaining the U.S. alliance.

SOCIALIST PARTY. Factional strife, plus a policy dispute over the Japanese-American treaty, split the Socialists into left and right wings. The left-wing Socialists, who retained the largest support including that of the General Confederation of Japanese Trade Unions (Sohyo), followed a Moscow orientation, pursued a militant anti-capitalistic line, and opposed rearmament. The right-wing group, who found strength in the Smaller Council for a Democratic Labor Movement, (Zenro), supported the peace treaty and limited rearmament. They espoused a more moderate line of gradual socialization similar to that of the British Labor Party. Both groups favored trade with Communist China and resented its restriction by the United States. While they remained divided, the Socialists presented little threat to the Conservatives and could gain power only by joining coalitions. Also, the Socialists' addition to opposition for opposition's sake limited their chances of becoming a responsible parliamentary party.

TWO-PARTY POLITICS. In October, 1955, however, the two Socialists groups reached a compromise on main differences and rejoined to form a single party. Combined, they commanded nearly one-third of the total votes. Hence, only by a coalition with the Liberals could Hatoyama retain power. In November, 1955, a merger resulted in the formation of the Liberal Democratic Party (Jiyu Mishuto). Conservative unity was achieved by a bargain that divided the cabinet posts and promised to make Liberal Party president Ogata the next premier. When Ogata died the following year, 73-year-old Hatoyama was finally succeeded by 72-year-old Ishibashi. In early 1958, however, ill health forced Ishibashi to relinquish the premiership to Kishi Nobushke who was 12 years younger. Kishi remained in office long enough to push the 1960 U.S.-Japanese Security Treaty through the Diet, but was forced out in the wake of subsequent demonstrations.

CONSERVATIVE ASCENDANCY. Ikeda Hayato, who succeeded Kishi, carried the Liberal Democratic Party to victory in the 1960 elections, winning 301 seats to the Socialists' 144. The Socialists continued futilely to try to break the "one-third barrier" that brought them only one-third of the votes in the elections of 1961, 1962, and 1963. Unquestionably, they were hurt by their insistence on sounding more leftist than the Communists and by their resort to violence. While other parties ranged from the Communists to a variety of more or less fanatical right-wing groups, no party aside from the Socialists appeared to seriously challenge the conservative Liberal Democratic Party. The 1963 elections, which brought the lowest voter turnout since 1947, saw the Liberal Democrats still firmly in the saddle, albeit with diminished strength. The Democratic Socialist Party, formed in 1959-60 by right-wing Socialists, showed surprising gains in 1963, while the larger left-wing party declined somewhat in strength. With the re-election of Ikeda to the premiership, the Liberal Democratic Party was free to pursue its policies on economic improvement.

Liberal Democratic Party Program. Despite its long period of power, the Liberal Democratic Party remains more a coalition than a unified party. Ikeda has retained control by balancing off various party factions and avoiding a showdown on any issue that might lead to serious intra-party dispute. This policy the Japanese call "low posture" as opposed to Kishi's "high posture" or high-handed methods of forcing issues. Ikeda's objectives are primarily economic and center around the ten-year income doubling platform he adopted in 1960. This program was so successful that Ikeda announced in 1963 that his goals would be reached in only seven and one-half years. Ikeda's plans for increasing social security and medical coverage have taken some of the thunder from the left-wing Socialists as evidenced by their relatively poor showing in the 1963 elections.

Religion in Politics. A new political phenomena is the rapidly growing Buddhist sect *Soka Gakkai*. Drawing over four million votes in the 1962 elections and winning 15 seats in the House of Councillors, Soka Gakkai overnight became the third largest group in the upper house of the Diet. Their victory is attributed to the tight discipline and strong organization of this militant sect which claims to represent the teaching of Nichiren Buddhism. Its founder Makiguchi died in prison during the war, but the cult was revived by his friend Toda Josei in 1945. Soka Gakkai's political objectives are obscure. It claims to be above party, and so entered elections for the upper house only. Its slogans oppose nuclear weapons and promise the doubling of welfare payments and the abolition of income taxes on wages and salaries. As a Japanese sect, it has a nationalistic appeal for the depressed, restless elements who see little hope in the conservatives' program and are repelled by the foreign materialistic doctrines of the Socialists and Communists. Although it has some adherents among intellectual groups and students, it has found followers especially among the sick and the poor, the less educated, non-organized labor, and especially, among women. It is too soon yet to see whether the cult's success in politics will be more than ephemeral, but already it has spread to several cities in Korea.

Japanese Labor Movement. One important postwar trend was the rapid growth of a powerful labor movement. Previously held down by unfavorable laws, labor organization was encouraged by SCAP, who induced the Japanese government to adopt laws similar to the National Labor Relations Act of 1935 in the United States. However, when the Communists seized union leadership and disrupted the economy by politically motivated strikes, SCAP encouraged the passage of laws resembling the Taft-Hartley Act. By 1964, the total of over eight million union members was largely divided between two major federations.

Sohyo. Larger of the two was the Sohyo, which claimed nearly one-half of all union members. Sohyo follows the Socialist Party in politics and leftist orientation, and provides 75 per cent of its membership. Although Communist influence declined steadily after 1955, Sohyo remains in the forefront of mass demonstrations against government policies, including "monopoly capitalism," which it claims is supported by American imperialism. Like the Socialist Party, Sohyo has been drawn into the Sino-Soviet dispute. Increasingly, however, Sohyo has devoted attention to economic goals.

Zenro. Second in importance is Zenro with about 20 per cent

of the total union membership. Zenro is moderate in politics and is allied to the right-wing Democratic Socialist Party. While Sohyo has been affiliated with the Communist-dominated World Federation of Trade Unions (WFTU), though flirting occasionally with the pro-West International Confederation of Free Trade Unions (ICFTU), Zenro has remained firmly with the ICFTU. Like the Democratic Socialist Party, Zenro advocates a Socialist state achieved through parliamentary means and favors friendship with the United States. Zenro has been notable for its devotion to economic advancement by its annual spring wage offensives. In 1962 right-wing labor's position was strengthened by the formation of the National Council of Labor Federations (Domei Kaigi) to improve liaison between right-wing labor groups, including Zenro.

Renewed Communist Agitation. After SCAP forced the Communist Party underground in 1950, it acted chiefly through its infiltration of the Socialist Party and the left-wing Sohyo. When the party was again legalized in 1955, its program emphasized non-violent political activity under Nozaka's leadership. Its membership was still less than 100,000 by 1964, and direct influence remained weak. Branded as a tool of foreign powers, it is unlikely to win power by legitimate political activity. It has exerted its influence by infiltration of various leftist unions and students groups, such as the Zengakukun that spearheaded the 1960 riots against President Eisenhower's visit. Party unity was severely disrupted by the Sino-Soviet cleavage. Many Japanese Communists sympathize with the Chinese, but they have avoided public commitments for fear of political effects. In the 1963 elections, the Communists polled less than 5 per cent of the vote and won only 5 of the 467 seats in the Lower House of the Diet. Their chief overt activity, therefore, continued to be stirring up demonstrations on such popular issues as opposition to the continued administration of Okinawa and the Bonin Islands.

Foreign Policy. The principal objectives of Japan's immediate postwar foreign policy have been to (1) help keep world peace, (2) maintain friendly relations with the United States, (3) conclude a peace treaty with Russia that would revive normal diplomatic relations and restore at least part of the northern islands lost to Russia, (4) be admitted to the United Nations, (5) achieve a favorable trade balance and expand foreign markets, and (6) regain Japan's lost prestige in Asia. To these, there is a growing tendency to add the re-establishment of normal trade relations with South Korea and mainland China and the return of the "lost islands" of the Southern Kuriles held by the Soviet Union and of the Bonins and Okinawa held by the United States. During the first postwar years under Yoshida and Hatoyama, Japan viewed herself as a small power seeking to rise above the isolation brought about by defeat and foreign occupation. During the Kishi administration, Japan rose in her policy to the level of a middle power seeking to establish its economic base in Asia. Finally, under Ikeda, Japan began to consider herself again a great power, aiming to cooperate as an equal partner with the other advanced industrial nations of the free world.

FOREIGN RELATIONS Through the conservative governments from Yoshida to Ikeda, Japan maintained that world peace and Japanese security are best protected through close alliance and cooperation with the United States. Throughout, this policy was persistently and noisily attacked by the Communists and left-wing Socialists. While there are many signs that Japan will pursue an increasingly independent foreign policy in the future, there is little likelihood that this will alter the fundamental relationship with the United States. Japan's anti-Communist, pro-American stance caused the USSR to veto Japan's first request for admission to the United Nations. Disputes over fishing rights and Japan's claim to South Sakhalin and Kuriles broke up talks begun in 1955. Finally, in 1956, a Soviet-Japanese protocol technically ended the state of war, but left conclusion of a peace treaty to a later date. Two months later, Japan was admitted to the U.N. by unanimous vote.

FOREIGN TRADE. With 95 million people crowded into an area the size of California with very limited mineral resources, Japan must trade to live. Since 80 per cent of her industrial raw material needs and 20 per cent of her foodstuffs must be imported, exports must be kept high to maintain a favorable balance of trade. The Japanese link this problem with the need both to regain lost prestige in Asia and to revive trade with China. In Southeast Asia, Japan has concluded reparations agreements with the nations she invaded. These provided credits, goods, machinery, and technical assistance, but they also served as opening wedges for increased trade.

JAPANESE FOREIGN AID PROGRAM. Under strong U.S. urging, Japan has entered the field of aid to underdeveloped nations. She cooperated with the Colombo Plan, made important contributions through ECAFE (Economic Commission for Asia and the Far East), and launched her own programs in many countries of Asia, Africa, and Latin America. Over 500 Japanese experts had served abroad and over 4,000 foreign trainees from all over the world had studied in Japan by mid-1963. This trend was bound to increase in view of Japan's spectacular industrial expansion.

TRADE WITH COMMUNIST COUNTRIES. Still, Japan's trade with the developing nations of Asia increased at a pace slower than her trade with the U.S. and Western Europe. Fearing exclusion from Europe by the rising trade barriers of the European Economic Community, Japanese businessmen yearn for the forbidden markets of Red China. For a time after the Korean War, China wooed Japanese trade with cultural and trade missions. Some private agreements were signed, but in 1958 the Chinese suddenly slammed the door closed over the destruction of a Red Chinese flag. For a time the Red Chinese vilified the Japanese government leaders as "fascists" and "running dogs of American imperialism," but most Japanese resented the attacks and again China reversed itself. Subsequently several private trade agreements have been concluded between China and various Japanese groups. Although the Japanese government avoids formal diplomatic relations with Red China, these agreements have greatly irritated the Nationalist Chinese government. Since Western nations like Great Britain and West Germany are carrying on profitable trade with Red China, however, Japan intends to follow suit. Japanese businessmen also have concluded numerous trade agreements with the U.S.S.R., East European satellites, North Korea, North Viet-Nam, and Outer Mongolia Negotiations for normalization of relations with South Korea still continued in 1964.

Economic Boom. Since 1950, Japan has experienced the most rapid industrial expansion of any modern nation, more than doubling her gross national output by 1961. Industrial growth averaged over 10 per cent annually. In steel production she exceeded France and Great Britain, and only the U.S., Russia, and West Germany surpass her in total industrial output. Her shipyards are the world's finest. Most of the postwar expansion has come in newer industries—heavy machinery, chemicals, plastics, synthetic fibers, optical instruments, household appliances, automobiles, and trucks. Conversely, the older industries such as textiles declined in importance.

IMPROVED LIVING STANDARDS. Living standards have risen almost unbelievably. Pre-war consumption levels were reached in 1954-55 and continued steadily upward, achieving a 17 per cent rise in 1961 alone. Television sets and other electrical appliances are enjoyed in greater number than in any European population. While the agricultural population has declined, Japan has increased her food production by mechanization and improved techniques. Educational facilities and social services have also expanded. While life expectancy has climbed to levels equal to those of the West, birth control has minimized danger of a population explosion.

PROBLEMS OF PROSPERITY. The enormous expansion of industry was achieved largely by pouring 25 per cent of the national income back into new investment. Japan received much less American aid per capita than Western Europe and has maintained restrictions on foreign investments. However, the whole structure has been called a "bicycle" economy: it must keep moving forward or it will fall over. The many new factories require vast imports of raw materials. Increased purchasing power has created an internal mass market that raises imports without increasing the exports to pay for them. There is a constant battle to keep the balance of payments from going too far awry. Periodically, the government must put the brakes on the runaway economy. While factories have mushroomed creating new jobs, housing has lagged. Building costs and land values have skyrocketed. Roads, railroads, and harbor facilities are far from adequate. Only 14 per cent of Japanese towns have sewers as compared with 100 per cent in Britain and France.

RATIONALIZATION NEEDS. New Japanese industry suffers from a labor shortage, while older industries burdened with outmoded employment practices are heavily overstaffed. But labor is becoming more mobile, men are changing jobs to advance themselves, and pay is becoming based on job classification rather than longevity. As a result, both worker and employer are gaining a new freedom necessary to rationalize Japan's factories so they can compete abroad. Japan, too, must lower her high trade barriers to gain equal concessions from the U.S. and Western Europe. This will force modernization of weaker Japanese industries.

RESTLESS JAPAN. The postwar boom and dislocation have created social ferment. Lacking deep roots in the past, the young search for new social ideologies and values but find Western ways not altogether satisfying. Older Japanese are shocked by the apparent social and political irresponsibility of much of the youth. There is a quest for a new self-identification and nationalism manifested in the mushroom growth of the Soka Gakkai and other cults, the erection of a tomb to Tojo, and the five million visitors annually to the Ise Shinto Shrine. Nationalism is especially manifested in the enormous effort which Japanese of all levels poured into the Tokyo Olympics which seems to symbolize a return to world leadership.

BIBLIOGRAPHY

Allen, G. C., *A Short Economic History of Modern Japan*, 1963.

Baerwold, H., *The Purge of Japanese Leaders Under the Occupation*, 1957.

Bisson, T. A., *Zaibatsu Dissolution in Japan*, 1954.

Brown, D. M., *Nationalism in Japan*, 1955.

Cary, J. *Japan Today; Reluctant Ally*, 1962.

Cohen, J., *Japan's Postwar Economy*, 1958.

Dore, R. P., *Land Reform in Japan*, 1959.

Kahin, G. M., ed., *Major Governments of Asia*, 1958.

Latourette, K. S., *The American Record in the Far East, 1945-1951*, 1952.

McNelly, T., *Contemporary Government in Japan*, 1963.

Mendel, D. H., *The Japanese People and Foreign Policy*, 1961.

Morris, I. I., *Nationalism and the Right Wing in Japan*, 1960.

Quigley, H. S., *The New Japan*, 1956.

Reischauer, E. O., *The United States and Japan*, 1957.

Scalapino, Robert A., *Parties and Politics in Contemporary Japan*, 1962.

SCAP Civil Information and Education Section, *Education in the New Japan*, 2 vols., 1948.

SCAP Government Section, *Political Reorientation of Japan: September, 1945 to September, 1948*, 2 vols., 1949.

SCAP, *Instructions to the Japanese Government from 4 September, 1945 to 8 March, 1952*, 1952.

Schwantes, Robert S., *Japanese and Americans*, 1955.

Swearingen, R. and P. Langer, *Red Flag in Japan . . . 1919-1951*, 1952.

Taeuber, I. B., *The Population of Japan*, 1958.

Wildes, H. E., *Typhoon in Tokyo: the Occupation and its Aftermath*, 1954.

Yoshida, S., *Yoshida Memoirs; the Story of Japan in Crisis*, 1961.

CHAPTER 15
Upheaval in China

NATIONALIST-COMMUNIST RIVALRY

Problems of Japanese Capitulation. The suddenness of Japan's capitulation created a political and economic vacuum in the areas Japan had occupied in China. Who would receive the Japanese arms and munitions surrendered on Chinese territory posed a serious problem. By the Sino-Russian Treaty concluded between Nationalist China and Russia on the day of Japan's surrender, the U.S.S.R. occupied Manchuria and received the Japanese surrender there. In his order of August 17, 1945, specifying the procedures for the capitulation of the Japanese forces, General MacArthur ignored the Communists. In conformity with this, the Japanese emperor ordered his troops in China proper to surrender to the Nationalists, but in fact a race took place to see whether Nationalists or Communists would arrive first.

CONTEST FOR CONTROL. In many regions, Chinese puppet government leaders quickly came to terms with Chiang K'ai-shek's forces. In the northern regions adjacent to the Communist-controlled areas, however, the Communist forces under Chu Teh made important gains and soon dominated one-tenth of China, including Chahar, Jehol, Shantung, Shansi, and portions of adjacent provinces. For the Nationalists, Chiang was able with the substantial assistance of American transport planes and ships, to gain control of the main railroads and the larger cities in east, central, and north China. In addition, 50,000 U.S. Marines were sent by General Wedemeyer to secure the ports and airfields in Tientsin, Peiping, and Tsingtao. This move aimed both to secure the Japanese evacuation and to assist the Nationalists to reoccupy the area. Not unnaturally the Chinese Communists complained of "American intervention."

COMMUNIST GAINS IN NORTH. The Communists, however,

gained advantages from Russian actions in Manchuria. After receiving the Japanese capitulation in that region, the Russians violated other aspects of the Yalta Agreement and Sino-Soviet pact by remaining after the deadline and treating Manchuria as occupied enemy territory. Factories were looted of their machinery which went to Russia as war booty and the surrendered Japanese were taken to Siberia instead of being evacuated to Japan. While Chiang's forces were prevented from using Manchurian ports to reoccupy the north, Chu Teh's men were allowed to filter into the area.

The Search for Peace. The quest for some basis for reunification was begun before the war's end by General Hurley, the special representative of President Roosevelt. American hopes to bring Mao's and Chiang's governments and armies together into a coalition government had been encouraged by the support Russia gave to Chiang throughout the war in preference to Mao Tse-tung, whose peasant-based Communist regime was viewed as heretical in Moscow. But while Russia's apparent lack of interest in the Chinese Communist Party convinced Chiang that he need not compromise, it made Mao no less uncompromising. In any "coalition" government the Communists were determined to control their own military forces and provinces, and to secure complete freedom to propagandize their doctrines throughout China. The Nationalists were equally determined that Chu Teh's forces should be brought under Chiang and that the Kuomintang should clearly dominate politically.

THE MARSHALL MISSION. After Hurley's resignation in 1945, General Marshall was sent to try to bring peace to strife-ridden China. In January, 1946, Marshall arranged a cease-fire that brought the two sides together for discussions. This conference laid plans for (1) the organization of a provisional government to include all political viewpoints, (2) the calling of a National Assembly in May, 1946, (3) the inauguration of economic, social, and political reforms, and (4) the unification of the Nationalist and Communist armies. In March, however, chances for peace were wrecked when the Russians timed their withdrawal from Manchuria to permit its occupation by the Communists. Thereafter, war continued on a large scale despite strenuous American efforts to achieve a reconciliation.

The Kuomintang Regime. The exigencies of fighting, combined with the rivalry with the Communists, gradually had silenced nearly all liberal voices within the Nationalist-held areas. The government continued to operate theoretically under the period of political tutelage during which local self-government was to build the foundation for constitutional democracy. In practice, China had become virtually a police state. Corruption and inefficiency threaded through the party and government fabric. Yet, Chiang, enjoying the prestige of victory, might have made his regime popular again. Militarily he controlled over 3 million troops, many of whom were battle-hardened and had received American arms and training.

NATIONALIST CONSTITUTION OF 1947. Faced with strong popular and foreign pressure for reform, the Kuomintang National Assembly drew up a new constitution in 1947. Though this document proclaimed the end of political tutelage and was very democratic in theory, it also reserved large and ill-defined powers to the president. There was little in the new constitution either to satisfy the liberals or to entice the Communists into the government. Furthermore, it was increasingly obvious that the Kuomintang was controlled by reactionary forces with no intention of liberalizing the government. In April, 1948, Chiang was elected president under the new constitution but his vice-presidential running mate Sun Fo was defeated by Li Tsung-jen, former warlord of Kwangsi.

The Communist Regime. At the time of the Japanese surrender, the Communist regime appeared to be in much the weaker position of the two Chinese governments. The poorly-equipped Communist forces were less than half the size of the Nationalists' and generally were widely scattered in small mobile guerrilla units. By capitalizing on the Russian withdrawal from Manchuria and the acquisition of Japanese equipment, however, the Communist army quickly gained strength. Moreover, attracted by the promises of reforms liberally made by the Communists, two Nationalist armies defected as early as November, 1945.

COMMUNIST OFFENSIVE. From 1945 to early 1947, the Nationalists, acting against U.S. advice though using American air and sea transport, launched an all-out effort to occupy all of North China and Manchuria. Although the Communists at first retreated, the Nationalists found they held only the cities while the Communists blocked the railroads and disrupted supply lines in the rural areas. Though able to supply his northern garrisons by costly airlift, Chiang could not expand his control. From early 1947, the Communists began to counterattack.

COMMUNIST PROPAGANDA CAMPAIGN. During the years of civil war, Communist morale was kept high by the combination of successful propaganda, efficient and inspired leadership, and increasing popular support. While the Communists promised land reforms and gradual socialization, returning Kuomintang armies were too often accompanied by landlords, who, having fled the Japanese, now reclaimed land the peasants had tilled freely for years. Unbridled inflation wrecked the middle class and salaried workers. Disillusionment and disgust swept the country as Chiang proved incapable or unwilling to make needed economic and political reforms. In protest, intellectuals, businessmen, peasants, and many officials became either neutral or even pro-Communist. Although military experts have stated that no battle was lost by the Nationalists because of lack of American military assistance, Chiang kept calling for more. Meanwhile, the Communists cleverly identified American aid with foreign interference and imperialism.

NATIONALIST DEFEAT. During 1948, the U.S. Congress voted $338 million in aid to China, but early in 1949, the U.S. National Security Council advised President Truman to halt arms shipments for fear they might fall into Communist hands. By then it seemed obvious that no aid could save the Nationalist regime. As Chiang appeared to have lost the "mandate of Heaven," defections in the Nationalist army multiplied. Many soldiers sold their guns while some generals seemed more concerned with profits than with victories. By November, 1948, Manchuria was lost to the Nationalists together with 300,000 of Chiang's best trained troops with their American equipment. In the following month, a great battle at Hsuchow claimed another 500,000 Nationalists. This defeat was followed by the fall of Peiping, leaving the road to the Yangtze open for the Communists.

Retreat to Formosa. Under severe criticism for these disastrous defeats, Chiang K'ai-shek resigned from the presidency in January, 1949. While he left his political responsibilities with vice-president Li Tsung-jen, Chiang retained control of the armed forces and the treasury reserves of 300 million U.S. dollars, which he shipped to Formosa. Without real power or money to pay the soldiers, Li Tsung-jen could not stem the retreat. In May, Chiang marched some of the main forces in central China into Shanghai and sailed them off to Taiwan. Vice-president Li tried vainly to keep the struggle going. In December, he flew to the United States while Chiang took refuge on Taiwan with the remnants of the government and army. All the Chinese mainland was then in the hands of the Communists who on October 1 had already proclaimed the People's Republic of China at Peiping with Mao Tse-tung as president.

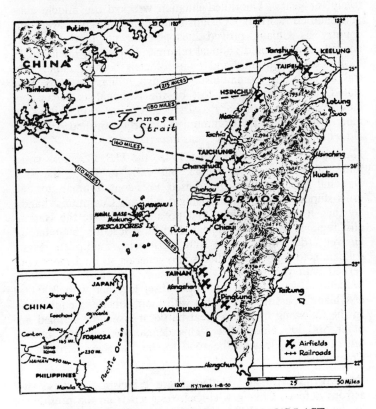

THE ISLAND OF FORMOSA, CHIANG'S LAST
STRONGHOLD

THE REPUBLIC OF CHINA IN TAIWAN

The Chinese Return. By 1945, the indigenous non-Chinese population of Taiwan (Formosa) was greatly outnumbered by Chinese despite a half-century of Japanese rule. Both the Cairo and Potsdam agreements promised Taiwan's return to China and Chiang's forces were given *de facto* control by General MacArthur after the Japanese surrender. Although the Japanese had been efficient rulers and brought many improvements in public services, their efforts to assimilate the Taiwanese to Japanese culture were resented. Hence, the Taiwanese genuinely welcomed the first Nationalist troops.

PROBLEMS OF REOCCUPATION. The islanders soon found, however, that they had exchanged one form of oppression for another. They were treated as conquered people by the new Chinese rulers whose rapacity and inefficiency led to an uprising in 1948 that was brutally repressed at the cost of 10,000 lives. Thereafter, an alarmed Nationalist government made some improvements, and later, anticipating the Nationalist retreat, Chiang made political concession to win Taiwanese cooperation. During 1949 more than two million civilians and soldiers fled to the island from the mainland, overstraining an already weakened economy.

Nationalist Rule on Taiwan. On Taiwan, Chiang K'ai-shek reclaimed the presidency he had abandoned. Vice-president Li protested, but prudently remained in exile. Upon evaluating the causes of his defeat, Chiang undertook a program of political, economic, and social reforms. His new government redistributed the land, settled refugees, increased power production, constructed fertilizer plants and other factories, and improved public health, housing, and education.

KUOMINTANG DOMINATION. In the political field, progress was less spectacular. The Kuomintang government and party structure brought from the mainland carried on more or less intact. The undemocratic 1947 constitution continued in effect, and few younger leaders not of the inner Kuomintang circles and virtually no Taiwanese could find important positions. The Kuomintang Party still dominates politics, but since the national legislators theoretically represent electoral districts in the Communist-held mainland, new elections are impossible. Taiwan itself is ruled as a province of China. Taiwanese participate only in "local" political offices, closely controlled by mainland Chinese and ever watched by over-zealous secret police. Control of the powerful police was taken over by Chiang's eldest son, who permits no significant dissident voices.

Economic Gains. President Chiang, elected by the legislature for his third term in 1960, showed no signs of relaxing his iron grip. The development of his country, however, was remarkable. The real national income doubled from 1952 to 1962, and current government planning aims at 8 per cent annual increase. During 1963, new manufacturing and processing industries combined with inflated prices and growing world demand for Taiwan's sugar brought new record export levels nearly 50 per cent above the previous year's. Unfortunately, population increases of 3.4 per cent annually threaten to wipe out these gains. Despite tremendous agricultural production increases, Taiwan is no longer self-sufficient in staple foods. Among the serious problems are the burden of the huge army that absorbs 80 per cent of the budget, the growing inflation, the continuing reports of corruption in government, and the large, dissatisfied, displaced intellectual class. Increased taxes have largely consumed the advantages that land reform brought to the farmers. During 1963 and 1964, friction with Japan developed as a result of Japan's increasing trade relations with Communist China. Since Japanese trade and investment have been important to Taiwan's development, the Nationalist government faced a dilemma of having to end economic cooperation with Japan or to accept what amounts to a "two China" policy.

Relations with the U.S. Much of the progress on Taiwan depended upon the more than one billion dollars in U.S. economic and military assistance provided over the years. It was expected to have a diminishing importance, however, as Taiwan progressively developed its own economic potential. When the Kuomintang leaders first fled to Taiwan, the U.S. policy was to "let the dust settle." Yet, barely six months had passed before the Communist invasion of South Korea in June, 1950. caused President Truman to order the Seventh Fleet to neutralize the 100-mile straits separating Taiwan from the mainland. Then the Chinese Communist entry into the war induced the U.S. to extend economic and military aid to the Nationalists. U.S. military assistance strengthened the defenses of Taiwan, the Pescadores, and other offshore islands held by Chiang's forces. It also helped Chiang to keep alive the hope that one day his army could reconquer the mainland.

U.S. PROTECTION. It became apparent, however, that Taiwan's independence rested upon United States support. Nationalist forces sporadically raided Communist-held territories, but the "unleashing" of Chiang K'ai-shek by President Eisenhower in 1953 produced no noticeable change. U.S. naval vessels continued to screen the island from invasion from the mainland, and Nationalist efforts seemed to be concentrated on defense. By the Mutual Defense Treaty of 1954, signed just after conclusion of the Southeast Asia Collective Defense Treaty, the U.S. promised aid in defending Taiwan and the Pescadores against foreign attack and internal subversion, but left open the question of legal title to the island and made no mention of the defense of the offshore islands of Quemoy and Matsu.

DEFENSE OF OFFSHORE ISLANDS. Communist China soon put this pact to the test by attacking the Tachens, the most northerly of the chain of offshore islands. After the Communists captured one island in January, 1955, President Eisenhower ordered the Seventh Fleet to cover the evacuation of the Nationalists from the remaining Tachens and secured authority to defend the other offshore islands. Facing the possibility of renewed war with the U.S., Chou En-lai backed down on his threats to take Taiwan by force. In 1958, the Communists opened new bombardments on Quemoy. These have continued sporadically, intensifying on such occasions as President Eisenhower's visit to Taipei in June, 1960.

U.S.-CHINESE FRICTION. As in Japan, friction arose concerning the legal jurisdiction over American soldiers and civilians involved in civil offenses. General civil unrest was brought to a head by the U.S. handling of a case involving the killing of a Chinese on an American base. This touched off a large anti-U.S. riot in Taipei in early 1957. Although the incident caused some soul searching, American support continued, and during Eisenhower's visit he was welcomed with spontaneous warmth.

CONTINUED SUPPORT FOR REPUBLIC OF CHINA. The United States has refused to recognize the Red Chinese government, despite their undisputed sway over the mainland. The U.S. is also opposed to the Communists securing China's seat in the

United Nations with the rich prize of the Security Council chair that goes with it. On the other hand, President Kennedy referred in 1962 to the "defense of Taiwan" and to U.S. commitments to the "government and people of Taiwan" rather than using only the term "Republic of China." French recognition of Red China in January, 1964, further complicated the situation. At that time, however, Secretary of State Dean Rusk reconfirmed U.S. support for Taiwan, stating that America "will never abandon the 12 million people on Taiwan to Communist tyranny."

COMMUNIST CHINA

The People's Republic. In September, 1949, the Communists established at Peking a new government for their People's Republic of China. A People's Consultative Conference, representing Communists and various collaborating non-Communists, rubber-stamped a Common Program and an Organic Law to provide a transitional government structure. The Common Program was a restatement of Mao Tse-tung's *New Democracy* concept advanced in 1940 (see page 168). The Organic Law combined these "united front" or "class coalition" concepts with another principle called "democratic centralism" to tightly organize all levels of government under central Communist Party control. As all previous laws were abrogated, the legal vacuum was filled with an *ad hoc* justice based on Socialist principles and expediency.

PERSECUTIONS. One of the first acts was the Agrarian Reform of June, 1950. This set off a brutal persecution of all landowners holding more than subsistence-sized plots. In the cities a parallel attack was launched on the industrial and commercial class and Kuomintang bureaucrats. Utilities, large industry, banking and foreign trade were nationalized immediately, and light industry and internal trade were progressively subjected to state controls. By such devices as the "five-anti movement" (anti-bribery, tax evasion, theft of state assets, cheating on state contracts, and leakage of state economic secrets), businessmen and industrialists were terrorized into "confessions" and charged heavy fines or worse. Revenues from this extortion were used to build state enterprises. State "enemies" were tried in mass public trials in which party workers stirred up crowds to a frenzy of hatred so they "demanded" the death penalty and watched the executions. During a four-year period, about fifteen million are estimated to have been executed and another twenty million sent to forced labor for "re-education." To destroy family loyalties, brother was turned against brother, son against father, and employee against employer. By massive propaganda, terror, and organization, the population was strictly regimented.

Constitution of 1954. After four years of steadily tightening their control, the Communists took their next major political move. In 1954, a popularly elected National People's Congress met at Peking to approve unanimously a constitution which had been drafted over a two-year period with great show of public discussion. Based partly on the Common Program and the Soviet constitution of 1936, it placed Red China in a transitional stage between "feudalism" and "bureaucratic capitalism" and the future goal of a Socialist society. The goal was to be reached gradually by a Socialist industrialization of the country. Peasant land ownership and small-scale capitalism were to be replaced gradually by ownership by the whole people. A liberal bill of rights was negated by a provision for suppression of "counter-revolutionary activities."

GOVERNMENT STRUCTURE. The highest government organ is nominally the indirectly elected National People's Congress (NPC). With 1226 members, it only approves legislation presented to it, while power is actually wielded by its standing committee. Mao Tse-tung was chairman until 1959 when he was succeeded by Liu Shao-ch'i. The executive branch is the State Council or Cabinet, headed by Chou En-lai. A Council of National Defense under Mao controls military policy, and a Supreme People's Court tops a hierarchy of courts. A network of People's Congresses or Councils reaches down into the local administrative units. Five autonomous regions occupied by non-Chinese peoples received separate governments. Behind this window dressing, all government became highly centralized in Peking. This was manifested in the 1954-55 purge of individuals and elements who had ridden to power independently of Mao but had been used by him for expediency, remaining virtually autonomous in areas under their control.

The Communist Party. The real power, however, was the Communist Party, its structure paralleling the government's.

According to the party constitution of 1956, responsibility is concentrated in the twenty-man Political Bureau (Politburo) and particularly in its seven-man standing committee. Like the government, it operates on the Communist principle of "democratic centralism." The "democratic" part is the hierarchy of party congresses representing the 15 million party members. "Centralism" involves the concentration of power at the top. Great effort is made at all levels to hold open discussions on issues, but decisions are made at the top and passed down as absolute orders. As party chairman, Mao is undisputed boss though since 1959 Liu Shao-ch'i succeeded him as chief of state. Chu Teh is nominally military head, but Mao retains authority as chairman *ex-officio* of the Military Affairs Committee. Chou En-lai seems to be the party's government expert. These and other top Communists have worked together for over thirty years since the Long March. Few have traveled abroad except to Moscow and their view of the world is markedly insular.

Thought Reform. From the outset, the Communists have exerted much effort and ingenuity to remold the thinking of China's population, particularly the educated. Best known is the technique Mao Tse-tung called "brainwashing." This emphasizes group meetings in which participants criticize each other and themselves to ferret out wrong thinking and create positive rather than passive acceptance of Communist ideology and techniques. When this fails to produce intellectual subsurvience, attacks are made on select individuals to make examples of them and thereby terrorize a whole group. But despite a general purge of one out of ten intellectuals, social and political unrest was openly manifested during 1956-57.

BLOOM-CONTEND CAMPAIGN. Either to release pent-up discontent or to bait a trap, Mao in early 1957 announced that contradictions between economic forces and between the masses and their Communist leaders were inevitable. "Let all flowers bloom and diverse schools contend," Mao advised. The flood of criticism from all classes both of Communist doctrines and action frightened the Communists. They quickly reimposed thought controls and launched their own counter-criticism of their critics. This rectification movement caused a party purge and sent a million bureaucrats to labor in factories and villages.

Thereafter the Communists demanded that intellectuals be "Red as well as expert." An upside-down situation resulted with loyal Communist workers becoming professors while professors became factory and farm workers, costing China dearly both in lost skills and academic standards.

Economic Planning. Meanwhile, the Communists had launched their first five-year plan (1953-58) to initiate the transformation of China into a modern industrial power. At great human sacrifice, over one-fifth of the nation's production was devoted to internal development. Russia aided with 10,000 advisors and $3 billion in loans to construct new industries. However, China paid for this aid by exports to Russia of agricultural products and raw materials often needed at home.

EARLY ACHIEVEMENTS. Discounting inflated statistics, the first plan probably swelled industrial production 460 per cent above that of 1949 and moved China up to ninth place in world steel output. Important new industrial bases were developed in northwest and southwest China. Consumer goods, light industry and such vital needs as fertilizer, however, were neglected. While the farmers were being asked to increase production 30 per cent and support much of the plan's cost, the Reds disrupted agriculture by progressive collectivization. Increased taxes, a grain monopoly and rationing were introduced, and farmers were forced to pool tools, labor and land in "mutual aid teams." A next step was the organization of "rural producers' cooperatives," followed in 1955 by the forcing of 90 per cent of the farmers into collective farms. Meanwhile, millions of city and farm workers were conscripted for vast flood control, irrigation and hydro-electric power projects. The failures of some of these badly engineered and constructed dikes and dams augmented the damage inflicted by natural disasters. Consequently, agricultural gains barely matched the 12 million a year population growth. The deficiencies of the first plan were initially hidden by an inflation of statistics at all reporting levels by over-zealous Communist cadre. This tendency had been encouraged by Peking's rulers who announced that statistical work is a political mission, not just a technical one.

The Great Leap Forward. Made over-confident by their own inflated statistics, the Reds ordered impossible goals for their second five-year plan (1958-62) under such slogans as "leap forward in industry and agriculture." Barely were initial goals announced than they were raised as the entire population was mobilized for frenzied activities such as the ill-conceived back-yard furnaces to produce iron and steel. Agriculture was further disrupted by conversion of the 700,000 collective farms into 26,000 multi-purpose county-sized communes, designed to combine small industry, commerce, local militia and government with agriculture. Men and women were herded into dormitories while children were tended in nurseries. Millions were resettled in border areas or driven from one massive project to another. Urban and rural workers were pushed long hours to achieve unrealistic production goals.

SUCCESSES AND COSTS. At first the Great Leap achieved notable progress in some fields. According to some Western estimates, China's gross national product grew about 18 per cent in 1958 and 12 per cent in 1959. In 1960, however, growth dropped to around 4 per cent. Thereafter Peking stopped publishing statistics but production apparently declined until 1963 which saw an upturn. Peking blamed the decline on natural disasters but Western observers believe the Communists' monumental blunders were responsible. To meet exaggerated goals, machinery was worn out producing slovenly goods, the transportation system was overworked, and by 1960 a large part of the country's machinery was idled by lack of spare parts. The dislocation of agriculture and neglect of basic rural needs sharply reduced production of food and raw materials needed by industry. Malnutrition and overwork undermined workers' health and morale, further slowing production. The famine years of 1961-62 reduced the population growth from over 2 per cent to 1 per cent annually. Peking's insensate drive to communalize agriculture and to surpass her great Communist neighbor and her insistence on creating her own nuclear bombs, antagonized the USSR. As a result, 10,000 Soviet advisors departed in 1960, leaving projects unfinished. The loss of Russian aid was catastrophic to China's industrial development.

Retrenchment. From 1961 onward, primary emphasis was turned to mechanization and improvement of agriculture. Twenty million urban workers were shifted to the farms though this increased the burdens on the communes to feed them. The communes also divided their huge work teams into smaller units. Farmers were allowed to grow food on private plots in their spare time and even to sell it in open markets. Thought controls were relaxed to utilize the skills of intellectuals and scientists, and the confidence of party radicals in the infallibility of Communist doctrine seemed shaken.

PROSPECTS. In 1961, the National People's Congress was not called and the 1962 session was closed to foreigners. No statistics on the second plan were published and no specific targets were set for the new ten-point plan. Still, this congress and that of 1963 showed the top leaders still entrenched and clinging to their "three Red banners" of "the general economic line," the "great leap forward," and "the people's communes" despite the failures of all three. By 1964 industry and agriculture were below the peak year of 1958 though population meanwhile had increased by 75 million to over 700 million. Moreover, as some improvements appeared by late 1963, partial reactivation of the communes was ordered and attacks were made on "peasant capitalists" who sold food grown on private plots.

Foreign Affairs. Since its birth, Red China has been an important power. The strongest Asian regime and second strongest Communist power, it was heir to an ancient tradition of cultural and political superiority. Most of her neighbors were former tributaries or held lands she once claimed. Maps published by both the Nationalists and the Red Chinese show that neither has forgotten this past glory. The reunification of China under strong government and the humiliation and elimination of Western powers brought a resurgence of national pride. Hong Kong and Macao alone are permitted to remain as windows to the West and as routes for extracting foreign exchange from overseas Chinese. The continuation of the Nationalist government on Taiwan provides both constant irritation and pretext for maintaining vast armies.

STRATEGY OF FOREIGN POLICY. The first phase of Red China's foreign policy was a "hard line" of belligerent self-assertion, openly hostile to the non-Communist world. During this period, China initially rejected British recognition, aimed abusive propaganda at the U.S., intervened militarily in Korea, Indo-China, and Tibet, threatened invasion of Taiwan, and backed militant Communist activities in other Asian nations. After the Korean

War, China shifted to a "soft line." Partly to devote more resources to internal development and partly to cope with the growing strength of other countries in East Asia, China began promoting neutralism and the five principles of co-existence: (1) mutual respect for national sovereignty and territory, (2) non-aggression, (3) non-interference in internal affairs, (4) equality and mutual benefit, and (5) peaceful co-existence. During the soft line period, China signed peaceful co-existence treaties with her Asian neighbors and asserted her leadership at the Afro-Asian Conference at Bandung, Indonesia, in 1955.

RENEWED BELLIGERENCE. In 1957, apparently as a result of overconfidence engendered by the first Sputnik and China's early economic successes, a hard line was resumed. Mao then announced that the "east wind will prevail over the west wind" and "the strength of socialism will prevail over imperialism." Initial achievements of the "great leap" increased China's arrogance, leading to the brutal subjection of Tibet, border conflicts with India, disputes with Indonesia concerning overseas Chinese, support of insurrection in Laos, an embargo of trade against Japan, and finally a serious split with the USSR.

DIPLOMATIC RECOGNITION. The People's Republic of China was recognized by the USSR and her European satellites in October, 1949. Thirteen Asian and non-Communist nations offered recognition in the next three months, but most countries held back. Great Britain received but insults for her friendly gestures. The U.S., by diplomatic tradition, usually recognizes *de facto* governments, but Chiang K'ai-shek still claimed his regime was the legitimate government and China's seat on the U.N. Security Council was at stake. In addition, Peking acted belligerently, charging the U.S. with all of China's troubles. This made recognition difficult and Red China's intervention in Korea made it virtually impossible. Recognition of Red China continues to be a difficult political issue in the United States and in the United Nations.

Sino-Soviet Relations. Moscow was slow in accepting the Chinese Communists as legitimate because Mao Tse-tung based his revolution upon the peasants rather than the city workers. However, having gained control of all China, the Reds sought to build power by industrializing. Being antagonistic to "imperialist" powers, China could expect aid only from Russia and then for a price. In February, 1950, a Sino-Soviet mutual assistance treaty bound both nations to take joint measures against new aggression by Japan. Since Japan was then disarmed and occupied, the treaty was at least partly aimed at the U.S. In addition, Russia returned railroads and other Manchurian properties she had seized and promised aid for China's development. In 1956, Khrushchev's de-Stalinization policy weakened this tie, and his subsequent refusal to provide materials and data for manufacturing nuclear bombs angered China more.

CLEAVAGE. Subsequently the cleavage widened steadily. In 1958 and 1959, Russia infuriated the Chinese by sympathizing with India in her border dispute with China. China's headstrong haste in pressing early communization of industry and agriculture contributed to the discord, hastening Russia's withdrawal of her technicians and economic support. Main elements in the dispute became (1) personal rivalry between Khrushchev and Mao, (2) rivalry over whether the USSR or China would lead the Communist world, and (3) the question as to whether the Communist parties in underdeveloped nations should cooperate with democratic elements in working toward ultimate socialism as recommended by Khrushchev, or should they try to achieve their goals by armed struggle as advocated by Mao.

Korean War. Barely had the Communists conquered China than they began to intervene in former tributary regions. Peking early proclaimed support of the North Koreans after their invasion of South Korea and charged the U.N. and the U.S. with aggression when they intervened. Threats to enter the war were used to try to force transfer of China's U.N. seat to the People's Republic. When U.N. forces reached the Yalu River on the Manchurian border, Mao sent large Chinese armies as "volunteers" to aid North Korea. In China the war provided pretext for stiffer controls and heightened production efforts. Anti-European and anti-American propaganda was intensified throughout Asia with such devices as spurious germ warfare charges. The failure of the U.N. to win a clear-cut victory enhanced China's prestige in Asia.

Tibet. Isolated by deserts and mountains, Tibet traditionally has been ruled by a theocracy dominated by the Lama form of

Buddhism. Since the Mongol conquest, China has claimed suzerainty over Tibet. For centuries two spiritual leaders—the Dalai Lama and the Panchen Lama—have been rivals for supremacy with the former usually in the ascendancy. The Ming, the Manchu, the Republican government and the Communists all have become involved in this rivalry, usually to pursue a divide and rule policy. When Nationalist China fell, the government of the Dalai Lama proclaimed independence, but no foreign power gave recognition. In October, 1950, the Red Chinese invaded Tibet to "liberate" Tibetans from American and British imperialism. No Americans and few British were in Tibet at the time. Indian protests were brusquely rejected. In May, 1951, Tibetan authorities signed an agreement accepting Tibet's incorporation into China. Though promised autonomy, Tibet's religion, government, and economy were encroached upon as Chinese settlers, garrisons and officials moved in. Revolt broke out in 1958 and 1959 but was crushed and the Dalai Lama fled to India. Subsequently, the Chinese redistributed the land and organized the Tibetan peasants into collectives.

Invasion of India. One of China's major concerns in Tibet was the construction of highways to link the area with China proper and to improve communications with the border regions facing India, Nepal and Bhutan and especially with Sinkiang where a major industrial complex was being constructed. The best route to Sinkiang happened to pass through Indian-held Kashmir. Even while signing with India the 1954 agreement emphasizing peaceful co-existence, the Chinese were building a highway in this remote frontier region without Indian permission. When the Chinese protested against the presence of Indian troops in the area, India withdrew them and made no public announcement for fear public outcry might spoil Sino-Indian relations and the possibility of a peaceful settlement.

OUTBREAK OF FIGHTING. In 1960, Chou En-lai offered to guarantee India's eastern border if India would cede the disputed territory in Ladakh but India refused. Border incidents continued until October, 1962, when the Chinese attacked at several points, but in greatest force in the east. After advancing deep into the eastern frontier region, the Chinese unilaterally declared a cease-fire and offered a partial withdrawal. The

Chinese objectives and the reasons for their withdrawal in the incident are uncertain. In attacking, the Chinese probably wanted to disrupt India's economic development which was becoming so successful that India was appearing a better model for other nations than China with its humiliating failures. Perhaps, too, China wanted to impress the other Asian nations with her military power. The quick response of Great Britain and the United States in providing aid and Russia's obvious irritation with this Chinese adventure unquestionably encouraged them to stop short of real victory. On the other hand, China could hardly have intended a long campaign since the attack was launched at the beginning of winter.

Foreign Relations Prospects. By 1964, both Russia and Red China had strengthened their garrisons along their vast common border. Russian consulates were closed by China in Harbin, and serious disputes appeared to be developing. As the split seemed to have become irreparable, Chinese propagandists began to put a new implication on the phrase "the east wind will prevail over the west wind." The Chinese apparently believe they are riding the crest of the future, and they are prepared to use any means—deceit, hard line or soft—to achieve their goals of total Communist victory under Chinese leadership. The Red Chinese believe their long experience of winning China by force and subsequent rapid Communization gives them a special message to carry to the "colonial and semi-colonial countries." What the recognition by France in early 1964 will mean is not yet clear. Red China obviously considered it a huge step in the direction of the U.N., and it is probable that some of the Western-oriented Asian nations may well follow the example. In February, however, the Nationalist government on Taiwan severed its diplomatic relations with France in protest.

BIBLIOGRAPHY

Ball, W. M., *Nationalism and Communism in East Asia*, 1956.

Barnett, A. D., *Communist China and Asia*, 1960.

Center for International Affairs, Harvard Un., *Communist China, 1955-1959. Policy Documents with Analysis*, 1962.

Chandra-sekhar, S., *Red China: an Asian View*, 1961.

Chen, T.H.E., *Thought Reform of the Chinese Intellectuals*, 1960.

Chu Y. C., *Communist China's Economy, 1949-1962*, 1963.

Fitzgerald, C. P., *Revolution in China*, 1952.

Hsieh, A. L., *Communist China's Strategy in the Nuclear Era*, 1962.

Hudson, G., A. V. Sherman, and A. Zauberman, *The Chinese Communes: A Documentary Review and Analysis*, 1960.

Hughes, T. J., and D. E. T. Luard, *The Economic Development of Communist China, 1949-1958*, 1959.

Kahin, G. M., ed., *Major Governments of Asia*, 1958.

Kuo, P. C., *China: New Age and New Outlook*, 1956.

Latourette, K. S., *The American Record in the Far East, 1945-1951*, 1952.

Linebarger, P. M. A., *Far Eastern Governments and Politics*, 1956.

London, Kurt, ed., *Unity and Contradiction; Major Aspects of Sino-Soviet Relations*, 1962.

Mac Farquhar, R., *The Hundred Flowers Campaign and the Chinese Intellectuals*, 1960.

Maki, J. M., *Conflict and Tension in the Far East, Key Documents, 1894-1960*, 1961.

Mao, T. T., *Selected Works*, 1954-6.

Mende, T., *China and Her Shadow*, 1960.

Morin, R., *East Wind Rising; a Long View of the Pacific Crisis*, 1960.

Mu, F. S., *The Wilting of the Hundred Flowers; the Chinese Intelligentsia Under Mao*, 1963.

Quigley, H. S., *China's Politics in Perspective*, 1962.

Richardson, H. E., *Short History of Tibet*, 1962.

Riggs, F. W., *Formosa Under Chinese Rule*, 1952.

Tang, Peter, *Communist China Today*, 2 vols., 1957-8.

Warner, D., *Hurricane from China*, 1961.

Zagoria, D. S., *The Sino-Soviet Conflict, 1956-1951*, 1962.

CHAPTER 16
Divided Korea and Viet-Nam

KOREA

Independence Promised. Korean independence was pledged at the Cairo Conference. However, at Yalta it was agreed that for military operations Russia should occupy North Korea, and the United States the South. At Potsdam, the 38th parallel was set as the dividing line, but this temporary demarcation was intended only to fix the responsibility for receiving the Japanese surrender. The American zone contained the best ports and agricultural lands and two-thirds of the population, but the Russian zone included most of Korea's heavy industries and mineral resources.

Independence Movement. Despite Japanese repression during their thirty-five year colonial rule, Korean nationalism had flourished, finding leadership among nationalist refugees abroad. A "Provisional Government" set up in 1925 under Syngman Rhee later moved to Chungking under Kim Koo, while Rhee sought support in the U.S. Many refugees fled to the U.S.S.R. where they trained for eventual return to Korea. Still other Nationalists and Communists worked secretly in Japanese-occupied Korea and Manchuria, maintaining contacts abroad. Near the war's end, the Communists formed a *de facto* government later called the "People's Republic," while rightist elements established the Democratic Party supporting the exiled

Provisional Government. Both groups named Syngman Rhee as their head, but Rhee rejected them both.

American Military Occupation. The American occupation forces under General Hodges brought few trained civil affairs officers or Korean specialists. In accordance with military orders to favor no political group, however, both the People's Republic and the Provisional Government were ignored. A more serious blow to Korean Nationalists was the Soviet-American decision of December, 1945, declaring a five-year trusteeship for Korea.

MILITARY GOVERNMENT. To facilitate the transition period, the occupation forces tried to retain much of the Japanese administrative structure. This aroused strong opposition and a host of political factions sprang up. Lacking recognition, the People's Republic fell largely under left-wing leadership, alienating it more from occupation authorities. Meanwhile, Syngman Rhee and Kim Koo became leaders of opposing right-wing movements. An effort by General Hodges to form an advisory council under Rhee elicited little popular support.

INTERIM GOVERNMENT. Despite political confusion and lack of Korean cooperation, the military authorities sought to establish democratic government under Korean administration. Responsible positions were turned over to Koreans with Americans acting only as advisors, and elections were held for an Interim Legislative Assembly in 1946. Because of the occupation's repression of the Communists and support of right-wing democratic elements, conservatives dominated the new assembly.

The Soviet Zone. In North Korea, leadership was divided among (1) the Yenan Communist faction returned from China, (2) the Russian Communist faction, (3) the domestic Communists, and (4) the non-Communist nationalists led by Cho Man-shik who received the Japanese surrender at Pyongyang. Although the Soviet army initially gave Cho Man-shik a top position, when the Russians arrived in strength they united all groups under the control of the Russian faction led by Kim Il-sung. Kim was a veteran of the Soviet army who had assumed the name of a noted nationalist. By using Korean Communists, backed by the Soviet army, the Russians achieved complete political control of the north without formally proclaiming military rule.

Two Republics. The 38th parallel soon became a boundary between rival governments. The Soviet-American joint commission to supervise the formation of a united government could not even agree on which Koreans could represent Korea. Although a United Nations commission recommended that

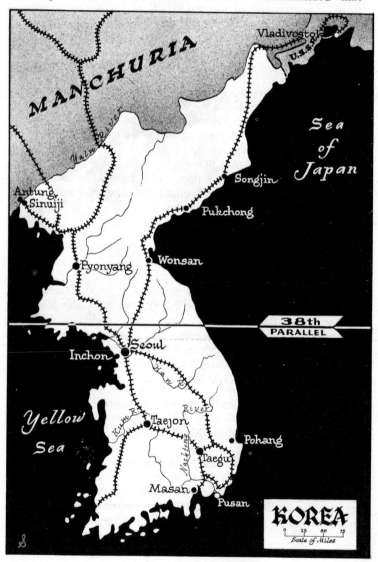

elections be held in 1948 for a united national assembly, the Communists refused to permit supervised elections, and they were held only in South Korea. The new assembly there adopted a constitution and chose Syngman Rhee as president. In August, 1948, General MacArthur transferred governing powers to the new Republic of Korea (R.O.K.). The Soviet-sponsored People's Republic of Korea in the north also adopted a constitution and claimed jurisdiction over all Korea although in December, 1948, the U.N. recognized the R.O.K. as the only lawful Korean government.

Military Withdrawal. Having launched and armed the North Korean regime, the U.S.S.R. withdrew her forces to Siberia, ostensibly in response to a U.N. appeal. Considering Korea a potential "Bataan," American forces departed in June, 1949, leaving only an advisory group to train the small R.O.K. army. Backstopped by U.S. air force units in Japan, the R.O.K. forces were deemed adequate to cope with foreign invasion. The North Korean army, however, continued a heavy build-up with Soviet assistance and soon began probing attacks along the border.

Party Politics. Bitter factional strife continued in the South. A series of political assassinations eliminated the leaders of both the former People's Republic and the Provisional Government. In the first independent elections in 1950, Rhee's conservative faction lost heavily as 2,230 candidates competed for 210 seats, and Rhee would have lost power except that 128 new assemblymen were independents. The new moderate assembly convened on June 19, 1950, in a hopeful spirit. Six days later the North Koreans launched a well-prepared invasion, claiming that they had been attacked by the South.

Korean War. The United Nations ordered a cease-fire, but to no avail. Two days later President Truman ordered U.S. forces into action under General MacArthur as the United Nations voted military sanctions. Well-equipped and led by Korean veterans of the Communist armies of China and Russia, the North Koreans drove the U.N. armies into a small perimeter around Taegu and Pusan. But when MacArthur landed forces at Inchon near Seoul, the Red offensive disintegrated. The U.N. units pushed rapidly into North Korea in October, 1950.

ENTRANCE OF CHINA. As the R.O.K. and U.N. forces neared Manchuria, Red China intensified its propaganda and threats. Then, suddenly, large Chinese "volunteer" armies attacked across the Yalu, almost engulfing the U.N. units. The U.N. invited Peking to negotiate a solution, but discussions seemed futile. While U.N. forces retreated over the 38th parallel, they inflicted enormous casualties on the enemy.

DISMISSAL OF MACARTHUR. As the fighting became a war of attrition, General MacArthur proposed introducing Nationalist Chinese forces and bombing Red China's Manchurian supply lines to break the stalemate. Fearing to provoke Russian intervention under the 1950 Sino-Soviet pact, Britain and France objected. When MacArthur persisted in publicizing his views, President Truman abruptly replaced him in all his commands with General Matthew Ridgway. A storm of partisan controversy ensued in the U.S., but relations among the Allies improved.

KOREAN ARMISTICE. After losing another 200,000 lives during the spring of 1951, the Communists proposed a cease-fire and truce talks. Negotiations at Kaeson and Panmunjon broke down in October over Communist demands for forced repatriation of prisoners, but were renewed after the death of Stalin. Agreement was finally reached in June, 1953, calling for voluntary repatriation of prisoners under the supervision of a neutral nations' commission and the drawing of a defensible truce line diagonally across the 38th parallel.

R.O.K.–U.S. Mutual Defense Agreement. Viewing any agreement not reuniting Korea a betrayal of South Korea after its sacrifices, President Rhee unilaterally released 25,000 anti-Communist prisoners and threatened to fight on alone. Only after the U.S. agreed to guarantee South Korea's defense did Rhee abandon his threat. Thus, after costing the lives of some two million North Koreans and Chinese, over 460,000 U.N. soldiers, and several million civilians, the war ended inconclusively. By the Mutual Defense Treaty of August, 1953, the U.S. and R.O.K. agreed to act together if either was attacked, and the U.S. retained 50,000 men in Korea to guard the truce line. In addition, the U.S. pledged large-scale aid for reconstruction.

Geneva Conference. The political conferences following the truce were turned into Communist propaganda sessions, possibly in retaliation for the fact that three-fourths of the Chinese prisoners screened by the neutral commission chose to go to Nationalist China while only twenty-one Americans elected to defect. The subsequent Geneva Conference in mid-1954 not only failed to unite Korea but added Viet-Nam to the list of divided lands. In Korea, the North Koreans blocked efforts of the U.N. Commission to supervise the truce and finally expelled the Commission after it reported illegal arms shipments. In 1956, the U.S. announced it, too, would rearm Korean forces with the latest type weapons.

Rhee Regime. By the war's end, President Rhee seemed solidly in control of South Korea. After maneuvering a constitutional amendment providing for direct election of the president, Rhee won a second term in 1952. Two years later after Rhee's Liberal Party won a two-thirds majority in the Assembly, they passed another amendment permitting a third presidential term. The 1956 elections brought victory for Rhee and his party, although opposition leader John M. Chang (Chang Myung) won the vice-presidency.

MALADMINISTRATION. Despite his political shrewdness, Syngman Rhee was a poor administrator. He was autocratic, changed his cabinet frequently, trusted few subordinates, and made all minor as well as major decisions himself. As the old man lost his mental and physical capacities, a coterie of corrupt guards, secretaries, and parties wielded increasing power. With the decline of Rhee's prestige, an enormous police force repressed the opposition and rigged elections in the Liberal Party's favor.

Student Revolution. Denouncing the 1956 elections as corrupt and unconstitutional, the opposition formed a new Democratic Party headed by vice-president John M. Chang. After the Democrats showed growing strength in local and national elections, the Liberal-dominated Assembly passed a security law severely restricting press and political freedom. The 1960 elections that gave the Liberals another victory were again marked by violence and corruption, and the Democrats rejected the results. Student demonstrations spread to all major cities, fanned by police brutalities. After the Seoul police were over-whelmed on April 19, military forces occupied the city, but remained politically neutral. As his supporters fled or turned against him, Rhee resigned and subsequently went into exile in Hawaii.

Democratic Party Government. A caretaker government un-der Huh Chang began cleansing the government and preparing for elections. New constitutional amendments limited presi-dential powers by introducing cabinet-style government. In the fairest elections Korea had seen, John M. Chang's Democratic Party won a solid majority. The new Assembly elected Yun Po-sun as president and he, in turn, named Chang as premier, but neither could exert adequate control. Factionalism hope-lessly split the Democratic Party, blocked legislation, and kept cabinets powerless or short-lived. With police repression lifted, much of the press proved unworthy of the freedom, corruption spread, and students demonstrated regularly.

Military Coup. Before the Chang government could be thor-oughly tested, however, on May 16, 1961, a military junta seized power. President Yun Po-sun gave official recognition to the new group, thus preserving diplomatic continuity. The junta moved rapidly, dissolving political parties, labor unions, and social organizations, and barring political activities and demonstrations. A provisional constitution centered power in a Supreme Council of National Reconstruction to rule until a new assembly would be elected at an unspecified date. The S.C.N.R. membership included the main revolutionary leaders. While Washington expressed regret over the suspension of democratic processes, American reaction was largely restricted to diplomatic pressures on the junta to accelerate a return to civil rule.

Military Government. The S.C.N.R. tried energetically to re-vitalize the nation. An overly-ambitious five-year development plan emphasizing industry was hastily drawn up. Fines were assessed against "illegal fortune makers." Thousands of "cor-rupt old politicians" were purged from political life. Steps were taken to reform the civil service, to abolish usury and tax abuses, and to rally the people behind the revolutionary pro-gram. But despite the disillusionment with the apparent failure of democracy in Korea and despite some real material improvements, the military government aroused limited popular support.

PROBLEMS OF S.C.N.R. Factionalism early split the junta group as General Do-young was superseded in power by Major General Park Chung-hee, who, with Colonel Kim Chong-pil, had masterminded the coup. Military men investigating illicit fortune makers were jailed for accepting bribes. In June, 1962, the economy was temporarily paralyzed by an ill-planned currency reform that failed in its goal of bringing to light hoarded capital. Next came a spectacular stock market rigging scandal popularly believed to be the work of the R.O.K. Central Intelligence Agency headed by Kim Chong-pil. The same agency was later accused of a variety of other malpractices and costly errors. These charges tarnished the image of the military group which had justified its coup through the need for integrity and efficiency in government.

Return to Civil Rule. In December, 1962, a new constitution was approved in a national referendum. When the ban on politics was lifted in early 1963, the first party to appear was Kim Chong-pil's Democratic Republican Party (D.R.P.). Opposition leaders charged that the party was organized before the lifting of the ban and even many military leaders opposed the strong position Kim created for himself. The dispute forced both Kim and his leading opponent into exile. As plots and counterplots weakened the coup group, Park Chung-hee announced he would hold a referendum on extending military power. When this aroused a storm of opposition, Park reversed himself and announced he would run for president. In hotly contested elections in late 1963, Park was elected with only 45 per cent of the votes and a bare plurality over Yun Po-sun. The D.R.P. won two-thirds of the assembly seats with one-third of the votes because of the divided opposition and a system of partial proportional representation. Thus, while Park Chung-hee assumed the presidency with a strong party majority as Korea returned to civil rule, his victory was obviously due to the division of the opposition rather than to broad popular support. This weakened his mandate for strong action. As his government pressed to settle the long-standing dispute with Japan in the spring of 1964, student demonstrations began again and the D.R.P. began to be weakened by factionalism.

Economic Problems. The new government faced serious economic problems. Two years of bad crops compounded an economic slump caused by maladministration under Rhee, chaos under Chang, economic errors under the S.C.N.R., and the fundamental ailments of a divided land. Despite the use of strong measures by the S.C.N.R., production gains in 1962 failed even to match the population increase of over 3 per cent. Little improvement was shown in 1963. Furthermore, U.S. aid declined because of Washington's global policy changes and growing unwillingness to continue to underwrite the failings of Korean governments. Following the restoration of civilian rule in 1964, food and foreign currency shortages grew more acute. With one of the highest literacy rates in Asia, this densely populated land continues to suffer from one of the lower per capita incomes, despite enormous infusions of American aid.

Foreign Affairs. Since independence, Korea's foreign affairs have been dominated by the problems of unification, foreign recognition, and relations with Japan. Unification remains the avowed goal of both North and South Korea as well as Peking, Moscow, and Washington, but the Communists have rejected unification based on fair elections and have wrecked every effort at negotiation, remaining as belligerent as ever at the Panmunjon truce talks.

R.O.K.-JAPANESE RELATIONS. Korean bitterness over Japanese rule remains strong. Korea demands reparations for losses incurred during Japanese rule, and seeks protection for her fisheries inside the so-called Rhee Defense Line, which was originally proclaimed by MacArthur. The Japanese also seek reparations for properties seized in Korea after World War II. Another point of difference is the Korean minority in Japan. South Korea was alienated by a repatriation agreement Japan concluded with North Korea under which over 150,000 Koreans were repatriated to the North. Subsequent letters from the early returnees describing conditions under Communist rule have slowed this flood to a trickle. Strong Korean opposition and hard bargaining by the Japanese disrupted R.O.K.-Japanese negotiations in the spring of 1964.

Politics in the People's Republic. About three million anti-Communists fled from North Korea to the South before and during the Korean War. This eliminated much opposition to Communist rule. Despite his Russian backing, however, Kim Il-sung could only gradually win complete control. First to be purged were nationalists who had collaborated with the Communists. Next followed a struggle among the various Communist factions, as Kim Il-sung extended the purge to eliminate first the internal Communists and then the Yenan group. Eventually even those Russian-trained Communists not part of Kim's personal faction were purged from leadership. Meanwhile, the party organization became centered in the Korean Worker's Party under the chairmanship of Kim Il-sung, who thus united control of party and government under one man after the pattern developed by Stalin.

SINO-SOVIET RIFT. Prior to the Korean War, Russia's dominance in North Korea was unchallenged. Red China's heavy sacrifices during that war and the exemplary conduct of the Chinese armies toward the people compared favorably to Russia's limited support and the raping and looting by Russian soldiers after World War II. Though North Korea relied heavily on Russian material and technical aid, Red China's prestige remained high. As an admirer of Stalin and Mao Tse-tung, Kim Il-sung was not sympathetic to Khrushchev's de-Stalinization policies, but he tried to walk a tight rope. In July, 1961, North Korea signed mutual assistance treaties with both China and the U.S.S.R., but as the Sino-Soviet cleavage widened, Kim sided more openly with Peking, while still receiving Russian assistance. In the spring of 1964, moreover, some 5,000 North Koreans studying in Russia were abruptly called home.

NORTH KOREAN DEVELOPMENT. While better endowed with industry and resources, North Korea suffered more damage from bombing during the Korean War than did the South. The exodus of the best farmers and the educated urban workers also hurt both agriculture and industry. Heavy emphasis on industrial development in the three- and five-year plans extending from 1954 to 1961 caused a shift of rural population to the cities, producing a rural labor shortage. At the same time, agriculture was being dislocated by collectivization of farming. Serious food shortages forced increased emphasis on rural development during the "shock absorption" year of 1960. The first four years of the seven-year plan (1961-67) emphasize mechanization of agriculture, development of irrigation, and other rural improvements. While North Korea boasts of trade with forty nations and has achieved notable advances in industry, exports have been achieved at heavy cost. Food shortages continue, and reports indicate that the average citizen is no better off than are his cousins in South Korea.

VIET-NAM

Japanese Occupation. The fall of France in 1940 cut French Indo-China adrift. Vichy recognized Japan's pre-eminence in Eastern Asia and granted her limited transit rights in Tonkin. When French field commanders stalled, Japan attacked, securing limited occupation rights and forcing the cession of three Cambodian and two Laotian provinces to Japan's ally Thailand. Unwilling to intervene, but recognizing Indo-China's strategic value as a Japanese base against the Philippines, the U.S. sought to neutralize the French colonies.

WARTIME DEVELOPMENTS. The Japanese left Indo-China's rule to French officials who were backed by a French army of 50,000. Cut off from France, the colonial administrators vigorously pressed the development of local industries and public construction to meet wartime needs. A Fascist-like youth corps encouraged nationalism and self-reliance among Vietnamese youth. Indo-Chinese nationals, especially Vietnamese, rose to higher posts in the colonial administration and the army.

INDEPENDENCE UNDER JAPAN. Near the war's end, some French officials secretly aided Allied intelligence. Fearing an uprising, the Japanese attacked French garrisons in March, 1945. As President Roosevelt had decided not to support French colonial ambitions, French pleas for aid went unanswered and her colonial forces and officials went into Japanese concentration camps. Under Japan's orders, Vietnamese Emperor Bao Dai proclaimed Viet-Nam's independence and its collaboration with Japan's co-prosperity sphere.

The Democratic Republic of Viet-Nam. Faced with Japanese interference, war devastation, and crop failures, Bao Dai's task seemed hopeless. The Viet-Minh made certain that it was. Organized in 1941 by Ho Chi Minh, the Viet-Minh was a coalition of Northern Vietnamese Communists and Nationalists. Ho had been a founding member of the Communist Party in France in 1920 and in Indo-China ten years later. During the war, his Viet-Minh followers worked with the American O.S.S., thus gaining an air of legitimacy. As the war ended, the Viet-Minh seized Hanoi and Saigon, and Communists led uprisings throughout the country hoping to win control before the British and Nationalist Chinese could occupy the country as planned at Teheran and Potsdam. Deserted by his officials, Bao Dai was forced to abdicate his ancient throne in favor of the Democratic Republic of Viet-Nam (D.R.V.) proclaimed in Hanoi. As D.R.V. president, Ho Chi Minh named Bao Dai his Supreme Councilor to maintain an air of government continuity. On September 2, 1945, the D.R.V. declared independence of France.

Allied Occupation. As planned, the British occupied South Viet-Nam, recovering Saigon and rearming the French. By the end of 1945, the reinforced French firmly controlled Cochin-China, and the British withdrew. In Hanoi, the Chinese Nationalists received the Japanese surrender but blocked French return to power. Many former French and Japanese weapons wound up in Viet-Minh hands. But, while favoring the Viet-Minh, the Chinese demanded many concessions before leaving Tonkin in February, 1946.

Viet-Minh–French Accord. While all Viet-Nam suffered floods and famine, the D.R.V. was wracked with internal strife. To win outside acceptance and capture Nationalist support, the Communists officially dissolved the Indo-Chinese Communist Party, although Communists retained the most important government posts. In January, 1946, elections were manipulated to keep Communists in control despite a weak Viet-Minh showing. Having abolished land taxes to win popular support, the D.R.V. had no income and Ho Chi Minh had to negotiate reasonably with the French. A provisional agreement of March, 1946, recognized the D.R.V. as a free state within the newly conceived Indo-Chinese Federation and the French Union.

Outbreak of War. D.R.V. leaders were outraged when French elements proclaimed a Republic of Cochin-China in the south and created a separate zone for the mountain tribes in central Viet-Nam. While Communist Vo Nguyen Giap organized Viet-Minh forces in Tonkin and ousted non-Communists from power, Ho Chi Minh went to France to negotiate. But French political turmoil precluded settlement, and Vietnamese and French constitutions adopted in 1946 differed sharply on Viet-Nam's status. Events moved rapidly. The French refused to meet D.R.V. representatives and a frightened French commander bombarded Haiphong. When the French ordered their disarmament, the Viet-Minh launched an attack, ending hopes of a peaceful solution. After initial victories, the French demanded almost unconditional surrender, but the Viet-Minh refused and military stalemate ensued.

Restoration of Bao Dai. As the war continued, some Vietnamese Nationalists, fearing the Communists, decided to work for independence by cooperating with the French. Bao Dai, who had fled to Hong Kong, became a rallying point. Driving a hard bargain, Bao Dai returned in March, 1949, as Chief of State of a Viet-Nam that was to include Cochin-China, Annam, and Tonkin. France still controlled foreign and military affairs, however, and the country was federated with Laos and Cambodia in the Associated States of Indo-China.

Viet-Minh Victory. After 1950, the Chinese Communists began material and technical aid to the D.R.V. Over-extended, the French were driven from upper Tonkin before able General de Lattre turned the tide. Resuming guerrilla tactics, the Viet-Minh won control of most of the delta outside the cities and paved roads. The death of de Lattre in 1952 reduced the French to despair of winning a war that cost twice the Marshall Plan aid from the U.S. French restrictions caused Bao Dai to leave governing to his ministers. Leaderless and disillusioned, Vietnamese intellectuals rejected commitment to either side. When their best forces were trapped in the isolated outpost of Dien Bien Phu in 1953, while Viet-Minh forces invaded Laos, France agreed to negotiate with Red China and the D.R.V. at Geneva.

GENEVA AGREEMENT. At Geneva in July, 1954, the new French premier Mendès-France moved for quick settlement. Chou En-lai, Molotov, and Anthony Eden represented China, the U.S.S.R., and Great Britain. The U.S. sent observers. The agreement ended French rule in Indo-China. Viet-Nam was divided along the 17th parallel between the D.R.V. and Bao Dai's state of Viet-Nam, but general elections under an international commission's supervision were projected for 1956.

Bao Dai and the U.S. refused to sign the agreement, but the U.S. agreed not to use force to disturb its implementation.

Republic of Viet-Nam. Bao Dai named as premier a ruggedly independent Catholic Nationalist, Ngo Dinh Diem, who had served as minister during Bao Dai's reform efforts in 1933. After winning powerful friends in the U.S., Diem returned to government office when Bao Dai gave him almost dictatorial power to save Viet-Nam. By a mixture of bribery, intrigue, and force, Diem won control of the Vietnamese army, defeated the para-military forces of the Hoa Hao and Cao Dai religious sects, and ousted the Binh Xuyen gangster organization to whom Bao Dai had turned over control of the Saigon-Cholon police.

DIEM AS PRESIDENT. From his French villa, Bao Dai opposed these measures, but U.S. support prevented Diem's dismissal. When Diem called a national congress to prepare for elections and a new constitution, Bao Dai again ordered his dismissal. Diem then held a national referendum that backed the ousting of Bao Dai. In October, 1955, Diem proclaimed Viet-Nam a republic with himself as president and premier. Recognition from the U.S. and leading Western powers followed quickly. A constitution adopted in 1956 provided for a strong presidency.

The Diem Regime. The elections called for by the Geneva Agreement were never held since free elections were not possible in the Communist D.R.V. With strong U.S. aid, Viet-Nam appeared to progress toward recovery, but Diem extended rather than relaxed his dictatorial powers. Civil liberties were violated and the legislature became a rubber stamp. Diem made his brother Ngo Dinh Nhu his chief advisor, and Madame Nhu, who organized Vietnamese women into a para-military organization, exerted great influence. Brother Ngo Dinh Can ruled central Viet-Nam like a fief, while another brother dominated the Catholic Church. Officials or others criticizing the family disappeared. Secret prisons were filled with political dissenters often jailed without trial.

ECONOMIC AND SOCIAL POLICIES. Diem's suspicion of foreign capital impeded economic development. Industry lagged as Diem favored agriculture, but his agricultural programs were generally ill-advised. As the Communists resumed terrorism, Diem sought to regroup the scattered rural populace into "agrovilles," larger new towns capable of self-defense. But these were built by forced labor, and the promised urban amenities such as electricity, schools, and clinics often never came. From 1962 to 1963, emphasis shifted to "strategic hamlets," which aimed at fortifying existing hamlets; but these, too, proved unsatisfactory.

Renewal of Terrorism. While they withdrew many forces from the south in 1954, the Communists left behind arms caches and thousands of hard-core guerrillas to melt into the population. Other thousands were recruited locally or filtered back from the north after the D.R.V. resumed guerrilla warfare in 1957. Known as Viet Cong, they sought to rule the countryside by terror. By 1964, some 15,000 local officials, doctors, teachers, youth organizers, and others cooperating with the Diem government had been killed and other thousands kidnapped. This loss of leaders caused irreparable damage, disrupting local government, closing schools, stopping malaria control, and other social services. Meanwhile, attacks on communication routes made all travel unsafe.

UNITED STATES MILITARY AID. At Diem's request, the United States increased its military advisory group from under 1,000 in 1961 to 15,000 by 1963, and the total aid bill rose to over $1,000,000 daily. Americans began accompanying on combat missions Vietnamese units they were training, with an increasing toll of American lives. Still, Diem failed to delegate adequate authority. He interfered with field operations, countermanded American advice, and promoted generals on the basis of their subservience to him.

TERRORISM BY DIEM. American protests over Diem's dictatorial policies and duplicity only increased his recalcitrance. A U.S. Senate committee reported in early 1963 that South Viet-Nam was further from democratic government than in 1956. As security disintegrated, opposition grew, and Diem's police filled the jails with 30,000 political prisoners. Unrest found focus in May, 1963, when Buddhists in Hué rioted in protest against discriminatory regulations against their ceremonies. Demonstrations spread. In June, Buddhist monks attracted world attention by killing themselves in flaming gasoline-drenched robes. These suicides, called "monk barbecues" by Madame Nhu, inspired more demonstrations which Diem brutally suppressed. The U.S. expressed its disapproval and withdrew its advisors from units used against the Buddhists. Meanwhile, the Viet Cong stepped up their attacks, using 1,000-man units with heavy guns to seize fortified hamlets. Vietnamese and American casualties mounted, and increasing numbers of planes and helicopters were lost. Over half of South Viet-Nam's population lived under the Viet Cong's direct or indirect control.

GROWING ANARCHY. In June, President Kennedy sent Henry Cabot Lodge, prominent Republican and diplomat, as ambassador to Viet-Nam. Just before Lodge's arrival, Diem proclaimed martial law and seized Buddhist pagodas in Hué and Saigon, claiming that the Buddhists were Communist tools. When professors and students demonstrated against the repressive and corrupt regime, Diem jailed hundreds and closed the universities. As more Buddhist suicides followed, the United Nations sent a mission to investigate charges of violation of human rights. While pressing for reforms, the U.S. slowed down the aid program and cut support for the special service troops Diem used as palace guards rather than guerrilla fighters.

Military Revolt. Up to this point, Diem's armed forces had generally remained loyal. In 1960 and 1962, coup attempts had failed, but as opposition spread, the army was inevitably affected. Finally, a group of disaffected generals led by Major General Duong Van Minh moved on November 1, seizing key ministries and police stations in Saigon and attacking the presidential palace. By nightfall, Diem and his brother Nhu had perished, killed by soldiers while held in custody.

CONTINUED STRIFE. A Revolutionary Council of Generals, who suspended the constitution, named vice-president Nguyen Ngoc Tho the premier of a caretaker government. But within three months, the military junta was overthrown by 36-year-old General Nguyen Khanh, who charged that some junta members were cooperating with foreign agents to neutralize South Viet-Nam. To gain public confidence and display unity, Khanh named General Minh Chief of State, while Khanh himself became premier. The Viet Cong severely tested the military government with large-scale attacks and terrorist tactics against Vietnamese and American military and civilian personnel. In early 1964, visiting U.S. officials found conditions very grave, despite the vast U.S. aid. It was uncertain whether General

Khanh could provide the inspired, aggressive leadership necessary to fuse new fighting spirit into the army and the people. No way had yet been found to stop the flow of supplies and reinforcements to the Viet Cong from the Communist North, but in Washington, under President Johnson, there was open talk of carrying the attack into D.R.V. territory in the North.

D.R.V. Since Geneva. Like Red China, the Democratic Republic of Viet-Nam claims to be a democratic people's republic. The 1946 constitution was a liberal document designed to attract broad nationalist support, but its guarantees of traditional liberties remained more completely dead letter than did those of Diem's constitution. The national legislature, after adopting the constitution, next met again for one day in 1953, and elections were not held until 1960. Meanwhile, a small coterie of top Communist leaders, forming the permanent committee of the legislature, actually ruled. Ho Chi Minh remained both president and premier until 1955, when his younger protégé Pham Van Dong became premier. The Viet-Nam People's Army has remained from its formation in 1944 under the control of deputy prime minister Vo Nguyen Giap.

POLITICAL ORGANIZATION. The largest political organization is the Lien Viet (Fatherland Front), a coalition of functional associations designed to regiment the entire population under the control of hard-core Communists. The Communist Party, officially "dissolved" in 1946 and reformed in 1951 as the Lao Dong (Worker's Party), is the real government. In 1960, following years of consultations and country-wide discussions, a new constitution was promulgated. This emphasized Socialist economic goals at the expense of traditional liberties. Again, a standing committee exercised the powers of the legislature when the latter was not in session and the president had strong powers. One unusual feature was the assignment of one-seventh of the legislature's seats to the minority peoples who constitute 2.5 million of the total 12 million North Vietnamese.

ECONOMIC DEVELOPMENTS. The Communists found it harder to build an economy than to sabotage one. Plundered by the Japanese and Chinese, bombed in World War II, and fought over by the Viet-Minh and the French, North Viet-Nam was in a bad condition by 1954. The exodus to South Viet-Nam of nearly a million persons cost a large part of the professional class and technicians. The French departed with much of the movable machinery. Normal trade with South Viet-Nam for food in exchange for coal, cement, and industrial products ended after Geneva. The flight of many peasants and small merchants increased the food deficit and brought normal business to a standstill. Pacts with France, Britain, Egypt and West Germany produced little trade, and shortages of all kinds caused unrest and riots. Nevertheless, the D.R.V. ruthlessly pressed a program of conformity, socialization, and industrialization.

LAND REFORM. Although over 90 per cent of the farmers already owned their tiny plots of land, the D.R.V. introduced a land redistribution program. Much of the redistributed land was that left by refugees to the South. In addition, 50,000 "rich" farmers and landowners were executed or sent to forced labor for owning two or three acres of land. This program ultimately was reversed after a serious rebellion in November, 1956. Thereafter, the Communists pressed the farmers to unite their minute holdings into larger cooperatives, which by early 1964 included nearly 90 per cent of all rural families. While the D.R.V. was much influenced by Red China, she has not rushed into premature development of rural communes. Despite strenuous efforts by the Communists to increase agricultural production, food deficits continued into 1964.

INDUSTRIALIZATION. D.R.V. planning moved on annual programs until 1957 when a three-year plan was launched. This was succeeded in 1960 by a five-year plan which made no public statement of goals. Industrial planning has aimed at exploiting the large coal reserves located close to harbors, the iron ore adequate for a significant steel industry, and other mineral deposits. Transportation and power shortages have handicapped industrial development. China, Russia, and the satellite nations have provided over $1 billion in economic aid of which over 60 per cent came from China. Indications in 1964 were that the sole source might become China as North Viet-Nam chose sides in the Sino-Russian dispute. While this aid has made possible the introduction of a variety of new industries, the D.R.V. has sought to avoid becoming "colonized" by her Communist allies. On the other hand, the aid has not yet provided significant improvement in the well-being of the average North Vietnamese over that he enjoyed before World War II.

BIBLIOGRAPHY

Allen, Richard C., *Korea's Syngman Rhee*, 1960.

Ball, G. W., *Viet-Nam, Free World Challenge in Southeast Asia*, 1962.

Berger, Carl, *The Korea Knot, a Military-Political History*, 1957.

Buttinger, J., *The Smaller Dragon: a Political History of Viet-Nam*, 1958.

Cady, J. F., *Southeast Asia, Its Historical Development*, 1964.

Chung, K. C., *New Korea*, 1962.

Fall, B B., *Street Without Joy; Indochina at War*, 1961.

Fall, B. B., *The Two Viet-Nams*, 1963.

Farley, M. S., and V. M. Dean, *Korea and World Politics*, 1950.

Fishel, W. R., ed., *Problems of Freedom: South Viet-Nam Since Independence*, 1961.

Goodrich, L. M., *Korea: A Study of U.S. Policy in the United Nations*, 1956.

Hammer, E., *The Struggle for Indochina*, 1954.

Honey, P. J., ed., *North Viet-Nam Today*, 1962.

Kahin, G. M., ed., *Government and Politics of Southeast Asia*, 1959.

Lancaster, D., *The Emancipation of French Indo-China*, 1961.

Leckie, R., *The Korean War*, 1963.

McCune, G. M., and A. L. Grey, *Korea Today*, 1950.

Mead, E. G., *American Military Government in Korea*, 1951.

Reeve, W. D., *The Republic of Korea, a Political and Economic Study*, 1963.

Rudolph, P., *North Korea's Political and Economic Structure*, 1959.

Trager, F. N., ed., *Marxism in Southeast Asia*, 1960.

U.S. Department of State, *North Korea: A Case Study in the Techniques of Takeover*, 1961.

Vatcher, W. H., *Panmunjon; the Story of the Korean Military Armistice Negotiations*, 1958.

Vinacke, H. M., *Far Eastern Politics in the Postwar Period*, 1956.

Vinacke, H. M., *The United States and the Far East, 1945-51*, 1952.

Whiting, A. S., *China Crosses the Yalu; the Decision to Enter the Korean War*, 1960.

CHAPTER 17
Postwar Problems
in the Rice Bowl Countries

CAMBODIA

Independence Movement. The pioneer of Cambodia's independence movement was Son Ngoc Thanh, who founded a nationalist and anti-French newspaper in 1936 and led an unsuccessful revolt in 1942 against the Vichy French rulers. When the young King Norodom Sihanouk followed Bao Dai in proclaiming independence in March, 1945, Thanh, with Japanese sponsorship, became first foreign minister and then premier.

RETURN OF FRANCE. The French return altered his fortunes. Alarmed by the aggressive Viet-Minh and by Thanh's growing popularity, King Sihanouk declared loyalty to France and signed a *modus vivendi,* which proclaimed Cambodia an "autonomous state within the French Union" but retained tight French control. Cambodia was partly appeased by Thailand's return of the western provinces ceded during the war. Thanh, however, was arrested, and many patriots fled to the jungle to form armed bands known as Khmer Issarak or Free Cambodians.

CONSTITUTIONAL MONARCHY. The elective legislature, created by the 1947 constitution, included many former Issaraks who had accepted a general amnesty. Ultra-nationalistic, anti-French, and often obstructionist, it refused to ratify both the *modus vivendi* and the subsequent treaty of 1949, by which France promised an unsatisfactory "independence." After new elections in 1951, the leading Democratic Party secured the return of the controversial Son Ngoc Thanh, whose inflammatory agitation for total independence aroused an outburst of nationalist fervor. When the French ordered his rearrest, he fled to the jungles to lead the remaining Issaraks, who now opposed both France and the monarchy. Sihanouk responded by dissolving the cabinet, proclaiming a three-year period of personal rule, and launching his own dramatic "Crusade for Independence."

SIHANOUK'S CRUSADE. Going into exile, Sihanouk proclaimed Cambodia's grievances against France in several foreign capitals. His campaign, which coincided with French collapse in Viet-Nam, won final concessions. In November, 1953, Cambodia gained control over its own armed forces. Complete independence followed the Geneva agreements in 1954. The next year, Cambodia formally withdrew from the French Union, leaving only French cultural and military training missions as the last links.

Personal Rule. Although a national plebiscite demonstrated his overwhelming personal popularity, Sihanouk still was handicapped by the opposing Democratic Party. He therefore proposed constitutional reforms to reduce the powers of opposition politicians. When these proposals were opposed both internally and by the International Control Commission, the king abdicated in favor of his father Norodom Suramarit. Sihanouk then organized his own party, the Sangkum (Socialist Community) which won overwhelming victory in the 1955 elections. For the next four years, "Prince" Sihanouk maintained party leadership, serving intermittently as premier. Following the dissolution of the Assembly in 1958 because of a suspected plot against the government, the Sangkum again won total victory. During this campaign, Sihanouk publicly stated his aversion to Communism.

Royal Chief of State. After King Norodom Suramarit's death in 1960, the constitution was amended to create a Chief of State chosen by national referendum. Sihanouk, who had just won national approval of his policies, assumed the new position, intermittently being premier also. In the 1960 elections, his Sangkum totally defeated the leftist Pracheachon Party, which was handicapped by the arrest of its main leaders on charges of plotting with a foreign government (presumably North Viet-Nam). Whatever his title, Norodom Sihanouk remains the real leader of Cambodia, inheriting the Khmer loyalty to their traditional kings. His leadership may well be challenged, however, by the rapidly growing body of unemployed young western-trained "intellectuals," who protest their lack of voice in the undemocratic government which they criticize as corrupt and inefficient.

Economic Evolution. Cambodia's 6,000,000 people are relatively well fed, clothed, and housed. Eighty per cent are farmers growing chiefly rice and rubber. Although economic development has not been spectacular, the postwar years have brought superficial evidences of prosperity: paved highways and roads, new hotels, street lights, banks, schools, and urban development projects. The French-financed new port of Sihanoukville on the Gulf of Siam is an important symbol of independence of South Viet-Nam, through which all commerce previously moved. It was linked with the capital city of Phnom Penh, 150 miles away, by an American-financed highway. The five-year plan adopted in 1958 aimed to diversify agriculture and encourage light industry. Development has been handicapped, however, by excessive government control and by the Cambodians' distaste for business and commerce. Foreign assistance has come from fourteen different countries. Communist nations have built factories for producing plywood, textiles, cement, and tin. American assistance totaling $360 million by 1964 went toward sawmills, power plants, public health, education, agriculture, industrial development, and roads, as well as military aid. Sihanouk's People's Socialist Community advocates a welfare state, and the government has enormously improved public health facilities and education at all levels for both the urban and rural dwellers.

Foreign Relations. While the Geneva Agreement of 1954 guaranteed her independence and banned foreign military bases there, Cambodia insisted on the right to arm and seek foreign alliances. Since being admitted to the United Nations in 1955, Cambodia has tended to vote with the neutralist bloc. While rejecting SEATO participation, Sihanouk accepted U.S. military assistance. Because of his Socialist inclinations, Sihanouk fears the U.S. as an imperialist power and admires China which he believes will one day win all Southeast Asia. He frequently visits Peking, which he recognized in 1958 and has sent some of his children to be educated there.

NEUTRALITY CAMPAIGN. Sihanouk took active leadership in

organizing and chairing the Geneva Conference which "neutralized" Laos in 1962. Thereafter, he appealed for a similar guarantee for Cambodia. When the U.S. tempered its reply, Sihanouk threatened to seek Chinese protection. Obviously alarmed by the violent death of Diem in South Viet-Nam, Sihanouk abruptly rejected further U.S. aid, and turned hopefully to France to pick up the $30 million annual tab. Still threatening to call in his Chinese neighbors, Sihanouk arrogantly demanded U.S. agreement to an international conference guaranteeing Cambodian neutrality.

BORDER TENSIONS. Cambodia deeply fears and mistrusts her traditional enemies Viet-Nam and Thailand, and U.S. aid to those countries increased that fear. On the other hand, Cambodia's friendliness with Red China has made the mistrust mutual. Several times the borders have been closed or diplomatic relations severed with both countries. Repeated claims of border violations by both South Viet-Nam and Cambodia mounted to charges of armed invasion in 1962. Yet in early 1964, Sihanouk invited South Viet-Nam to reject its U.S. alliance to join Cambodia in a neutralist confederation. With Thailand, differences over a disputed temple were settled when the International Court of Justice awarded the ruin to Cambodia. Nevertheless, Cambodia's increasing Socialist orientation has aroused Thai fears, resulting in public statements which prompted Cambodia to ask the U.N. to investigate suspected Thai subversive activities. Cambodia also embarked on a major program of building its border defenses.

LAOS

World War II and the Associated States. The Kingdom of Laos is a post-World War II creation. An ethnic hodgepodge, its two million people consist of the valley-dwelling Lao and a variety of mountain tribal peoples, roughly divided before World War II into two kingdoms. The French directly ruled the former kingdom of Champassak, maintaining a protectorate over the northern kingdom of Luang Prabang. In 1942, the Vichy regime recognized King Sisavong Vong of Luang Prabang as king of all Laos, and in the spring of 1945 he reluctantly followed Viet-Nam and Cambodia in proclaiming independence.

LAO ISSARA MOVEMENT. Moreover, the Lao Issara (Free Lao),

led by Souvanouvong and Souvana Phouma, cousins of the king, were determined to resist French return. They even briefly deposed Sisavong Vong and declared a republic. But they fled to Bangkok when the French returned and reinstated the king in 1946. With the adoption of a constitution in 1947 and the incorporation of Laos into the Associated States in 1949, the Lao Issara movement so thoroughly collapsed that one of its leaders, Prince Souvana Phouma, could serve as prime minister.

Pathet Lao Challenge. Prince Souvanouvong, however, fled to northeastern Laos where, with Viet-Minh support, he organized the Pathet Lao that harassed the French with guerrilla attacks. Operating in national politics as the Neo Lao Hakxat or Laotian Patriotic Front Party, the Pathet Lao pretended to be purely nationalistic, whereas it was clearly Communist in inspiration and goals. The mountain tribal people provided the indigenous fighting force since the lowland Lao have little interest in fighting, whatever the purpose. For real battles, Pathet Lao forces have been heavily stiffened with Viet-Minh "advisors." The Pathet Lao has also shrewdly used to its own advantage the historic cleavages between the lowland Lao and the upland tribal people.

Geneva Agreement. At Geneva in 1954, Laos, France, and North Viet-Nam agreed to permit the Pathet Lao to concentrate their million forces in two northern provinces, to be administered jointly with the royal government. The Pathet Lao army was to be integrated into the royal army and nation-wide elections were to be held. Laos could make no foreign military alliances and all foreign troops except a French military advisory group were to be withdrawn. An International Supervisory Commission of Indian, Canadian, and Polish representatives was to supervise the agreement's implementation. Although the Royal Lao government and the French maintained that Laos was not legally partitioned, in actuality the Pathet Lao never permitted the central government to operate in its provinces.

INDEPENDENCE AND CONFUSION. Despite internal problems, Laos achieved full independence in January, 1955, and was admitted to the U.N. the following December. After national elections, which the Pathet Lao boycotted, Prince Souvana Phouma formed a coalition cabinet including his Communist half-brother Prince Souvanouvong. The Pathet Lao, however, rejected integration of their forces and provinces into the Royal Lao government until November, 1957, when a second Pathet Lao minister joined the cabinet. Communist strength was clearly manifested in the May, 1958, elections when they won nine of the twenty-one contested legislative seats.

Right Wing Resurgence. When U.S. aid failed to stem the Communists, a series of political maneuvers caused the compromising neutralist Prince Souvana Phouma to be replaced by the militant anti-Communist General Phoumi Nosavan. With the Pathet Lao in retreat and Souvanouvong jailed for treason, the rightists won a sweeping victory in the 1960 elections. That August, however, the neutralist paratroop Captain Kong Le engineered a coup which reinstated Souvana Phouma as premier in Vientiane. General Phoumi Nosavan retreated southward to Savannakhet.

INTERNATIONAL RIVALRIES. Kong Le's victory initiated a new phase as he received Russian support while Phoumi's forces continued to get U.S. aid despite American recognition of the neutralist government. By December, 1960, Phoumi had pushed Kong Le back to the Plain of Jars where the Pathet Lao joined forces with him. Neutralist Prince Souvana Phouma headed a government in exile in Cambodia, while General Phoumi Nosavan set up a new rightist government under Prince Boun Oum. Quickly defeated by a combined Pathet Lao and neutralist army supported by the Viet-Minh, Phoumi's forces beat a frightened retreat to the Thai border. By the spring of 1961, the Pathet Lao controlled two-thirds of Laos, and U.S. Marines moved to Thailand's northern border to discourage a possible Viet-Minh— Pathet Lao invasion.

Geneva Conference—1962. Finding three rival governments in Laos and no right-wing forces willing to fight, the Kennedy administration accepted the suggestion of Cambodia's Prince Norodom Sihanouk of a second Geneva Conference to negotiate a settlement. A coalition cabinet formed by right-wing Prince Boun Oum, neutralist Prince Souvana Phouma, and leftist Prince Souvanouvong sent a delegation to Geneva to sign a fourteen-nation agreement guaranteeing the independence and neutrality of Laos. Laos pledged not to make any military alliance, not to recognize the protection of any military coalition, and not to permit foreign military bases on her soil. All foreign forces were to be evacuated under the supervision of an International Control Commission.

PRICE OF NEUTRALITY. The neutrality policy bought neither true neutrality nor peace. The shaky coalition government, strong only on its left flank, soon recognized Communist China and North Viet-Nam among other Communist nations. The Pathet Lao resumed its attack on both right-wing and neutralist forces, and opportunistic General Phoumi concluded aid agreements with both Peking and Moscow. The tendency has been toward polarization of the neutralists to either the left or the right while Souvana Phouma blames the political turmoil on the Communist-controlled Pathet Lao. The Communist position, however, grew more unclear as the Sino-Soviet split grew more bitter.

Economic Conditions. The heavy infusion of American aid brought many dislocations to Laos, scarcely out of a barter economy. A *nouveau riche* and many of the old ruling families prospered, but little trickled down to the villages. Inflation became rampant. When aid was cut off during the Geneva Conference in 1962, General Phoumi ran the government by printing more money. By early 1964, insecurity had virtually paralyzed all foreign assistance programs — Japanese, Chinese, North Vietnamese, and French, as well as American. However, since Laos is still an underpopulated land and its people produce most of their own needs, the economic elements of the city do not so seriously affect the bulk of the population as equivalent situations would in most countries.

THAILAND

Postwar Reorganization. Although Thailand had quickly capitulated to Japan and declared war on the Allies, many officials such as Pridi had secretly aided the Allies. At Japan's defeat, these patriots imprisoned Pibun and other collaborators and claimed the Thai declaration of war had been illegal. Though the U.S. readily accepted this position, the British and French resented Thailand's wartime annexation of portions of British Malaya and French Indo-China. Not until these territories were returned was Thailand able to gain admission to the United Nations.

FAILURE OF PRIDI. The liberal Pridi directed the first postwar government. Newly legalized political parties contested for seats in the national legislature which after 1946 had an elective House of Representatives. The mysterious death of the young king that same year forced Pridi's resignation. His supporters continued in control, but were unable to meet the pressing economic problems or to control the rampant official corruption.

Pibun's Return. In November, 1947, a group led by Pibun, who had been freed from prison, seized control of the government. Until Western recognition was won, however, Pibun remained in the background. Not until April, 1948, did he assume official leadership. The following year Pridi was exiled following an unsuccessful insurrection which only more firmly entrenched Pibun and Police Colonel Pao. Under Pibun's dictatorship, political activities were closely restricted, though elections were held and the national assembly continued to meet.

NATIONALIZATION AND MODERNIZATION. Pibun resumed and extended the nationalistic social and economic program he had pressed between 1938 and 1944. Again, education was used to promote national pride with Thai as the only language of instruction. Although some relaxation came after 1953, Pibun's government aimed to reduce foreign control over Thai industry. Chinese-owned industries were ordered nationalized, and Chinese and European managers replaced with Thai. Government industries were expanded to include textiles, cement, wine, cigarettes, rubber, and a monopoly over rice exports. A Buddhist revival brought discrimination against Moslems and Christians, although Westernization was encouraged. Transportation facilities were expanded and modernized.

REALIGNMENTS WITHIN MILITARY OLIGARCHY. Pibun's power rested on military support, though jostling among the army, navy, and national police for top positions brought cabinet shuffles. An abortive navy coup in December, 1951, shifted the power balance to Police General Pao and army heads Phin and Sarit Thanarat. In 1955, another cabinet shuffle weakened Pao and the police force lost its purely military equipment such as tanks. General Phin also lost stature, while Field Marshal Sarit became minister of defense as well as army chief of staff. Meanwhile, Pibun remained prime minister to the popular young king, Phumipon Aduldet, whose nominal duties left him adequate time to pursue his musical hobby.

POLITICAL ORGANIZATION. In 1949, a new constitution was promulgated, and subsequent elections gave Pibun's government a solid majority. The 1951 coup, however, reinstated the original constitution of 1932 which provided for a unicameral half-appointive House of Assembly. Following a world tour in 1955, Pibun announced the resumption of "normal political activity"; but public meetings were banned and voting closely controlled in the 1957 elections. Pibun's Seri Manangasila (Conservative) Party retained power only with the support of the Thai army commanded by Sarit.

Army Coup of 1957. After the elections, Marshal Sarit grew increasingly at odds with General Pao. Since Pibun supported Pao, opposing political leaders aligned with Sarit, and in September, 1957, Sarit organized a bloodless coup that forced Pao and Pibun into exile. Marshall Sarit, while unquestionably controlling Thailand, named as prime minister Pote Sarasin, a diplomat who had been Secretary-General of SEATO. Elections in December gave an overwhelming victory to the pro-Western Democratic Party and the 1957 coup leaders. General Thanom Kittakachorn became the new prime minister, while Sarit journeyed to the United States for medical treatment.

DICTATORSHIP OF SARIT. Another coup by Sarit in October, 1958, ended all semblance of democracy. Claiming drastic action was needed to stem Communism, Sarit declared martial law, abrogated the constitution, disbanded the assembly, and forbade political parties, except for a "Revolutionary Party," composed of army, police, and government officers. King Phumipon approved an interim constitution and appointed a predominantly military Constituent Assembly which named Sarit premier. Following Sarit's death in December, 1963, Deputy Prime Minister Thanom Kittakachorn became premier, while his old associate Praphas Charusathien became his deputy.

ANTI-COMMUNIST CAMPAIGN. After the 1958 coup, hundreds of suspected Communists were arrested and ten newspapers were closed. The campaign was intensified following the disclosure of a Communist plot to seize the northeastern provinces bordering Laos in July, 1961. To offset Communist influence, the government launched intensive development programs especially in the Communist-infiltrated northeastern provinces.

Economic Expansion and Social Change. Large U.S. purchases of rice for relief of Japan, the Philippines, and Korea, and of rubber and tin for stockpiling brought a surge of prosperity punctuated by the end of the Korean War. Thereafter, the Thai economy gradually stabilized, and except for the northeastern area, the Thai generally enjoy an adequate living. Agricultural diversification has made Thailand the world's fourth largest grain exporter. The six-year development plan of 1960 emphasized the basic infrastructure — transportation, power, and communications, but also stimulated growth in the mining and oil industries. The projected annual growth of 5 per cent was actually achieved, while population increase averaged 3 per cent.

FOREIGN ASSISTANCE. Since 1962, the government has encouraged foreign and private investment and has ended Pibun's policy of displacing Chinese entrepreneurs. Foreign aid has played an important but not vital role in Thai expansion. Between 1950 and 1960, $500 million in U.S. aid was received, more than half of which was military. Comparable aid levels continued into the mid-1960's. Other assistance has come from U.N. organizations, the Colombo Plan, and Japanese war reparations.

SOCIAL CHANGE. The Thai modernization movement began long before World War II but the negative fruits of industrialization became more evident in the postwar years. Crime rates rose sharply. Mounting juvenile delinquency prompted the Sarit government to open nineteen youth centers in Bangkok. The rapid growth of Bangkok created appalling slums and transportation problems that have been attacked by large housing projects, improved social welfare facilities, and street building. Extending education to seven years has required training of many new teachers and an energetic classroom building program. To Bangkok's five universities was added the first provincial one in Chiengmai.

Foreign Relations. Postwar Thailand has maintained a firm pro-Western and anti-Communist policy. A member of the United Nations since 1946, she sent forces to fight against the

Communists in Korea. She was an original member of SEATO in 1954, and in 1961, joined the Philippines and Malaya to form the Association of Southeast Asia (ASA), designed to foster economic and cultural cooperation among the three countries.

INVOLVEMENT IN LAOS. Thailand has clashed with her neighbors on all sides. Most serious has been the Communist infiltration and efforts at subversion of the populace of the northeastern Thai provinces. Sarit publicly supported the royal Lao government and the rightist Prince Boun Oum and General Nosavan, and was angry with the U.S. for backing neutralist Prince Souvana Phouma. Although Thailand bitterly opposed the establishment of a coalition government in Laos, she signed the fourteen-nation Geneva Agreement of July, 1962. To bolster Thai security against possible Communist invasion from Laos, U.S. troops have periodically been sent into the menaced border regions for maneuvers.

CAMBODIAN DISPUTE. The traditional enmity between Cambodia and Thailand intensified after Sarit's coup, which was probably in part stimulated by Cambodia's recognition of Red China in 1958. Sarit claimed that Cambodia was a potential springboard for a Communist take-over of Southeast Asia. Diplomatic relations, broken in 1958 and restored the following year, were again severed in 1961. When the U.S. gave fighter planes to assist in Cambodia's defenses against Viet Cong forces spilling over from the Vietnamese war, Thailand protested that this supported Cambodia's claims of Thai aggressive intentions. Tensions continued as both countries charged border infractions.

U.S. REASSURANCES. Shaken by U.S. support of a coalition government in Laos, Thailand publicly wondered whether the U.S. didn't treat so-called "neutral" countries better than she treated proven friends. In March, 1962, the U.S. offered reassurances by stating that it would defend Thailand against Communist aggression regardless of whether or not the other SEATO signatories agreed upon such defense. Despite this and the actual employment of U.S. forces in Thailand, the Thai continued to re-examine their position, and a growing nationalistic self-consciousness is emerging.

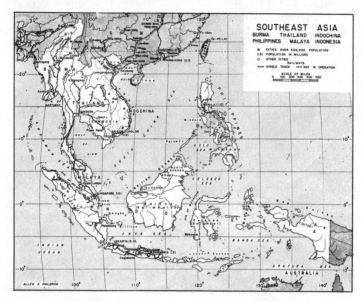

Courtesy of Human Relations Area Files, Inc., Yale University New Haven, Conn., under whose auspices this map was prepared for the *Area Handbook on Malaya* by the University of Chicago (Norton S. Ginsburg, Editor).

BURMA

Gaining of Independence. In 1943, the Japanese puppet government of Burma proclaimed independence. While independence proved a sham, the proclamation, combined with other Japanese policies, stimulated Burmese nationalism. As disillusionment with Japanese exploitation grew, however, formerly pro-Japanese nationalists like Aung San and Thakin Nu organized the Anti-Fascist Peoples Freedom League (A.F.P.F.L.) and the Burman National Army which collaborated secretly with the Allies.

BRITISH RECONSTRUCTION PLANS. The war devastated Burma's economy and destroyed its government. To effect recovery, the British proposed a three-stage plan: (1) direct rule of a governor, to be followed by (2) a return to the prewar semi-autonomous status, and (3) finally complete self-government

within the British Commonwealth. In general, Burmese propertied interests favored strong government during reconstruction, but political leaders preferred immediate independence.
When negotiations for gradual transfer of power failed, the
British Labor Government determined to grant independence
within or without the Commonwealth.

Republic of Burma. In the subsequent elections, the A.F.P.F.L.
under Aung San emerged victorious and dictated the writing
of the new constitution. Despite a series of assassinations, including that of Aung San, preparations for transfer of power
continued. A major problem concerned the status of minority
groups. The Shans and Kachins preferred British rule, and the
Christian Karens feared persecution by the Buddhists. The
1947 constitution, which established a British type parliamentary government, attempted to resolve the problem by an
elected Chamber of Nationalities to represent the five minority
states of the Shan, Kachin, Karen, Chin, and Kayah. Rejecting
membership in the British Commonwealth, the Republic of the
Union of Burma was inaugurated on January 4, 1948, with
Thakin Nu (U Nu) as prime minister.

POLITICAL STRUGGLES. As the head of the A.F.P.F.L., U Nu
dominated Burma's political life for its first decade of independence. However, when the party split in 1958 and expelled
U Nu both as president and party member, he resigned the
premiership to army strong man General Ne Win. Military officers promptly took control of all major cities and dominated the
central government. Although U Nu again became premier following his faction's victory in the 1960 elections, the army
remained dominant and numerous problems plagued the government. A constitutional amendment making Buddhism the state
religion aroused the minorities, and a major rebellion was
threatened in the Shan states. In addition, U Nu's new Union
Party (the "Clean" faction of the A.F.P.F.L.) split into new
factions and elected left-wing officers.

MILITARY GOVERNMENT. At this point on March 2, 1962,
Ne Win led a bloodless military coup. U Nu and his chief
officials were arrested, the constitution was abrogated, and the
parliament and cabinet were replaced by a Revolutionary Council of military officers. Buddhism was disestablished, and the

Revolutionary Council moved quickly to control the state councils while recognizing minority rights. Left-wing student riots were brutally suppressed and the universities temporarily closed. A government proposal for a union of the three major parties into the Burma Socialist Program brought only the left-wing National Front into the movement. Seeking a neutral path, Ne Win arrested leading A.F.P.F.L. members in October, 1963, and a month later rounded up known Communist leaders (435 in all), following the failure of peace talks with Communist insurgents.

Problems of Internal Security. Postwar Burma has been plagued with internal strife, banditry, and rebellion. Forced underground, rival Stalinist and Trotskyite Communists launched separate revolts in 1948. Great confusion followed, with army mutinies and revolts by Karens and other minorities, costing tens of thousands of lives and driving many peasants into banditry. At times the government had little control outside of Rangoon and Mandalay. Even though the major rebel forces were largely subdued, minor bands consumed a disproportionate amount of the government's resources. As late as November, 1963, some 8,000 Communists and many thousands of other scattered bandit and minority bands remained at large despite a variety of measures used by both U Nu's and the military government.

Socialism and Nationalism. Burma's economic policy combines Marxist and Buddhist concepts. Suspicious of capitalist countries, Burma welcomed aid from Communist China and the USSR, while opposing Communists at home. Economic policy has tended generally toward nationalization of industry, commerce, and national resources, including agriculture. The four-year plans of 1957 and 1961 provided for cooperation between private industry and government with the aim of eventual nationalization. Since 1963, the military government has moved toward rapid economic socialization. Nationalization and redistribution of farm land owned by absentee landlords was especially pressed. But development is slow. Socialism has brought little prosperity. Nationalization and anti-foreign, anti-capitalist policies have driven out foreign capital and much needed technical skill. Agriculture has yet to reach the 1930 production levels. Although she has received extensive foreign aid both from the Eastern and Western blocs, foreign assistance has declined. Following conclusion of a peace treaty in 1954, Japan also provided considerable aid in reparations and technical assistance.

Foreign Relations. In foreign policy, Burma remains committed to neutralism. Although she supported U.N. action in Korea in 1950 and voted against the Communist bloc on the Hungarian issue, Burma has favored admitting Red China into the U.N. In 1954, Burma adhered to the five principles of peaceful co-existence as jointly enunciated by Nehru and Chou En-lai, and in 1955 supported neutralism at the Bandung Afro-Asian Conference. While an active member of the Colombo Plan, Burma rejected participation in the Southeast Asia Treaty Organization (SEATO). Increasingly nationalistic and anti-foreign, Burma forced out foreign groups such as the Ford and Asia Foundations and closed down international educational exchange programs and news agencies. In 1963, however, she signed the limited nuclear test ban agreement with Russia and the U.S., despite Red Chinese opposition.

BORDER DISPUTES. Burma has had border disputes with all her neighbors, but especially with Communist China. Following Red Chinese incursions in 1956, Burma ceded 100 square miles in Kachin to secure Chinese withdrawal to the line defined by the Anglo-Chinese Treaty of 1941. A 1960 agreement combined with a 10-year non-aggression pact involved minor concessions on both sides but returned much of the area lost in 1956. Burman minority unrest and distrust of the Chinese force the Burmese to maintain heavy border garrisons.

CHINESE NATIONALIST GUERRILLAS. The flight of a Chinese Nationalist force into North Burma in 1950 created problems that long embittered U.S.-Burman relations. The Chinese were charged with maintaining themselves by smuggling opium and arms, and the U.S. was accused of supporting them indirectly from Taiwan. After Burmese government forces captured American carbines in 1961, Burma formally complained to the United Nations. Subsequently, the Taiwan government admitted airlifting arms to Chinese guerrillas in Burma, and with Thai assistance arranged for the withdrawal of 4,400 Chinese to Taiwan.

BIBLIOGRAPHY

Berval, R., *Kingdom of Laos, The Land of the Million Elephants,* 1959.

Blanchard, W., *Thailand, Its People, Its Society, Its Culture,* 1958.

Byles, M., *Journey into Burmese Silence,* 1962.

Cady, J. F., *A History of Modern Burma,* 1958.

Cady, J. F., *Southeast Asia, Its Historical Development,* 1964.

Champassak, S. N., *Storm Over Laos. A Contemporary History,* 1961.

Elsbree, W. H., *Japan's Role in Southeast Asian Nationalist Movements, 1940-1945,* 1953.

Fall, Bernard, *Crisis in Laos,* 1962.

Furnivall, J. S., *Governance of Modern Burma,* 1960.

Hall, D. G. E., *Burma,* 1960.

Herz, M. F., *A Short History of Cambodia from the Days of Angkor to the Present,* 1958.

Insor, D., *Thailand; a Political, Social, and Economic Analysis,* 1963.

Jacoby, E. H., *Agrarian Unrest in Southeast Asia,* 1961.

Johnstone, W. C., *Burma's Foreign Policy,* 1963.

Kahin, G. M., ed., *Government and Politics of Southeast Asia,* 1959.

Kahin, G. M., ed., *Major Governments of Asia,* 1958.

Le Bar, F. M., and A. Suddard, ed., *Laos: Its People, Its Society, Its Culture,* 1960.

Pendleton, R. L., *Thailand, Aspects of Landscape and Life,* 1962.

Purcell, V., *The Chinese in Southeast Asia,* 1951.

Pye, L. W., *Politics, Personality and Nation Building: Burma's Search for Identity,* 1962.

Steinberg, D. J., C. A. Bain, et al., *Cambodia: Its People, Its Society, Its Culture,* 1959.

Tinker, H., *The Union of Burma,* 1961.

Trager, F. N., ed., *Marxism in Southeast Asia,* 1960.

von der Mehden, F. R., *Religion and Nationalism in Southeast Asia,* 1963.

Walinsky, L., *Economic Development in Burma, 1951-60,* 1962.

Wilson, D. A., *Politics in Thailand,* 1962.

CHAPTER 18
The Malay Arc

INDONESIA

Nationalism and the Japanese Occupation. During the last two decades of Dutch rule in the Netherlands East Indies there had been a steady growth of national consciousness and agitation for self-government under such leaders as Sukarno, Mohammad Hatta, and Sutan Sjahrir. World War II accelerated the movement. Dutch resistance quickly crumbled, and the Japanese, having limited occupation forces, encouraged anti-Dutch feelings by promising independence. Indonesians were trained in self-defense militias and given government posts formerly prohibited to them. Following discussions among nationalist leaders, some, including Sukarno and Hatta, appeared to collaborate with the Japanese while actually working with the underground resistance forces organized by Sjahrir. Those Indonesian nationalists who genuinely cooperated with the Japanese were ultimately alienated by Japanese brutality and excessive demands for food, raw material, and forced labor, which reportedly took the lives of about 4 million Indonesians.

Republic of Indonesia. Withal, the Indonesians did not welcome the return of their Dutch overlords at the war's end. On August 17, 1945, Sukarno and Hatta broadcast a stirring proclamation of independence for the Republic of Indonesia. Throughout the islands, Indonesian nationalists, spearheaded by students, rose up. When the British forces landed six weeks later, the Republic of Indonesia was a functioning reality. Although the British worked with the Indonesians in the disarmament of the Japanese and repatriation of Allied prisoners, they also permitted the return of some Dutch troops in late 1945. Subsequent clashes between the Dutch and Indonesians caused the British to urge a quick settlement. Lacking strength to put down the Indonesians, the Dutch offered a vague sort of commonwealth status, at the same time hastily setting up a series of independent federal states on the outer islands.

FAILURE OF COMPROMISES. The Linggadjati Agreement concluded in 1946 satisfied neither side. A federal state, the United States of Indonesia, to be organized by January 1, 1949, was to have equal status with the Netherlands under the Dutch crown. Continued tension and armed clashes mounted to war dimensions with the Dutch invasion of Java and Sumatra in July, 1947. Although another compromise, the Renville Agreement, was concluded in January, 1958, following a cease-fire resolution by the United Nations Security Council, this too failed of implementation. A Dutch blockade continued to keep out food and even medicines from Republic-held areas. Then Indonesian Communists, following Moscow's instructions for

1-REPUBLIC OF INDONESIA	5-STATE OF MADURA	9-AUTONOMOUS AREA OF S. E. BORNEO	13-STATE OF BILLITON
2-STATE OF SOUTH SUMATRA	6-STATE OF EAST JAVA	10-AUTONOMOUS AREA OF BANJAR	14-STATE OF BANGKA
3-BANTAM, UNDER PROV. FED. GOVT.	7-STATE OF EAST INDONESIA	11-STATE OF GREAT DAYAK	15-STATE OF RIOUW
4-STATE OF PASUNDAN (WEST JAVA)	8-AUTONOMOUS AREA OF EAST BORNEO	12-AUTONOMOUS AREA OF WEST BORNEO	16-STATE OF EAST SUMATRA

Courtesy of The New York Times

UNITED STATES OF INDONESIA AT THE TIME OF
ITS ESTABLISHMENT, DECEMBER 28, 1949

general uprisings in Southeast Asia, revolted against the Republic. Capitalizing on Indonesian weakness following the quelling of this revolt, Dutch forces seized the Indonesian capital of Jogjakarta and imprisoned the leaders. This resort to violence alienated world opinion from the Dutch.

Indonesian Independence. Pressed by the U.N. and the United States, then aiding Dutch recovery in Europe, the Netherlands agreed to effective negotiations, and in December, 1949, the Republic of the United States of Indonesia officially gained its sovereignty. The new nation consisted of a much reduced Republic and fifteen federated states, excluding West New Guinea or Irian, which remained a Dutch colonial possession, leaving a festering sore in Indonesian pride.

UNITARIAN MOVEMENT. Independence proved precarious, threatened by uprisings in the various partially autonomous states. Though Indonesians were convinced that the federal structure was a Dutch tactic to "divide and rule," they had accepted it to gain independence. However, harassed by continuing clashes, Indonesian leaders in August, 1950, replaced the federation with a unitary Republic of Indonesia divided into ten provinces. Sukarno became president and Hatta vice-president. The cabinet was to be responsible to a projected House of Representatives.

SECURITY PROBLEMS. Independence and unitary government did not bring peace to the far-flung island republic, impoverished by a decade of wartime disruption of agriculture, industry, and trade. For many Indonesians, fighting had become a way of life and dissidence or banditry a profession. Serious revolts—some led by religious extremists, some by genuine political dissenters, some by opportunists, some by Dutch sympathizers—flared up throughout the islands but especially in the Celebes, the South Malaccas, and Sumatra. The forces of Darul Islam, an extremist Muslim movement infested with bandits and opportunists, gave the most persistent trouble.

POLITICAL DISUNITY. The central government, dominated by a small Western-trained elite, was rent by political disunity. The fact that neither the parliament nor President Sukarno had been elected by popular vote weakened the central government's authority and even led to army-instigated demonstrations in 1952. When elections were finally held for a constituent assembly in 1955, more than forty political parties, ranging from extreme right to extreme left, gained representation. Four of these—the Muslim Masjumi, the Indonesian Nationalist Party, the Nahadatul Ulama (Muslim Scholars), and the Communist Party (P.K.I.)—emerged as leaders. Only by a coalition could a cabinet be formed, and each succeeded the other in rapid succession. None could stay long in power without Communist backing, as the P.K.I. gradually became the largest party. Moderate vice-president Hatta resigned in December, 1956, following a dispute with Sukarno. Continuing revolts required heavy military expenditures and disrupted production and trade, further reducing government income. No cabinet could take the strong measures necessary to relieve the situation. The constituent assembly succeeded only in approving a national anthem, flag, and language before it was dissolved by Sukarno.

FOREIGN POLICY. Newly independent Indonesia sought to follow neutralism in foreign affairs. One cabinet fell in 1952 for signing an American aid pact pledging support of the free world. SEATO was rejected in 1954 and a year later Indonesia sought prestige by hosting the first Afro-Asian Conference held at Bandung under the sponsorship of the Colombo powers.

Guided Democracy. On his return from an extended tour of Russia and Communist China in 1956, Sukarno introduced what he called "guided democracy." This plan involved creating (1) a national cabinet representing all major political groups, and (2) a top level advisory council representing a cross section of Indonesian society. As government ideals were the *Pantja Silla,* the five humanitarian principles first pronounced by Sukarno in 1945: nationalism, internationalism, social justice, representative government, and belief in God.

RISING OPPOSITION. All major parties except the Communists opposed the plan. In March, 1957, martial law was proclaimed, giving Sukarno powers to curb the wide-spread local uprisings with the help of a "non-party" cabinet of "experts" under the premiership of Djuanda. Later that year, several Masjumi Party leaders, three of them former prime ministers, fled to Sumatra. There they joined with local army units in proclaiming the Revolutionary Government of the Republic of Indonesia (PRRI). They appealed for popular support to "protect Indonesia from becoming a Soviet satellite."

SUPPRESSION OF PRRI. By August, 1958, the Indonesian army had quelled the main rebel forces, though guerrilla activities continued for two more years. The end of the revolt was hastened by Sukarno's leniency in merely banning the rebels from political activity. This was hardly a serious punishment, however, since during the struggle Sukarno had dissolved the assembly, ordered reduction of political activity generally, and proclaimed a return to the 1945 constitution to further implement his "guided democracy."

Gotong Royong Parliament. Using the vast presidential powers of the 1945 constitution, Sukarno appointed a parliament representing all parties except the banned Masjumi and its allies. The Communists received one-fifth of the seats though they had held only about 5 per cent in the elected assembly. Fourteen functional groups, including the armed forces, received representation. As his *Gotong Royong* (Mutual Aid) Parliament convened, Sukarno defined their task as the creation of an Indonesian Socialist state. Controversial issues would be decided by discussion, not by vote, and when no decision could be reached, Sukarno would decide.

Triangular Power Balance. The army's victory in Sumatra left a three-way power balance: (1) Sukarno, who alternately leaned to right or left, (2) the Communists, and (3) the strongly anti-Communist army headed by General Nasution. Shortly after the new parliament's opening, the army closed the Communists' leading newspapers for criticizing the government and arrested several Communist leaders. While the army denounced the Communists, however, Sukarno told his parliament that the Communists and he shared some views. Before the power struggle could worsen, Sukarno threw into high gear his campaign to win West Irian.

West Irian Campaign. In 1945, Sukarno stated his ambition for a Pan-Indonesia to include all the island world between Southeast Asia and Australia. During the Sumatra revolt, Sukarno had raised the Irian issue at the United Nations, hoping to bring the rebels into a united fold by a program of "confrontation" against the Dutch. The "confrontation" involved an accelerated campaign of diplomatic pressures, propaganda, mobilization of public opinion, the threat of force, and actual guerrilla infiltration. A steady build-up of the armed forces consumed 30 per cent of the national budget in 1960 and nearly 80 per cent in 1961. Military aid poured in from Communist nations, Russia alone furnishing $800 million in equipment. National mobilization was ordered in February, 1962.

ANNEXATION OF IRIAN. As Sukarno's confrontation campaign gained momentum, the wheels of international diplomacy moved faster, and the Dutch agreed to negotiate. A formula reached in mid-1962 transferred New Guinea to the U.N. and then to Indonesia, and the Indonesian flag was raised over West Irian on December 31. In view of Sukarno's attitude, there seemed little likelihood the people of New Guinea would receive the right of self-determination promised in the 1962 agreement.

Internal Tension. Once Irian was won, it was expected that Indonesia would concentrate on her serious economic problems, but Sukarno, a self-styled romantic and revolutionary, had little patience with such matters. Moreover, he found himself in a dangerous position internally. Communist leader Aidit threatened war unless Sukarno fulfilled an earlier pledge to include Communists in a special cabinet with nationalists and religious groups. The powerful armed forces violently opposed giving Communists cabinet posts. As a clash appeared imminent at the end of 1962, foreign issues provided new diversion.

Confrontation Against Malaysia. When Malaya accused Indonesia of instigating a rebellion in neighboring Brunei, Sukarno directed a "confrontation" against the forthcoming Federation of Malaysia, following the pattern used against the Dutch. Thousands of volunteers were recruited as "freedom fighters" for guerrilla activities aimed at disrupting federation plans in Sarawak, Brunei, and North Borneo. The armed forces, never demobilized after the Irian crisis, were ready for battle. While disclaiming territorial ambitions in Borneo, Sukarno and General Nasution declared that Malaysia was a neo-colonialist threat to Indonesia. Despite a series of apparent agreements to do so, including the Sukarno-Kennedy cease-fire in early 1964, Indonesia did not relax its confrontation program.

Economic Decline. Although the Dutch left a basically sound economic structure, Indonesia's economy steadily declined after independence, except briefly during the Korean War. Only foreign-produced oil has reached pre-1939 levels. Important crops such as sugar cane, rubber, coffee, and tea are 15 to 70 per cent below prewar levels. The intermittent crises have reduced most industry to 50 per cent capacity production, with a resultant drop in exports, government revenues, and foreign exchange holdings. Decline in food production despite an annual population increase of over 2,000,000, brought large-scale starvation and serious anti-government riots in some areas.

FRUITS OF NATIONALIZATION. Between 1957 and 1963, Dutch, Belgian, British and other foreign properties and industries were progressively nationalized. Thousands of badly-needed technicians were expelled, and ships vital to inter-island transportation were driven out. In 1958, the Indonesian government seized the assets of Chinese residents and prohibited Chinese from operating shops as they had done for centuries. In 1963, trade with Malaysia was barred. This dealt a devastating blow to Indonesia's faltering economy since most of her tin and crude rubber had been processed in Malaysia and much of her trade had channeled through Singapore. Alarmed by the "crush Malaysia" policy, the United States froze new economic aid and the International Monetary Fund suspended assistance.

INFLATION. The net effect was catastrophic. Inflation skyrocketed the cost of living index from 100 in 1953 to 2000 in 1962. Issuance of currency doubled in 1963 alone. To service the billion dollars owed to Communist bloc countries, mostly for munitions, required nearly half the foreign exchange received from exports, but the blockade against Malaysia has virtually stopped all trade except in oil.

Communist Party. The economic chaos most benefited the Communist Party (P.K.I.) which recovered most remarkably from its defeat in 1948. In 1964 it claimed over 2,000,000 members with a following of another 10,000,000 in various labor groups, youth organizations and other fronts. Sukarno finally gave cabinet rank to two Communist leaders, Aidit and Lukman, but withheld the reality of power they demanded, perhaps fearing the army that would like to crush the Communists again. Meanwhile, Sukarno relies on his great personal prestige and political acumen to balance these forces.

SINO-SOVIET FACTIONS. The Communists themselves have been split by the Sino-Soviet dispute. The Chinese-oriented group, led by Lukman, is supported by the wealthy Chinese minority whom Sukarno alienated by his nationalization program. The Russian-oriented group, led by Aidit, received a boost with a 1964 Russian promise to aid six new development projects.

MALAYA

Japanese Occupation. The bitter war years aroused a new sense of nationalism in Malaya, for the Japanese permitted some local self-government and propagandized for Asian cultural unity. While many Malays cooperated with the Japanese, the Chinese generally resisted. They formed the nucleus of the Malayan Communist Party and the Communist-dominated Malayan People's Anti-Japanese League and associated army, which worked with British Intelligence in harassing the Japanese in Malaya. At the war's end, this group briefly seized power and wreaked vengeance upon Malays who had collaborated in Japanese rule.

Federation of Malaya. When a British-proposed Malayan Union aroused a general boycott by all classes and races in 1946, the British negotiated a more acceptable federation. In February, 1948, the Federation of Malaya was finally inaugurated. All Malaya, except Singapore which remained a crown colony, was to be administered by a British high commissioner assisted by appointive executive and legislative councils and a conference of the sultans, who transferred some powers to the federal government. In 1954, following Malayan agitation, the British permitted an elected majority in the Federal Legislative Council. Non-Malays, especially Chinese, received only limited opportunities for citizenship and government positions.

Malayan Independence. One weakness of the Federation was the plural nature of Malayan society which divided into nearly separate Malay, Chinese, and Indian communities. To gain full independence, however, the leading communal parties joined in 1953 to form the Alliance Party under Tengku (Prince) Abdul Rahman. Having won control of the legislature in the first federal elections, Tengku Rahman's government achieved independence for the Federation within the British Commonwealth in August, 1957. The Malay states then elected as supreme ruler Sir Abdul Rahman, head of Negri Sembilan and no relation to Tengku Rahman. Following the supreme ruler's death in 1960, the Sultan of Selangor, Sir Hisamuddin Alam Shaw, was elected Head of State.

ALLIANCE PARTY RULE. The Alliance Party controlled the Malayan government from independence to the creation of Malaysia. It is a coalition of (1) the United Malays National Organization with solid Malay support, (2) the Malay Chinese Association representing urban Chinese businessmen, and (3) the smaller Malayan Indian Congress. Except for a few months in 1959, Tengku Abdul Rahman has been chief minister.

ECONOMIC PROGRESS. Having received a strong new mandate in the 1959 elections, the Alliance government pressed a conservative but efficient policy of national development. The five-year plan of 1961 aims to increase national productivity and diversify the economy, which depends too heavily upon rubber and tin, by improving agriculture, resettling landless farmers, promoting industry, and expanding roads, railroads, communications, and social services.

Communist Pressures. Independence accelerated national development programs that increasingly won popular support away from the Communist terrorists who had disrupted Malayan affairs for more than a decade. The Communist Party dates back to the 1920's in Malaya. Then and throughout, membership remained largely Chinese. Until 1948, except for the abortive effort to seize power in 1945, the Communists concentrated on organizing and fomenting unrest within labor and youth groups.

THE EMERGENCY. In 1948, the Malayan Communists launched a campaign of terror. The British declared an "Emergency," but for years thereafter, a few thousand Communist guerrillas occupied 250,000 government troops. By resettling into protected villages a half million Chinese squatters from the jungle areas and marginal rubber plantations and by controlling food stocks, the British starved out many of the terrorists. Moreover, an intensive campaign of psychological warfare and new jungle warfare techniques nibbled away at the Communist strength. Not until 1960, however, was the Emergency officially ended.

Singapore. Part of the Straits Settlement colony until World War II, Singapore became a separate crown colony thereafter. By the constitution of 1954, Singapore gained some self-government and a largely elective assembly. The first elected Chief Minister David Marshall, representing an all-party alliance called Merdeka (Freedom), negotiated for independence. To strengthen Singapore's position, Marshall also proposed federation with Malaya. Fearing the added Chinese voting strength, Tengku Rahman offered a larger federation to include Sarawak, Brunei, and North Borneo with their largely non-Chinese populations. At that point, however, Communist agitation among Singapore's Chinese destroyed possibilities for either independence or federation.

STATE OF SINGAPORE. Lim Yew Hock, who succeeded Marshall in 1956, so weakened the Communist position that in June, 1959, Britain created the State of Singapore with greatly increased internal self-government. Surprisingly, the first elections brought victory to the leftist People's Action Party headed by the Cambridge-educated Socialist Lee Kuan Yew. Recognizing that Singapore's 1.6 million people cannot exist alone, Lee launched a reform program aimed to win Malayan approval for federation. In reaction, the left wing of the P.A.P. split off to found the Barisan Socialis (Social Front), a Communist front party led by Lim Chin Siong. These events stimulated Tengku Abdul Rahman to rush the creation of Malaysia including Singapore with the hope of thus containing the Communists.

MALAYSIA

Malaysia Proposed. Though Tengku Rahman's first suggestion for federation of Malaya, Singapore, Brunei, Sarawak, and North Borneo brought no action, his official proposal in 1961 aroused favorable British response. By a painstaking interview system, a British commission determined that the great majority in the Borneo colonies favored federation and therefore recommended merger in the fall of 1963.

British Borneo. British Borneo consisted of the protected Sultanate of Brunei and the crown colonies of Sarawak and British North Borneo. Brunei once ruled most of Borneo (called Kalimantan by Indonesians), but now has an area slightly larger than Delaware. Sarawak was carved out of Brunei by an English adventurer James Brooke, first of the "White Rajahs." The Brookes accepted British protection in 1888 and ceded their domain to the British crown after World War II. North Borneo (Sabah) was secured from Brunei and the Sultan of Sulu (in the southern Philippines) by concession hunters who passed it on to the British North Borneo Company in 1881. It became a crown colony in 1945. In the two colonies, the British have cautiously directed the backward population toward self-government.

INSURRECTION. In Brunei, the sultan promulgated a constitution in 1959, but delayed holding elections until 1962. At that time, the Brunei People's Party, headed by Azahari, a leftist Malay immigrant from Indonesia, showed strong opposition to federation with Malaysia. When the sultan continued plans to join Malaysia, Azahari organized an insurrection with suspected Indonesian support. British forces quelled the uprising quickly, but raids from Indonesian-based guerrillas began to plague Brunei and neighboring Sarawak and Sabah as Indonesia pressed her confrontation program.

Obstacles to Malaysia. In June, 1962, Philippine President Macapagal reacted to Malaysia by claiming North Borneo on the basis of Sulu's former dominion there. He also proposed a Confederation of Greater Malaya, including the Philippines. Neither the claim nor the proposal received favorable hearing, and plans for Malaysia progressed, despite the Brunei insurrection and Indonesia's confrontation. Pressed by his larger neighbors, Tengku Rahman finally agreed to discussions. At a Manila conference in June, 1963, President Macapagal proposed a three-state confederation called Musjarawah Maphilindo. Indonesia and the Philippines also agreed to welcome Malaysia if a U.N. survey affirmed that the people of Borneo genuinely supported it.

PROGRESS TOWARD MERGER. Before the survey could get under way, Tengku Rahman continued merger negotiations. Brunei then decided against joining, but Malaya and Britain formally agreed to the merger of Sarawak and North Borneo and Britain surrendered her sovereignty there. When Sukarno and Macapagal protested, Rahman met them again in Manila and firmly agreed to the U.N. Mission. The U.N. speedily concluded a survey which showed definite support for Malaysia in Sarawak and North Borneo.

Malaysia Achieved. Before the U.N. survey results were published, Britain and Malaya set September 16 as the date of

Malaysia's inauguration, and the schedule was met. Indonesia and the Philippines recalled their ambassadors from Kuala Lumpur and refused to recognize Malaysia. Sukarno dedicated himself to "crush Malaysia" and proceeded with his destructive confrontation program. Though Sukarno showed no sign of relenting, Macapagal sought face-saving ways to renew diplomatic and commercial ties. To help mediate, U.S. Attorney General Robert Kennedy flew to the Far East in January, 1964. Discussions brought a cease-fire agreement along the long Borneo border, but it was almost immediately violated.

ECONOMIC FUTURE. As Malaysia was born, Malaya and Singapore boasted the highest per capita incomes in Southeast Asia, though the gap between rich and poor remained wide and population growth largely cancelled agricultural and industrial development. According to Malaysia's broad plans, Malaya and Singapore will contribute heavily to develop Sarawak and Sabah. Confrontation has been costly, not only from heavy loss of trade and profits from processing Indonesian rubber, but also from increased defense expenditures. These costs place serious strains on Malaysia's economy.

PHILIPPINES

Legacy of War. The quick Japanese victory in 1941 unnerved the Filipino leaders who remained to face the conquerors when President Quezon yielded to American pressures to head a government in exile in Australia. The Japanese made many concessions to secure support for their "Co-Prosperity Sphere," and in 1943 declared Philippine independence. Many Filipinos collaborated with the Japanese—some to protect their people, some for personal profit, and others to aid U.S. intelligence.

GUERRILLA FORCES. Philippine and American soldiers who escaped capture formed guerrilla forces who were joined by increasing numbers disenchanted by Japanese brutality. Socialist and Communist-led forces, organized as the Anti-Japanese People's Liberation Army, better known as the "Hukbalahap" or the "Huks," particularly attracted the depressed peasant tenants. Since many landlords were collaborators, the Huks attacked them along with the Japanese, sometimes clashing with other forces led by U.S. officers and sons of prominent families.

At the war's end, the Huks retained both their arms and organization in their strongholds in central Luzon. Their bitterness against the landlord-dominated government increased when partly because of wartime frictions they did not receive official recognition and the back pay and G.I. Bill rights accorded most guerrillas.

Independence. Though World War II interrupted the projected period of training in self-government, independence came as promised. Sergio Osmeña, who had succeeded to the leadership of the Nacionalistas on the wartime death of Quezon, attempted to form a government free of collaboration taint. Nevertheless, Manuel Roxas and Elpidio Quirino, who had collaborated in the Japanese puppet government but whom MacArthur had cleared for unspecified wartime services, became the first President and Vice-president when the Republic was inaugurated on July 4, 1946. Their victory split the Nacionalista Party which had dominated Philippine politics for decades.

CIVIL STRIFE. The expulsion from the Philippine House of Representatives of Huk leader Louis Taruc and six others elected with Huk support instigated renewed guerrilla warfare against the landlords and the Roxas government. An offer of amnesty coupled with a demand to surrender arms by President Quirino in June, 1948, following Roxas' death, provided pretext for a resumption of fighting coincident with the general Communist offensive in Asia. The mobile guerrillas whose forces numbered 10,000 plus some 30,000 "irregulars" harassed central Luzon for years. Despite the civil disorder and further splitting of parties, Quirino was re-elected in the 1949 elections, elections so corruption-riddled that public confidence in democracy was badly shaken.

Rehabilitation. Added to devastating wartime damages, the Philippines suffered serious natural catastrophes. The islands had also to reorient a predominantly agricultural economy which had been geared to American and then Japanese needs. Between 1945 and 1950, the U.S. poured in over $2 billion in aid, but much seems to have been lost or misspent. Ambitious development programs to exploit the very ample agricultural and mineral resources remained largely paper plans.

BELL MISSION. The U.S. Bell Mission, sent in 1950 in re-

sponse to an appeal for new assistance, frankly criticized the
Philippine government as corrupt and inefficient. They recommended $250 million in U.S. loans over five years provided
that the Manila government: (1) reformed fiscal policies and
equalized taxes; (2) improved working conditions, increased
minimum wages, and expanded social services; (3) executed
land reforms; and (4) ended graft by officials and businessmen.
An agreement was soon concluded and legislation enacted to
fulfill these requirements. The following year, a U.S. Economic
Cooperation Mission was established in Manila.

Ramon Magsaysay and Regeneration. To lessen civil disorders, the Querino government named wartime guerrilla leader
Ramon Magsaysay Secretary of Defense. Using relentless guerrilla tactics, Magsaysay routed the rebels. He also taught the
army to enlist peasant cooperation by alleviating discontent and
ending army exploitation and abuse of villagers. Huks who
surrendered received homesteads. Moreover, free and fair elections in 1951 brought significant victories to the opposition.
These moves gradually decimated the Huk forces and forced
their leader Louis Taruc to surrender. Splitting from the Querino government, Magsaysay ran for the presidency on the
Nacionalista ticket in 1953. Swept into office, Magsaysay
brought new vigor and imagination to the presidency.

POPULAR REFORMS. Magsaysay opened his office to all, invited citizens to telegraph or write their complaints, and personally visited the towns and villages. In July, 1954, laws were
passed providing for government expropriation or purchase of
large estates to be sold to tenants and landless workers and
for resettling landless families in frontier regions on Mindanao
and Palawan. A revision of the Bell Trade Act of 1946 helped
regain Philippine economic strength. The Nacionalist Party's
victory in the congressional elections of 1955 voiced popular
approval for Magsaysay's program.

President Garcia. On Magsaysay's tragic death in early 1957,
vice-president Carlos Garcia pledged to continue economic and
political reform and to cooperate with the U.S. Though Garcia
lacked Magsaysay's color, aggressiveness, and common touch,
he was a thoroughly experienced politician. Re-elected in 1957,
he pursued a conservative, though solid, program of develop-

ment and reform with special emphasis on industrialization. Accused of being too pro-American, Garcia associated himself with a "Filipino First" policy aimed to reduce the economic hold of aliens, primarily Chinese and American, who dominated 80 per cent of the domestic trade and 50 per cent of the foreign trade.

Macapagal Administration. Elected Vice-president on the Liberal ticket in 1957, Diosdada Macapagal began immediately to campaign for the 1961 presidential contest. Following Magsaysay's grassroots approach, Macapagal visited nearly all of the 28,000 Philippine barrios. Supported by the United Opposition, Macapagal snatched victory from the incumbent President Garcia and was inaugurated December 30, 1961. Though faced by a Nacionalista majority in congress, Macapagal managed to get much of his program enacted.

SOCIO-ECONOMIC PROGRAM. Macapagal initiated his "new era" by (1) presenting a five-year Integrated Socio-Economic Program (1962-7) to Congress, (2) restoring a free economy by abolishing currency controls, (3) securing $300 million in U.S. loans for monetary stabilization and economic development, and (4) raising tariffs on many non-essential and luxury imports. The Socio-Economic Program aimed to increase the national growth rate from 5.5 per cent to 7 per cent to provide adequate growth beyond that needed to meet a 3.3 per cent annual population increase. Characteristically, private enterprise and foreign investment were stressed. Though both foreign and domestic investment were sluggish in 1962, some improvement was subsequently realized. Macapagal's administration was criticized for poor use of U.S. loans and for failure to halt inflation, achieve self-sufficiency in rice and corn, and its inability to establish a favorable trade balance.

ANTI-CORRUPTION CAMPAIGN. Macapagal had promised to finally eliminate graft and corruption and to limit himself to one term. He early suspended some middle-grade officials, but action against high officials was slow in coming. In March, 1962, an American businessman, Harry Stonehill, was arrested and subsequently deported with three associates on charges of wholesale corruption of public officials and defrauding the government. Investigation of Stonehill's files during 1963 produced a startling list of Filipinos, including many top political figures.

POLITICAL OPPOSITION. Macapagal was hard put to maintain control of his party, especially after a bad showing in mid-term elections. By 1964, the Liberals had split into three factions and the president was feuding with Vice-President Pelaez, as Macapagal vacillated regarding his self-imposed limit of one term.

Foreign Affairs. A charter member, the Philippines has actively participated in the U.N. on the Free World side. Philippine forces fought in Korea, and the Philippines signed the Japanese Peace Treaty in 1951. While cooperating with the U.S., Filipinos have aimed to establish an anti-Communist Southern Asia bloc. Together with the U.S., Australia, New Zealand, Britain, Thailand, and Pakistan, the Philippines formed the Southeast Asia Treaty Organization (SEATO) in Manila in 1954. SEATO aims to resist external aggression and internal subversion, and to encourage economic and social improvements in Southeast Asia. In 1956, Japan agreed to pay the Philippines war reparations of $800 million.

U.S. RELATIONS. Friction developed over maintenance of U.S. military bases and Philippine demands for an additional $1 billion for war losses and other claims. In 1959, the U.S. finally agreed to reduce the 99-year bases to 25-year terms and to permit greater Philippine control over their use. Not until August, 1962, did Congress finally pass a claim bill providing only $73 million. Angered by an earlier defeat of the bill, Macapagal had canceled a scheduled visit to America. Coincidentally, the Philippine Independence Day was changed from July 4 to June 12, the date of Aguinaldo's proclamation of independence in 1898.

MALAYSIA AND MAPHILINDO. Although in July, 1961, the Philippines and Malaya, together with Thailand, launched the Association of Southeast Asia (ASA) for economic and cultural cooperation, Macapagal formally claimed North Borneo a year later. Great Britain flatly rejected the claim, but Malaya's Tengku Rahman did sit down to confer with Sukarno and Macapagal. The three agreed in principle to Macapagal's proposal for Maphilindo. However, its future dimmed when the Philippines and Indonesia refused to recognize Malaysia. Macapagal's close relations in this dispute with the erratic Sukarno aroused grave concern in both the Philippines and the U.S.

Top-level discussions following the Kennedy peace-making mission faltered, but the Philippines did offer to resume consular relations with Malaysia in February, 1964.

BIBLIOGRAPHY

Allen, G. C., and A. G. Donnithorne, *Western Enterprise in Indonesia and Malaya*, 1957.

Bernstein, David, *The Philippine Story*, 1947.

Brimmell, J. H., *Communism in South East Asia*, 1959.

Bro, M., *Indonesia: Land of Challenge*, 1954.

Cady, J. F., P. Barnett and S. Jenkins, *The Development of Self-Rule and Independence in Burma, Malaya, and the Philippines*, 1948.

Cady, J. F., *Southeast Asia, Its Historical Development*, 1964.

Elsbree, W. H., *Japan's Role in Southeast Asian Nationalist Movements, 1940-1945*, 1953.

Emerson, R., *Representative Government in Southeast Asia*, 1955.

Feith, H., *The Decline of Constitutional Democracy in Indonesia*, 1962.

Fifield, R. H., *The Diplomacy of Southeast Asia: 1945-1958*, 1958.

Golay, Frank H., *The Philippines: Public Policy and National Economic Development*, 1961.

Hanna, W. A., *Bung Karno's Indonesia*, 1960.

Harris, G. L., et al., *North Borneo, Brunei, Sarawak*, 1956.

Jacoby, E. H., *Agrarian Unrest in Southeast Asia*, 1961.

Kahin, G. M., ed., *Governments and Politics of Southeast Asia*, 1959.

King, F. H. H., *The New Malayan Nation*, 1957.

Malcolm, G. A., *The First Malayan Republic: The Story of the Philippines*, 1951.

Mills, L., *Malaya: A Political and Economic Appraisal*, 1958.

Mintz, Jeanne, *Indonesia: A Profile*, 1961.

Pye, L. W., *Guerrilla Communism in Malaya*, 1956.

Ravenholt, A., *The Philippines: A Young Republic on the Move*, 1962.

Romulo, C. P., and M. M. Gray, *The Magsaysay Story*, 1956.

Salosoemardjan, *Social Change in Jogjakarta*, 1962.

Smith, R. A., *Philippine Freedom*, 1958.

Thomson, I., *Changing Patterns in South Asia*, 1962.

Trager, F. N., ed., *Marxism in Southeast Asia*, 1960.

von der Mehden, F. R., *Religion and Nationalism in Southeast Asia*, 1963.

Woodman, D., *The Republic of Indonesia*, 1956.

INDEX

DATE DUE

MY 22 '69		
MR 28 '93		

GAYLORD   PRINTED IN U.S.A.